GW00493878

DISTRIBUTED IN CANADA BY JAGUAR BOOK GROUP

TO ORDER IN CANADA
Manda Group | info@mandagroup.com

**DISTRIBUTED IN THE U.S. BY
BAKER & TAYLOR PUBLISHER SERVICES**

TO ORDER IN THE U.S.
Please contact your Simon & Schuster rep or customer service
email: purchaseorders@simonandschuster.com
phone: 1-866-506-1949

UNDERWATER

UNDERWATER

THE GREED-SOAKED TALE

OF

SEXUAL ABUSE

IN USA SWIMMING

AND AROUND THE GLOBE

Irvin Muchnick

Published by ECW Press
665 Gerrard Street East
Toronto, Ontario, Canada m4m 1y2
416-694-3348 / info@ecwpress.com

Editor for the Press: Michael Holmes
Copy-editor: David Marsh
Cover design: [tk]
Cover image: [tk]

LIBRARY AND ARCHIVES CANADA CATALOGUING
IN PUBLICATION

[place CIP data block]

This book is funded in part by the Government of Canada. *Ce livre est financé en partie par le gouvernement du Canada.*
We acknowledge the support of the Canada Council for the Arts. *Nous remercions le Conseil des arts du Canada de son soutien.* We would like to acknowledge the funding support of the Ontario Arts Council (OAC) and the Government of Ontario for their support. We also acknowledge the support of the Government of Ontario through the Ontario Book Publishing Tax Credit, and through Ontario Creates.

PRINTED AND BOUND IN CANADA

PRINTING: [ADD WHEN KNOWN]   5   4   3   2   1

CONTENTS

PARTIAL LIST OF CHARACTERS IN THIS BOOK

THE SURVIVORS

Kelley Davies

Deena Deardurff

Debra Denithorne

Sarah Ehekircher

Melissa Halmi

"Ivory"

"Julia" (Irish division)

Ariana Kukors

Suzette Moran

Brooke Taflinger

Jancy Thompson

THE NON-SURVIVORS

Sarah Burt

Fran Crippen

Louis Lowenthal

Noel Moran

THE SKETCHY COACHES

Charles Baechler (defrocked judge division)

Paul Bergen

Linck Bergen

Joe Bernal, aka Hugo Bernard Calderon

Flavio Bomio (Swiss division)

Simon Daniel "Danny" Chocrón
(U.S.–Venezuelan division)

Rick Curl

Brandon Drawz

George Gibney (Irish division)

Sean Hutchison

Mitch Ivey

Andy King

Scott MacFarland

Jack Nelson

Derry O'Rourke (Irish division)

*James Pantera, aka Robert Michael Binkin,
James David Land, James Wallace*

Dustin Perry

Alex Pussieldi (U.S.-Brazilian division)

Cecil Russell (Canadian division)

Mark Schubert

Dick Shoulberg

Jesse Stovall

THE WHISTLEBLOWERS

Tony Austin, swimmer and blogger

Peyton Bailey, swimmer

Chris DeSantis, coach and podcaster

Sarah Kwon, masters swimmer

Jeffrey Linder, coach

Dia Rianda, coach

Ken Stopkotte, coach

THE FUNCTIONARIES

Tim Bauer, coach and USA Swimming board member

Paulette Brundage, FBI agent turned
USA Swimming "investigator"

Nancy Fisher, FBI agent turned USA Swimming "investigator"

Richard Foster, USA Swimming lawyer

Michael Henry, U.S. Center for Safe Sport
"director of legal affairs"

Pat Hogan, USA Swimming club development director

John Leonard, American Swimming Coaches Association
executive director

Lucinda McRoberts, USA Swimming lawyer

Dale Neuburger, national and international swimming
board member

Sharon Robb, Florida "journalist"

Travis Tygart, USA Swimming lawyer turned
U.S. Anti-Doping Agency CEO

Chuck Wielgus, USA Swimming executive director

Bruce Wigo, International Swimming Hall of Fame CEO

Susan Woessner, USA Swimming director of Safe Sport

Richard Young, USA Swimming lawyer

THE FLUNKING POLITICIANS

Jerry Brown, governor of California

George Miller, U.S. congressman

Jackie Speier, U.S. congresswoman

PROLOGUE

Water has erotic properties. As H_2O ripples off the human body, in bubbled molecules, it sends flattering light reflections off exposed flesh. And swimsuits expose a lot of flesh. And lissome athletes cloaked in them give off another level of pleasant vibes with their gracefulness, skill, and power. Swimming is sexy.

But sports aren't supposed to be about sexiness — especially when many of the athletes are underage. And as they say, rape isn't about sex. This helps explain why in 2017, after years of fits and starts, blue-ribbon advisory panels, and lawyers' studies of the insurance and liability implications, the United States Center for Safe Sport opened an office across from a strip mall just outside downtown Denver.

One of the challenges for the center was to exude stern independence — spiritual and operational autonomy, if not the actual and legal sort — from the U.S. Olympic Committee. Known today as the U.S. Olympic and Paralympic Committee, or USOPC, it was headquartered 70 miles south of Denver, in Colorado Springs, and had affiliated and scattered individual sport national governing bodies, or NGBs. The Safe Sport agency was there to serve as what police departments call their internal affairs divisions — the arbiter of disputes over allegations of misconduct in the ranks. For the center, this meant sexual abuse by coaches against the athletes, often underage, they supervised.

Safe Sport had a rocky start. While chief executive officer Shellie Pfohl (previously director of the President's Council on Physical Fitness under Barack Obama) worked on perfecting the reporting procedures and the organizational flowchart, and figuring out how to subdivide the office space for investigators, the biggest abuse scandal in sports history erupted. Its subject was Dr. Larry Nassar, an osteopath who, starting in 1996, had been national medical coordinator for USA Gymnastics. Through almost that entire period, he was also on the faculty of Michigan State University's College of Human Medicine.

For years, stories bubbled up about Nassar's heinous misconduct with young female gymnasts, all the way down to earliest teenagers (if that old). Some of the anecdotes stretched back to before his elevation to top physician of the national team, when he was just an athletic trainer. In 2016 the newspaper in the headquarters city of USA Gymnastics, the *Indianapolis Star*, published the first account of these allegations in a major newspaper, through on-the-record statements by victim Rachael Denhollander. The *Star* is part of the Gannett newspaper chain, whose flagship is *USA Today*. A Gannett outlet guaranteed that the story would get a national megaphone and legs, in *USA Today* and several hundred other Gannett papers large and small.

Though USA Gymnastics and Michigan State soon cut ties with Nassar, the scandal only worsened. By the time Shellie Pfohl and Safe Sport got up and running, publicly circulated nuggets of Nassar information were already metastasizing. They ranged from borderline inappropriate behavior to evidence of his hundreds upon hundreds of instances of perverse acts during medical examinations. The accusers backstopping Denhollander were a who's who of gymnastics superstars, a veritable roll call of America's sweethearts from quadrennial Summer Olympics: McKayla Maroney, Aly Raisman, Gabby Douglas, and Simone Biles, among others. The first state criminal charges against Nassar were filed in Michigan in November

2016. The next month, while free on bail, he was hit with federal charges of child pornography, including images of him molesting underage girls, and ordered held without bail. Back in Michigan state court in late 2017, Nassar pleaded guilty to ten counts of first-degree sexual assault.

And that was just the opening act. What really blew things up, in January 2018, were revelations that an astounding number of women had persistently tried to bring Nassar's abuses to the attention of both Michigan State and USA Gymnastics officials, and been met with bureaucratic indifference. Once so exposed, the university ejected president Lou Anna Simon and athletic director Mark Hollis. (Simon would be unsuccessfully prosecuted for covering up known malfeasance.) Eventually Michigan State would dole out around half a billion dollars to settle claims by more than 300 victims of Nassar incidents on campus.

Meanwhile, the Olympic gymnastics NGB accepted the resignations of chief executive Steve Penny and the entire 18-person board of directors. Within a month, Scott Blackmun, CEO of the Olympic Committee for eight years, was following them out the door.

Such was the maelstrom Pfohl waded into. As she settled in, *Harper's Magazine* published the latest in a succession of "exclusive" accounts in major magazines of the Olympic sports abuse issue. For this particular author, an urgent topic of discussion seemed to be interior design: "SafeSport's décor is spartan, a reflection of its newness. Most of the main room is empty space under the glare of fluorescent lights."

In April 2018, Pfohl conducted her first television interview, a live sit-down on the nightly evening newscast of hometown Denver's KUSA, Channel 9. Simultaneously, congressional hearings were spotlighting the gymnastics scandal and the need for a new sheriff for youth sports. This background made Pfohl's cheerful presentation all the more incongruous. The boss of the agency policing abuse chose to appear on air clad in a pullover bearing the U.S. Center for Safe Sport logo. It was as though she were some kind of corporate marketing brand extension spokesperson announcing a new social media presence, rather than the face of a purported fix of a pressing moral problem.

In lieu of a somber mien, Pfohl adopted a scripted chirpy and positive tone in her answers to the news anchors' softball questions. Rather than underscoring her determination to eradicate sexual abuse in the Olympic movement, she put emphasis on assuring viewers that this goal would not in any way impede the main objective — which of course was to continue, unabated, America's international athletic dominance and quest for gold medals. On her first public stage, Pfohl wasn't just acknowledging the reality of commercial interests; she was doubling down on them. To top it all off, she looked like a deer in the headlights.

Before 2018 was over, Pfohl would resign, abandoning her three-year contract.

≈

Shellie Pfohl's brief and beleaguered experience founding the U.S. Center for Safe Sport grew out of what one of the most visible national sport governing bodies, USA Swimming, called its Safe Sport program. Swimming's version of Safe Sport had launched in 2010.[1] In the intervening years, national Olympic head Blackmun had liked to cite swimming as its model sport for promulgating new and enlightened abuse policies and practices.

Blackmun's assertion was ridiculous, given how very little the new Safe Sport administrations, in swimming and elsewhere, actually

---

[1] All these entities and departments are sometimes rendered in the run-together neologism "SafeSport." Here and throughout, I've chosen to separate the words in a bid to keep their meaning from drowning in corporate speak.

changed about the handling of allegations and about authorities' purposefulness in protecting juvenile athletes from predatory coaches. This book will get into all that. But first, it's important to note that while the Safe Sport concept and verbiage were originally in evidence in the work of task forces within swimming in the early 2000s, the decision of USA Swimming executive director Chuck Wielgus to enact the first Safe Sport department, including the appointment of a dedicated administrator with that portfolio, had been prompted by a specific and spectacular public relations fiasco. That was Wielgus's disastrous performance as a spokesperson in a segment on the ABC News investigative program *20/20*.

The date of the fateful broadcast was April 9, 2010. Chief investigative correspondent Brian Ross began with the story of Brian Hindson, a coach in Kokomo, Indiana. One of Hindson's swimmers, Brooke Taflinger, told of how Hindson used to steer her and fellow female swimmers to a section of the locker room where, it turned out, he'd installed a hidden video camera, through which he captured them undressing. For his peeping and his possession of child pornography, Hindson would land a 33-year prison sentence. The *20/20* broadcast revealed that he was one of 36 coaches nationwide who'd been banned by USA Swimming for various forms of sexual abuse. Another coach in the same state, Ken Stopkotte, did a whistleblower interview with Ross expounding on the sport's widespread problem of coach misconduct; and almost immediately, the report noted, Indiana Swimming, the regional NGB affiliate, retaliated by opening an investigation not of what Stopkotte had reported, but of Stopkotte himself. (He was accused of falsifying his swimmers' times in meet entries.)

The ABC program revealed the state-to-state movements — always a step ahead of local efforts to hold him to account — of Andy King, another abuser coach. Ray Mendoza, the California prosecutor who finally put King away for a litany of crimes, including impregnating a 14-year-old girl, called him "a monster," responsible for sex offenses against at least 15 victims all along the West Coast over the course of three decades. King's conviction on 20 counts of child molestation in California sent him to prison for 40 years.

Though not detailed on *20/20*, seven King survivors would eventually come forward from San Ramon Valley Aquatics alone. Historically, the story there of swimmer Debra Denithorne (now Debra Grodensky) serves as a kind of apotheosis of a coach's form of twisted passion for and control over teenage girls, in defiance of professional ethics and the law. (One might say that a question raised by the persistence of these practices is whether they actually run afoul of societal conventions, as well.) King began abusing Grodensky in 1980, when she was 11; five years later, the coach, by now 37, asked her to marry him — leading to her temporary departure from the sport.

All this, a national TV audience learned, was enabled by a USA Swimming coach background-check system that was lackadaisical and unprofessional; by a culture of exploitation and objectification of young people; and by a national office that blew off complaints. One mother who spoke on the broadcast about her futile attempt to garner traction for an official investigation of her daughter's coach's inappropriate conduct got contacted by USA Swimming hours before *20/20* went on the air. And as with whistleblower coach Stopkotte, this was not to investigate the complaint at long last, but rather to interrogate the complainant herself, antagonistically, about why she'd talked to *20/20*.

Following a commercial break, the ABC piece's second segment proceeded to a broader examination, kicked off by the observations of 1972 gold medal swimmer Deena Deardurff. She recalled her years-long abuse, beginning when she was a preteen, by then Cincinnati-based coach Paul Bergen, a member of the International Swimming Hall of Fame. (She'd first named Bergen as her abuser in a public statement more than two years earlier.)

The climax of the nearly 20-minute report was an embarrassing interview of Chuck Wielgus. He insisted USA Swimming was doing "an awesome job" of combating abuse. He argued for a sense of proportion in stacking the group's 36 proven bad actors up against a total national pool of 12,000 swim coaches. "I'm not seeking to minimize [the problem]," Wielgus said in answer to a follow-up question from Ross. "You're seeking to accentuate it."

Most damaging of all, the reporter shared a secret audio of a meeting with other leaders of the sport, in which Wielgus was caught privately saying something quite different. "This happens almost every week," USA Swimming's chief said on the tape. "We get calls at the office. I get informed about it. One of my greatest fears is someone's going to start linking all this together."

On air, Ross asked Wielgus, "Have you apologized to any of the women victims?"

The camera captured an indignant grimace from Wielgus before he replied, "You feel I need to apologize to them?" Then he sputtered:

> I think we have done . . . I don't . . . Look, this is a
> tragic situation. And I think it's unfair for you to ask
> me individually or me as the head of an organization
> to apologize for something, when all we are trying to
> do is do everything we possibly can to create a safe
> and healthy environment for kids who are participat-
> ing in our particular activity.

The blowback from *20/20* (and a similar report the same season on ESPN's investigative program *Outside the Lines*, in which Wielgus was grilled by correspondent T.J. Quinn) was swift and devastating. The membership ranks of USA Swimming ebb and flow, diminishing in summer months and spiking after things like Summer Olympics publicity. But every year somewhere around half a million kids and their families participate on a regular or seasonal basis. In an open letter to the swimming community, Wielgus expressed regret for his clumsy demeanor on national television; he blamed it not on the content of his message but on his lack of media savvy. In the rhetorical equivalent of a flip turn at the wall, he averred: "In a way, I hate to say this, but there may be some fated reason why USA Swimming was put in this position, because we have the commitment and wherewithal not to shy away from an issue, to embrace an opportunity to make things better." Over the next seven years, Wielgus would specialize in such word salads, dressed up as a qualified, yet ultimately unaccountable, remorse.

Their earliest version culminated in Wielgus's announcement of the start of USA Swimming's Safe Sport program, weeks after *20/20*. As part of the initiative, Wielgus announced, the organization would begin posting on its website the names of and findings against all banned coaches. (By the time of the writing of this book, that initial list of 36 had swelled to more than 200.) In September 2010, Wielgus hired Susan Woessner as "athlete protection officer." Later her title would be changed to "director of Safe Sport." Woessner had been a teammate, and close friend on the Indiana University swimming team, of Brooke Taflinger, the accuser of Brian Hindson on *20/20*.

≈

2010: USA Swimming Safe Sport program commences . . .

2017: U.S. Center for Safe Sport launches . . .

2020: Congress authorizes the Commission on the State of the U.S. Olympic and Paralympic Committee to field and address complaints about USOPC operations . . .

The years roll off the calendar. The mechanisms for tackling abuse change acronyms but never add effectiveness. The lawsuits mount. Yet another generation of (mostly female) swimmers deals with the contradictions of enjoying expanded athletic opportunities in the era of the 1972 equity legislation known as Title IX — while still having to navigate the same old sexual politics, and wondering how deep the damage goes in their relationships and lives.

The general public, for the most part, shrugs. One feature of individual sports, especially those with short athletic career spans peaking in the late teens and early 20s, is the constant turnover in the cast of characters. What these sports sell, above all else, is a fortnight of feel-good nationalism every leap-year summer in television packages for USOPC broadcast partners and sponsors.

Personally, I came to this grim subject — far more vast and money-saturated than most people realize — through an accident of timing. I happen to have had a young daughter who swam competitively for more than five years with our local USA Swimming–sanctioned club. Thankfully, she wasn't a victim. In any event, I believe, victim-centricity isn't the right lens through which to critique sexual abuse in swimming; the problem is much more diffuse and insidious. A better way to view things is to start by considering that this sport became a recreational staple of Americana thanks to a regimen of intense after-school practices and far-flung, weekend-long meets. After which, somehow, by default and in a wrinkle of American exceptionalism, it all got grafted onto the ambitions for Olympic glory and riches. The question posed by this book is: Are there no better alternatives for running kids' swimming programs?

Full consideration of this question requires an unblinkered look at the tragically flawed system we have now — how it codifies the casual commodification of kids, turning physical education and mastery of a life skill into the developmental arm of professional-ized sports. Unexamined, these objectives splash around in public subsidies and in exaggerated and wrongheaded assumptions about their positive impact on our society.

One of the system's costs — little more than a cost of business in defending lawsuits, either sporadic or frequent — is widespread sexual abuse. The resulting damage scars its victims, and in individual cases we can debate into the night who are and aren't the genuine victims in what often become bottomless he-said/she-said scenarios. But regardless of the specific criminal and administrative findings in individual cases, we need to understand better not only how abuse adversely affects direct victims and all those around them, but also how abiding such a system diminishes the rest of us in untold ways.

My daughter Mara was eight years old when she began swimming with the Berkeley Bears. Her mother and I have four kids, and we were thrilled when our older girl was the one who turned into the family jock. I myself was what's known as a "sinker"; in my youth, I'd learned to overcome fear of the water and to get around in it, but I never mastered technique. Inspired by Mara's example, I decided to take some lessons of my own, and I finally got the hang of freestyle side breathing... sort of. One day, on a family vacation, I found that I could make it the whole distance of the 137-meter-long saltwater pool off Kitsilano Beach in Vancouver, Canada. Through our children, we learn.

Mara was a very good little swimmer. Never Olympic-class or athletic scholarship–bound, mind you, nor so aspirational. But she excelled at breaststroke, butterfly, and distance freestyle. At meets, Mara racked up prize ribbons: lots of 3rd places, 4ths, 5ths, and 6ths, the occasional 2nd, the very rare 1st. One time she got disqualified, and we proudly displayed the DQ slip on the corkboard on the wall of her bedroom, along with all the participation ribbons; after all, they said you weren't a real competitive swimmer until the first time you got busted for an illegal turn. I chaperoned Mara to daily practices, and once a month or so, we got up as early as 5 a.m. for drives to meets as far away as Santa Rosa and San Jose. At the end of her first year, she won the Most Improved Swimmer award at the team banquet.

The head coach was a former University of California backstroke specialist named Jesse Stovall. He was good at stroke-coaching, even if he was inept at organization, always hid his eyes behind sunglasses, and behaved immaturely. Near the beginning of one season, the Bears staged a poolside ice cream social to gather all the athletes and their families. I expected Stovall to welcome everyone with some community-building remarks. Instead, he just stood off to the side, flirting with the high school–age girl swimmers. At the time, I didn't think much of it.

I was further nonplussed by a bizarre incident at a large end-of-summer meet. This was what's known as a "trials and finals" meet: instead of just culling best scores from the various earlier heats to determine placement, the swimmers with the top times in each event moved on to a head-to-head competition in a late-afternoon session. This meet was close to home, and Mara had a full family contingent of cheerleaders, including her visiting aunt from out of town. Preparing for a final in the warm-up pool, she didn't notice that the sequence of events had been scrambled out of numerical order. The result was that she found herself still in the warm-up pool, instead of being on the starting block of the main pool, at call time for the final heat. She was disqualified.

As I always did, I lurked outside the team's E-Z Up tent to listen to the post-race words of wisdom imparted to Mara by an assistant coach. Usually they involved advice about pacing her race lap to lap, or some similar technical tip. This time I heard the assistant, Rick, say to Mara, "Pacific Swimming has an automatic $50 fine when a swimmer misses a final. It's to keep swimmers from cutting out and no-showing after the trials round. Pacific Swimming sends us the fine, and we put it directly onto the bill for your team membership dues the next month."

I thought this gazebo was kidding around. But Mara obviously internalized what he said: when we got home, she opened her piggy bank, which held her income from recent babysitting jobs, to see if she could scrape together the fifty bucks. Fining an 11-year-old kid who, in her exuberance to prepare for her final heat, simply got confused about procedures? She wasn't, for god's sake, a New York Yankees player who'd missed a hit-and-run sign. Surely this little sports league didn't actually impose monetary consequences for such mistakes, and the coaches in it didn't shove them in the faces of little kids, in lieu of discreet conversations with their parents? Yet when I confronted Rick the next day, he confirmed, with a deadpan, that he'd spoken for real. I told the head coach, Stovall, that this was unacceptable, and pointedly alerted fellow parents by email. The team backed down. We never again heard about the $50 fine.

≈

Our Bears got more and more disorganized and joyless. One Sunday we showed up for the heavily promoted "swim-a-thon," an annual fundraising event in which the swimmers raised money for the team with family and friend contributions pegged to how many practice laps they swam. Not one of the top coaches or older swimmers was even there. Rumors were spreading that the club was months in arrears in rent payments to the local community college aquatics center where practices were held. Later, I'd learn that Stovall was accused of pilfering funds.

Then came the day when we noticed that the Bears' star swimmer, a 16-year-old girl (also a top student, and pretty), was no longer there. The official story was that she and her family had decided to switch to another team, a short distance away, with better facilities and training resources.

By this time, Mara was approaching 13, and she was winding down her own competitive swimming career. Along with one of her friends, she soon moved to another team, whose coach had a healthier, laid-back attitude and style. There Mara put in another year of practices and meets. I was hoping she'd continue to swim on her high school team, because I'd heard that kids with years of club swimming experience often dominated at that level, but Mara wasn't interested. She'd had a nice run, but she'd also had enough. Henceforth, she would just be a skilled swimmer.

It was later that year, 2009, when someone forwarded to me an email chain involving our former coach Jesse Stovall. He'd been ousted from the Bears club, presumably because of the financial improprieties, and now he was coaching an adult group, called a masters team, on the university campus. The startling information from the emails was that one day recently he'd been arrested on Sproul Plaza on a fugitive warrant from Orange County, Florida.

What was that about? I decided to explore.

Police records from Orlando told the whole sordid story. It turned out that the Bears' top swimmer, that 16-year-old girl (whom I'll call "Ivory"), hadn't left on a whim or simply to improve her college athletic scholarship prospects. Rather, she'd stomped off the Bears' practice pool deck after a shouting match with Stovall, days after they returned together from a national invitational meet in Orlando. Stovall, who was married and had a baby daughter, had told Ivory's parents that they could stay home and he'd chaperone her to Florida himself. While in Orlando, Stovall performed cunnilingus on Ivory in two separate incidents. When they got back, she told a friend about it. The friend told her own therapist — who in turn, as a mandatory reporter of child sexual abuse under California law, informed Berkeley police.

Stovall was arrested. He'd cop a plea to the criminal charges in Florida and get banned by USA Swimming.

Our local alternative weekly newspaper, the *East Bay Express*, did a cover story on the scandal. I was the main source, on the record. One other former team parent spoke to the reporter, not for attribution. A team board member, a professor at Cal, either denied to the *Express* that the episode had been covered up or justified the decision to cover up, depending on how you interpreted his remarks. He vilified me as a disgruntled troublemaker.

≈

I thought that was the end of it. A week later, however, I tuned into *20/20* on ABC. That's when I realized that what I'd witnessed with Jesse Stovall and the Berkeley Bears was just the local precinct of a national problem. I corresponded with USA Swimming boss Wielgus and others in Colorado Springs. They were cagey. Wielgus touted to me the start of his Safe Sport program.

Two years later, during a lull between writing projects, I decided to check in on the progress of Safe Sport. Immediately, it became clear that the program was a sham and that the scandals of the sport were profound and far-reaching. Numerous lawsuits, substantial and revealing, were in the pipeline — many of them managed by an attorney in San Jose, Bob Allard (who'd been interviewed on *20/20*), and another in Indianapolis, Jon Little.

One of their clients was a former swimmer in California, Jancy Thompson, who was suing over USA Swimming's exposure in the actions of her coach, Norm Haverford. In the Thompson case, USA Swimming was in the middle of defying multiple California lower court discovery orders to produce the organization's internal documents; in lieu of complying, the group was writing checks totaling tens of thousands of dollars to pay off contempt sanctions, as if they were parking tickets. Litigation of this stonewalling reached the California Supreme Court, which USA Swimming asked to vacate discovery orders. In July 2012, the court refused, compelling enforcement. Later in the year, USA Swimming finally submitted, under seal, thousands of pages of papers memorializing discussions of abuse, with dossiers on scores of accused coaches. Many exploded with seedy information. That massive filing, in turn, got subpoenaed by the field office of the Federal Bureau of Investigation in Campbell, California, outside San Jose. Copies of this tranche of documents were later leaked to my reporting partner at the time, Tim Joyce in New York, and myself. (Thompson and USA Swimming would reach a monetary settlement of her lawsuit in 2014.)

These documents exposed corruption and big money. They detailed insurance fraud and the most reprehensible mistreatment of young people. Additionally, they trickled out anecdotes of gullible parents who'd outsourced the supervision of their children to Svengali coaches who were purportedly their tickets to athletic success, college scholarships, and Olympic medals.

These cases were set in California, Florida, New York, and almost every state of every size in every region. When caught, some of the bad guys fled to the more obvious enclaves, the bordering North American countries of Canada and Mexico. (Or, like Jesse Stovall, they found refuge in U.S. Masters Swimming, a kind of old folks' home for some of the sport's shadow-banned perverts.) But that was far from the geographical extent of the bigger story. The Caribbean island nation of Barbados — home of swimming's captive self-insurance subsidiary, "the United States Sports Insurance Company" — was key. Other foreign locales making appearances were Spain, Venezuela, Brazil, Colombia, Peru, Australia, Kuwait, and the United Arab Emirates.

At one point I traveled to Ireland to find out more about the background of the most notorious at-large sex criminal in sports history: George Gibney, powerful coach of the 1984 and 1988 Irish Olympic swimming team. Gibney had fled the country in 1994 after getting the Irish Supreme Court to toss his indictment on dozens of sexual molestation charges, thanks to a controversial statute-of-limitations technicality. Gibney moved to the U.S. and briefly coached in suburban Denver before his Irish past caught up with him; moved again, and again; and as this book was being written, was still playing out the string, in senescence and obscurity, in a central Florida suburb. Nazi concentration camp gate guards used to enjoy unobtrusive second acts by embedding themselves into American middle-class communities. George Gibney, whose past included not the massacres of people but serial violation of them, did the same.

For television sports fans, swimming is a spectacle of glory, the setting where athletes like Michael Phelps and Katie Ledecky break world records, garner gold, retail backstories of grit and overcoming personal obstacles, and stir upswells of patriotic pride.

Treading under the surface of the water, for generations, has been a darker narrative. It's time to tell that tale, in all its global slime. And past time to appreciate that youth sports coach abuse isn't one of those problems that will be solved by law enforcement breakthroughs or any single new insight out of academic ethics handbooks. The only real fix is cultural, and it will need to be owned by all of us.

CHAPTER 1

THE PUBLIC EYE

At 5:45 a.m. on October 1, 2010, the private detective for Horseman Investigations of Huntington Beach, California, reviewed the details of his assignment. He'd performed this kind of surveillance numerous times before, most notably in divorce cases. After a little experience, it was a piece of cake. All you had to do was follow the man and the woman suspected of illicitly consorting (or the man and the man, or the woman and the woman), discreetly set up the video and still-photo cameras, and capture the evidence. The investigator began his task by driving to the Janet Evans Swim Complex in Fullerton, another Orange County city, which was the site of early morning practice at what was being labeled as USA Swimming's innovative new post-graduate training facility (or professional "center of excellence") for veteran Olympians and for the most elite Olympic aspirants. It operated under the banner of the club there, Fullerton Aquatic Sports Team (FAST).

The subject of the investigation was a 39-year-old man, Sean Hutchison, a successful coach from Seattle's King Aquatic Club who'd been brought down to direct the pros at Fullerton. As the investigator's report would put it: "Caucasian male . . . with wavy, brown hair, prescription glasses and attired in a white green cap, black sweater jacket, white T-shirt, and olive green shorts."

The female subject was Hutchison's star pupil from the Pacific Northwest, 21-year-old Ariana Kukors. The previous year — during a fluky period when world records were getting broken left and right with the aid of controversial new tech swimsuits, whose polyurethane design marked a breakthrough in aerodynamics — she'd swum an out-of-nowhere world record time in the 200-meter individual medley. While not known as one of the most dominant athletes in the sport, Kukors was credited with versatile skills in all four strokes, as well as competitive drive. She was a top prospect.

The investigator's payoff came on the second day of his project, a Saturday. At 6:00 a.m., he noticed that Kukors's parking space was empty at the building where she was known to be living in nearby Irvine. This was about five minutes from Hutchison's dwelling in the same city. The private eye continued to that upscale condominium complex, where he saw the Kukors car parked in space 45 of the underground garage. Hutchison's own black BMW was in space 29.

"With both vehicles present at an early hour," the dry language of the Horseman Investigations report would extrapolate, Hutchison and Kukors must have spent the night together. This inference was reinforced at 7:23 a.m., when the investigator snapped the two on camera with a long-range lens as they simultaneously exited the elevator of the complex at the garage level. Each was pulling a suitcase.

Only later would the world learn who'd effectively hired Horseman Investigations, and why. The who was Mark Schubert. He'd been head coach of the U.S. Olympic swimming team in Beijing in 2008. Hutchison had been one of his assistants both then and when Schubert coached the U.S. women at the 2009 World Championships in Rome. Technically, Schubert didn't commission the detective agency himself; he'd merely informed the CEO of the Fullerton club, Bill Jewell — his old assistant at the University of Southern California — of his suspicions about Hutchison and Kukors, and Jewell had proceeded to retain Horseman. Conveniently,

Schubert's wife worked there. Years earlier, Horseman's president, Patrick Carroll, had dated their daughter. However you sliced it, Schubert had personally instigated this little piece of spy craft.

Now, if you're wondering why coaches of a predominantly youth-serving organization were snooping on each other's partners in bed, you're not alone.

Never mind that, from the perspective of many observers, Schubert had long had all the dirt he should have needed on Sean Hutchison. Inside the swimming world, where incestuousness verged on hillbilly hell, it was an open secret that Hutchison and Kukors were closely linked, personally as well as athletically. (Later *American Swimming*, the magazine of the American Swimming Coaches Association, would publish a feature article, including photos, that focused on their special coach-athlete bond around training techniques.) At major meets going back as far as when Kukors was 16, Schubert had witnessed what he thought was Hutchison inappropriately touching her. One instance was at the 2006 Pan Pacific Swimming Championships. Another was at the 2007 Worlds.

If accurate, this information was actionable and Schubert was obligated to report it to law enforcement. But Schubert seemed to have no interest in doing that. His only objective was to leverage the surrounding gossip for the resolution of his own employment dispute with USA Swimming, which was in its climactic phase. Earlier in 2010, Schubert had butted heads with board members over funding of his vision of new "centers of excellence," of which Fullerton was expected to be only the first. The last straw in the deterioration of Schubert's relationship with the powers-that-be was said to be his emotionally abusive treatment of swimmers leading up to the Pan Pacifics in Irvine that August. The upshot was that USA Swimming suspended Schubert from the head coach job.

In November — just weeks after the spying on Hutchison and Kukors — USA Swimming fired Schubert for good. He sued for wrongful termination, and the two sides commenced negotiations for what would resolve in a $625,000 settlement package.

Whatever his motives, Schubert was the confirmed leaker of the private eye's findings to Amy Shipley, a *Washington Post* reporter. When the story broke in December 2010 — "prominent coach Sean Hutchison appears to be sleeping with an unnamed athlete under his supervision at swimming's new Fullerton professional development center" — USA Swimming boss Chuck Wielgus and his newly appointed functionary, Susan Woessner, had the first full-blown, high-profile crisis of their new "Safe Sport" regime. Only months earlier, ABC's *20/20* report had challenged them to do better in policing sexual abuse by coaches. Wielgus and Woessner proceeded to do no such thing.

Under Wielgus's public relations–driven management, the Hutchison crisis was quickly downgraded to a kerfuffle. It blew over with a familiar disposition, a cryptic announcement by USA Swimming that its investigation found no evidence of coach conduct code violations — yet Hutchison was choosing to resign from the excellence center leadership anyway. USA Swimming called the *Washington Post* rumors of an irregular coach-athlete relationship "malicious lies." Even so, Hutchison left not only FAST but the sport as a whole. He became an entrepreneur of medical infusion therapies. USA Swimming would officially ban him on October 5, 2018.

Not long after suing USA Swimming in his own employment dispute, Mark Schubert found himself on the other side in the same type of litigation. An assistant coach of his new club program sued *him*. That coach, Dia Rianda, helped expose swimming's culture of widespread abuse, and she went on to an activist role on behalf of reforms that have yet to be realized. It was the discovery in her case against Schubert that revealed his plot to spy on Hutchison and Kukors, as well as several offshoots of bad behavior by other USA Swimming officials. The full nature and history of this relationship between coach and star swimmer, however, wouldn't unfold publicly for another seven years.

Through it all, Chuck Wielgus and Susan Woessner were just two of the several officials in Colorado Springs who, while not themselves guilty of directly perpetrating abuse (though, as we'll see, there were plenty of that ilk at headquarters, too), landed squarely into membership in swimming's rogue's gallery of disgraced enablers.

≈

Mark Schubert stood alongside such figures as George Haines and James "Doc" Counsilman on the Mount Rushmore of American swimming coaches. Schubert was a titanic authority, the alpha male of a hitherto much more minor sport that by the 1980s had burgeoned into a multimillion-dollar industry. One of the many Olympic legends mentored by Schubert was Janet Evans, namesake of the Fullerton pool.

Schubert's Mission Viejo Nadadores in Southern California won 44 different forms of national championships between 1972 and 1985. According to his biography at the International Swimming Hall of Fame, Mission Viejo swimmers during this period captured 124 individual national championships, ten Olympic gold medals (plus six silvers and one bronze), five individual world championship titles, 88 American records, and 21 world records.

But the Nadadores' real breakthrough was their business model. Mission Viejo was where Schubert conceived and perfected a high-powered program with the resources and commitment to draw coveted aspiring teenage swimmers from far and wide. This was the first true "destination" club for which kids and their families abandoned home lives and schools elsewhere for the purpose of immersing themselves in the quest for Olympic glory. When Schubert started, barely more than 50 swimmers competed out of their Southern California pool. A decade later there were several hundred. The Nadadores' investors also established quasi-satellite programs in other locales.

Not coincidentally, this single-minded rush to athletic excellence and commerce would be joined to some of the most prominent cases of coach abuse. Across decades, "the Mark Schubert coaching tree" would be littered both with proven sexual predators and with what could only be termed the interstate trafficking of girl swimmers who became abuse victims.

In July 2011, with his $625,000 USA Swimming settlement in hand, Schubert set up shop as head coach of the Golden West Swim Club, out of the community college of the same name in Huntington Beach. He brought along his old majordomo Bill Jewell, the elderly former chief of the program in Fullerton. Shortly after helping Schubert pull off the detective agency investigation of Hutchison consorting with Kukors, Jewell had found himself out of a job, too, when FAST fired him. He was under investigation on Safe Sport charges, which involved improper touching and "massages" of female swimmers. (Claiming to be a victim of age discrimination, Jewell unsuccessfully sued FAST for wrongful termination.)

Additionally, Schubert hired Dia Rianda, a long-time coach in central California, for his Golden West staff. In the swimming world, Rianda was more than just a respected mentor at two high schools in Salinas, among other places. With her husband Mike Rianda, who'd built Coastal Tractor, a successful farm equipment supplier, she'd also engineered a half-million-dollar donation to Carmel High School toward the construction of its new pool. The couple donated many hundreds of thousands of dollars more to the USA Swimming Foundation. At Golden West, Dia Rianda soon concluded that it would be impossible to balance her coaching duties in Monterey County with her work for Schubert in Orange County. So she moved full-time to the Southland.

There, Rianda was horrified when she almost immediately witnessed or fielded from parents multiple fresh misconduct complaints about Jewell. (In all likelihood, few if any of the people in the Huntington Beach program were aware that there was an ongoing Safe Sport investigation of Jewell based on his previous tenure less than 20 miles up the road in Fullerton.) These included allegations of some of the identical misconduct reported at FAST — inappropriate touching and massages — and added a few more for good measure: charges that he was seen making out with a young female swimmer in a truck on the parking lot, and that his practice supervision was strewn with profanity and sexually charged remarks ("You have small breasts," he told one girl). Furthermore, Rianda learned, both Jewell and Schubert were giving some swimmers rides to practices; that was illegal.

Rianda brought the information to her boss in the expectation that Jewell would be removed. Instead, Schubert fired *her*. Rianda's subsequent lawsuit against Schubert settled in 2014. It included reports of alcohol consumption by underage swimmers at Golden West, plus other scandalous lapses. But by far the most significant information was the Horseman Investigations report on Hutchison and Kukors, and Schubert's role as its catalyst and as the leaker of its findings to the *Washington Post*. By the time *Rianda v. Schubert* settled, USA Swimming had already suspended Jewell for three years for Safe Sport violations.

≈

After the *Post* story, Ariana Kukors went on to win the 200-meter individual medley at the 2011 Worlds. At the 2012 London Olympics, she placed fifth in that event, barely missing the medal podium. The next year, she retired.

Early in 2018, as the USA Gymnastics scandals went into high gear, and with explosive congressional hearings swirling, Kukors chose her own website as the platform for sharing the full story of her grooming and abuse by Sean Hutchison. Her extended memoir began:

> Any swimmer will tell you about the black line on the bottom of every pool . . . the line that we follow day after day. We develop a relationship with that line; it holds our hopes and our dreams, but it also holds our fears. If only that black line could talk, it would tell you of my nightmare.
>
> To those in the swimming community, if you've heard the rumors about me, you may have been wondering if and when I'd find the courage to speak my truth.
>
> This is the truth.

Kukors discoursed about growing up outside Seattle, the middle of three water-crazy sisters, all of whom competed at Olympic Trials. Hers was a template of fleeting joy on a collision course with lasting damage. "When I was 13, just on the cusp of making the USA National Team, I was handed off to a new coach, Sean Hutchison. Sean was an up-and-coming coach with a great reputation and we were excited to have him at King Aquatic Club. He was personable, well-liked, charismatic, and an incredibly convincing leader. We hung onto every word he said."

In Kukors's account, Hutchison's grooming started on day one. The first step was mandatory handshakes with the coach after every practice, an initial hint of gratuitous body contact that would become routinized. Hutchison's hold over his female swimmers progressed to a ritual of being served coffee and a scone by them before early morning practice. When Ariana was 15, she got a cell phone, on which she and the coach began exchanging increasingly suggestive text messages. One day he approached her on the parking lot outside the Mt. Rainier pool and asked if she was wearing underwear.

From there, the post-race hugs "lasted just a little too long," Ariana recalled. When they were alone, he had her sit on his lap. He kissed her on elevators, touched her through her clothes, gave her a paper ring he'd made with the label "My beautiful Ari." He said he wanted to spend the rest of his life with her. He was 34 and she was 16 when their relationship, or whatever you called it, turned overtly sexual.

When Kukors graduated high school, Hutchison pressured her to stay close to home, at the University of Washington, and to continue to train with him. After one year, the Washington swim program was disbanded and she transferred to Chapman University in California. That state now became her swimming base. Reconnecting in training with the other top national swimmers under Hutchison when he got hired at FAST was a natural move.

Post-*Post*, during which time Kukors said she lied to a USA Swimming investigator in an interview that took just a few minutes, their time as a couple of sorts progressed with ugly turns. As Hutchison struggled to set up his new business, his finger-pointing at Kukors escalated over the demise of his swimming fortunes — as did his emotional manipulation of and control over her. From Olympic Village in London, she sent back home to her erstwhile coach the daily reports he demanded from his protégé. They were accompanied by nude photos, also mandatory.

In 2015 Kukors met her future husband, Matthew Smith. Her desire to unburden herself to him helped give her the courage to go public about Hutchison.

In May 2018, Kukors sued USA Swimming in Orange County Superior Court on counts of sexual abuse of a minor, negligence, and intentional infliction of emotional distress. The co-defendants were Hutchison, Schubert, Hutchison's holding company, and the regional

USA Swimming affiliates of King Aquatic. The next year, Schubert was dropped from the case, which proceeded against the others.[1]

The lawsuit settled two years later. The size of the monetary settlement, paid by USA Swimming and its insurer on behalf of all the defendants, wasn't disclosed. USA Swimming used the settlement announcement to tout a festival of abbreviations whose circularity defined self-parody: its Safe Sport Club Recognition Program (SSCRP), its Minor Athlete Abuse Prevention Policy (MAAPP), and the most recent creation, a $5 million Keeping Athletes First Action Plan (KAFAP). The latter included a "customer relations management" (CRM) system and the appointment of a Keeping Athletes First Working Group (KAFWG), tasked with coordinating with staff on "a five-year plan to lead future development and implementation of the initiative."

Meanwhile, multiple police entities investigated Hutchison for statutory rape and other crimes. The Department of Homeland Security was one of the agencies that raided his home in Washington State, where physical evidence was uncovered, including indecent photos of Kukors when she was underage. The efforts of law enforcement were hindered, sources close to the criminal investigation believe, by the fact that Dia Rianda, Mark Schubert's estranged assistant, had already filed a complaint against Hutchison with the new U.S. Center for Safe Sport. Tipped that he was "hot," Hutchison was nowhere to be found by the time police investigators got organized and obtained a search warrant for his home. (Sources believed he moved away for a time to Brazil.)

---

1   Among the allegations were that Schubert and other officials within the swimming bodies had conspired to protect Hutchison from a rigorous background check. Chapter 4 covers USA Swimming's background check shortcomings and ruses.

Ariana Kukors headlined the inaugural and dysfunctional session of USA Swimming's professional training center. Though her story was replicated many times over the years and since, Kukors was a unique case in the sense that, here, a coach's predation of a swimmer under his stewardship made its way into major media coverage while she was still an active star. Then her lawsuit laid out a public record, scant years after she left the sport; that, too, was an extraordinarily truncated exposure timeline.

If Kukors was the one who generated the FAST headlines, it was Dagny Knutson, a girl from Minot, North Dakota, who became the historical footnote of the "center of excellence."

Kukors was Exhibit 1 of the abuse and the damage done. Knutson was Exhibit 1-A: a victim of the more subtle pressures reflecting the same skewed priorities of organized swimming. These don't always take the form of sexual abuse per se.

Smart and talented — and unassuming, except in the water — Knutson in the late 2000s was American swimming's next ticketed female superstar, a seeming can't-miss successor to the line of Debbie Meyer, Janet Evans, Natalie Coughlin, and Summer Sanders. The capstone of Dagny's legendary junior career came in 2008, when at 16 she broke Katie Hoff's American record in the 400-yard individual medley. Her time, less than a second over four minutes, would stand as the national age-group standard for 14 years, a veritable eternity in this sport. In May of the following year, Knutson even bested Hoff, who swam at Michael Phelps's North Baltimore Aquatic Club and had won three medals at the Beijing Games, in the 400-meter freestyle at the Charlotte UltraSwim meet in North Carolina. Dagny made the U.S. team for the world championships, where she garnered a medal in a relay.

A *New York Times* article about this phenom noted that she soon faced a fork in the road of her Olympic ambitions: "Does she stay home and attend classes at a local college, turn professional and keep her inner circle intact? Or does she go away to college on a swimming scholarship?" The story added that her parents, Jim and Ronda, who could have been expected to be steering her, instead spoke as if they were "being towed by Knutson's ambition." Ronda, once an elite high school basketball player in Kentucky, had been a walk-on one year for the team at the University of Louisville; she mused to the *Times* reporter, Karen Crouse (herself a former elite swimmer), that she might have snared a Division I scholarship had she only enjoyed Dagny's drive and instincts. "I think Dagny passed me mentally and physically a long time ago. . . . I don't think [my parents and I back in the day] knew what it took."

Dagny at first chose a swimming scholarship at Auburn University. But USA Swimming officials, eager to lock down a dominant team fully prepared for 2012 in London, prevailed upon her to change course. They were opening the Fullerton excellence center and they preferred direct supervision of their emerging wunderkind. In deals brokered by Mark Schubert but later disavowed by USA Swimming, Knutson and another swimmer, Kate Ziegler, were promised that the organization would underwrite almost all their expenses. Dagny and her parents acceded. This was the era before NIL (name, image, likeness) revenue for amateurs. Turning pro meant Dagny could focus on her athletic career while holding out the promise of lucrative sponsorship deals.

The Fullerton decision proved disastrous, and not only because of the publicity and chaos surrounding Hutchison and Kukors. (The FAST excellence center would soon shut down.) In her first extended experience away from home, in a milieu of older young athletes, Knutson was a fish out of water. Friends said she was unnerved by the culture of sexual promiscuity among the swimmers there. She developed an eating disorder, which overwhelmed her in the months following her singular success in the pro ranks, a gold in the 400-meter freestyle relay at the 2011 Worlds in Shanghai. At one point she was hospitalized for bulimia.

At the same time, floods were devastating Minot, and Ronda and Jim Knutson ran up heavy debts to cover the expenses of their daughter's career launch. Wanting to revert to plan A, Dagny asked the NCAA to restore her amateur status. Her petition was denied. She retired from competitive swimming, briefly unretired, then retired for good and began coaching at a North Dakota high school at 21. Finally, in what was more a humanitarian gesture than a competitive maneuver, the swimming coach at Grand Canyon University in Phoenix, Steve Schaffer, went to bat for Dagny and got the NCAA to relent and permit the university to issue her a scholarship. She assisted on the Grand Canyon coaching staff and trained a bit, but never again made a splash in the swimming world.

Knutson filed a fraud lawsuit against Richard Foster, the lawyer who'd represented her in the collapsed deal with USA Swimming to cover her expenses. He was ordered to pay her $617,800 in restitution. Foster had long represented swimming in various matters, a conflict of interest he'd failed to disclose to Knutson. Bob Allard, Knutson's lawyer, also lodged an ethical misconduct complaint against Foster, and the California State Bar suspended Foster's law license for a year.

Like many young women, Dagny Knutson encountered watersheds of athletic accomplishment, as well as varied experiences away from the field, court, or pool. In every walk of life there are best-case and worst-case scenarios; there are both amateur passion and professional business. The problem with the youth swimming system is that it doesn't bother with youth-centered or even neutral guidance through this process. USA Swimming runs the show for elite athletes and for the hundreds of thousands of casual ones alike; the latter are far more indispensable than the public realizes, for they provide the economies of scale to fill out the lineup cards for weekend meets and keep the water desalination equipment operating. For swimming's power players, the whole superstructure is nothing more or less than a U.S. Olympics vessel. Sifting through Knutson's choices, you could fairly reach the conclusion that organized swimming failed her as much as it did Ariana Kukors. Knutson didn't endure known sexual abuse. What she did suffer from was a scarcity of balanced values.

In one interpretation, she had a gift, which in the end cursed as much as blessed her. She positioned herself to play the system, by the rules laid out for her and with eyes wide open, and for random reasons fell short of the success she sought.

In the alternate interpretation, Dagny Knutson was a ripple in life's pool of damaged American girls — aspiring Olympians or collegiate stars or not — who were burdened daily and similarly by a system that elevates commercial goals over humanistic and developmental ones. Swimming failed them. It fails all of us.

CHAPTER 2

THE REST OF THE STORY

The Ariana Kukors narrative was powerful and damning. In terms of USA Swimming's history of abuse, most especially the ham-handed and willfully ineffective corporate measures to mitigate it, the most important aspects of her lawsuit were the dominoes. The larger problem implied by her public testimony and lawsuit long predated Kukors and Sean Hutchison; and in its aftermath, no avalanche of court claims and insurance adjusters could significantly stem it.

Mark Schubert's predecessor as national team director had been Everett Uchiyama, a coach from California. But Uchiyama never got a chance to coach at the 2008 Summer Olympics. The reason that opportunity came about for Schubert, instead, was that a former club swimmer, Tracy Palmero, contacted USA Swimming on January 24, 2006, with allegations that when she was 16 years old, some 16 years earlier, Uchiyama had committed sex acts with her when he coached her age-group program. It took all of three days for Uchiyama to tender his resignation. The Colorado Springs pooh-bahs didn't publicize Uchiyama's sacking — indeed, Chuck Wielgus didn't even tip the board of directors in advance.

The key passage of the severance agreement was its hush clause: "USA Swimming agrees that in consideration of the promises and commitments made by Uchiyama it will not move forward with any further investigation into the allegations set forth."

Through the same period, Uchiyama's wife Helen also held down a job at USA Swimming, as a field services assistant on the staff of Pat Hogan, the club development director. That was just the start of Hogan's largesse toward the Uchiyamas. Wanting to stay in the area after USA Swimming bounced him, Everett applied for a new job at the Country Club of Colorado, all of five miles from USA Swimming headquarters at 1 Olympic Plaza. Interviewed by the country club's Rose Snyder as part of the vetting, Hogan whole-heartedly endorsed Uchiyama, calling him a "great people person," according to the notes from Snyder's interview of Hogan, which later surfaced in litigation. Rose Snyder was a swimming coach and administrator who held various leadership positions at USA Swimming over the years. Her husband, Charlie Snyder, was the organization's communications director from 1990 to 2000.

In that character reference interview, Hogan graded Uchiyama's attendance on the job as "acceptable." Same for his "dependability," "initiative," and "ability to get along." Why did Uchiyama leave USA Swimming? Hogan was asked. "Personal choice."

The paperwork was vague as to the position for which Uchiyama was being vetted. Desk clerk? Towel boy? What's known is that within a year he was the country club's aquatics director. In that job, he enjoyed a franchise in the American Swimming Coaches Association's "SwimAmerica" program.[1]

Because of the Country Club of Colorado's convenient location and well-equipped business center, USA Swimming regularly used it for board meetings. On January 23, 2010, and again on May 1, 2010, directors gathered in the country club conference room could gaze

---

[1] Chapter 12 explores the special ways the American Swimming Coaches Association (ASCA) — a trade group separate from USA Swimming – has performed troubleshooting and kept some of the sport's most notorious abusers gainfully employed in the aquatics industry.

down through the window to the pool below — either unaware or not caring that their disgraced former national team coach had effortlessly slid over to running the show there.

In late May 2010, with the *Colorado Springs Gazette* closing in on coverage of the whole sordid affair, Everett Uchiyama resigned from the country club. Three years later, I asked Rose Snyder about Uchiyama's soft landing there. She began our email exchange platitudinously: "My heart and focus has always been on the grassroots of swimming. We need to work together to improve not only our sport, but all sports to make them a safe place for our children."

I asked Snyder if she'd been duped by USA Swimming's Pat Hogan. She replied: "Everett was hired for the position of Desk Attendant and per the HR required procedures, Pat Hogan was contacted as a reference. I left in early summer of 2007. I'm not certain what happened after that or when Everett was made Aquatics Director. To say 'duped' would infer that Pat Hogan knew about Everett's reason for leaving USA Swimming and I just don't know if that was the case."

≈

Pat Hogan offered up his own case study in both sexual abuse and swimming's indefatigable logrolling to cover it up. As a coach for the Dynamos club in Atlanta, Hogan first started dating a girl named Julie Ginden Sears when she was in high school. They married when he was in his late 20s and she was 18. Her father was a banker, and Hogan worked for a time as a branch manager for First Atlanta Bank. At the 1983 Junior Nationals in Indianapolis, Hogan was involved in a murky incident with one of his swimmers. Traumatized — sources close to the swimmer say she was sexually assaulted — the girl abruptly scratched all her events.

Like historical abuser Mitch Ivey (about whom more later), Hogan had a stint coaching at Trinity Prep in Winter Haven, Florida;

both of their jobs were likely arranged by John Leonard, the American Swimming Coaches Association boss. In Ivey's case, it was part of ASCA's efforts on his behalf in the wake of his dismissal by the University of Florida in 1993 on the eve of a report by ESPN about his serial abuse of swimmers there. When Hogan's wife, eventually ex-wife, Julie was coaching at Jacksonville Episcopal High School in the 2000s, she lined up Ivey as an unpaid assistant. This arrangement suited Ivey, who was trying to duck child support payments for the twin children he had with one of his abuse victims.

With Mitch Ivey, as with Everett Uchiyama and others, and like John Leonard, Pat Hogan always had a soft spot for colleagues who he thought had gotten raw deals from the abuse police crowd. Hogan, it seems, was the original "great people person."

And Hogan's modus operandi was part of the culture at USA Swimming headquarters of turning a blind eye to such scandals. Not even the very community in which its office dwelled was exempt from this disinterest in protecting children — as could be seen in the case of Hogan's predecessor as club development director, Will Colebank.

In 1998 Colebank was fired and secretly ushered out of the building, and his office computer was locked down. In the first public accounting for this incident some 16 years later, USA Swimming said in a statement that it had "terminated" Colebank "for improper communications with a male athlete and having pornographic images on his USA Swimming computer." The full story: Colebank was smitten with a 12-year-old male swimmer at a swimming camp, with whom he took up a lurid email correspondence. At that time, Colebank was 46 years old.

Swimming authorities disclosed none of this. As a result, Colebank soon found a new job — as a teacher at Carmel Middle School in Colorado Springs.

In 2007 Colebank's wife and son informed on his multitude of ongoing sex crimes. Police in Woodland Park, the Colorado Springs suburb where they lived, investigated. On October 31, the police told the Harrison School District, which compelled Colebank to resign. He was arrested five days later. In 2008 he was convicted on a felony count of promotion of obscenity to a minor, and in 2009, on one of sexual exploitation of a child. Colebank's wife had told police she came across a bag of disturbing CDs in the trunk of the family's Hyundai. She explained that she routinely searched the car at intervals for contraband alcohol (Will was an alcoholic as well as a generally troubled individual). The disks contained pornographic images of males in sex acts, some appearing to be as young as six. Discovering that his material was missing on a weekend when his wife and son were out of town, Colebank abruptly moved out of the family house.

In its 2014 statement, USA Swimming said it "followed the law and was not a mandatory reporter under Colorado law" in 1998. "However, if faced with similar circumstances today, USA Swimming would handle this differently and report [the Colebank conduct giving rise to his firing] to law enforcement."

≈

In the months prior to Kukors's 2018 lawsuit over Hutchison, attorney Bob Allard cleared out some of this underbrush. In February, he confronted USA Swimming with evidence that Susan Woessner, its founding director of Safe Sport, had herself had a relationship with Hutchison. This aligned with my own information from two separate sources inside the organization.

"We are hereby demanding that you fire Susan Woessner and Pat Hogan immediately," Allard wrote to Wielgus's successor as USA Swimming chief executive, Tim Hinchey, and to chief counsel Lucinda McRoberts. (Chuck Wielgus died of cancer in 2017, after 20 years on the job.) "They both have major blood on their hands as the information I am hereby sending to you makes clear. Further, based on information which has recently been made available to us, Susan Woessner was presented with about as clear a conflict of interest as it gets when she oversaw the investigation into Sean Hutchison in 2010–11. I will let you ask her what this information is and see if she tells you the truth. Suffice it to say, she has an intimately personal relationship with the very person who was being investigated. If Susan does not tell you the truth about this, I suggest you give her a lie detector test. . . . Multiple writers are actively looking into [the] gathering evidence."

Woessner hadn't directly conducted the 2010–11 investigation occasioned by the *Washington Post* story. That was the task of Paulette Brundage, a 27-year veteran of the FBI. Brundage was one of the bevy of retired FBI agents who double-dipped on their G-person pensions with freelance consultancies for USA Swimming. (In almost all cases, their exquisitely legalistic findings amounted to internal plumbing operations more than information useful to the public in cleaning up the mess of coach sexual abuse in youth sports.) But, of course, the report that Woessner had slept with the subject of her department's very first major controversy made for horrible optics.

On the Indiana University swimming team, one of Woessner's best friends had been Brooke Taflinger, who wound up fingering coach Brian Hindson for his creepiness in Kokomo, up to and through the Peeping Tom locker room cameras that landed him in jail. Another Woessner friend was Taflinger's boyfriend at the time, Jon Little, a track and field distance runner who would become an attorney.

Woessner's ineffectiveness in fighting abuse from her inside leadership role — and worse, her corruption as an official enabler of systematic misconduct — broke the hearts of her ex-friends. Her decisions didn't do competitive swimming's hundreds of thousands of families much good, either. Like Everett Uchiyama, Woessner played the nepotism game skillfully: her sister Geri also got hired by USA Swimming, in the marketing department. Indeed, it was sometimes hard to tell where Susan's Safe Sport work ended and Geri's brand polishing began.

For anyone paying attention, Woessner's conflict in the Hutchison matter was only the most dramatic proof that the USA Swimming Safe Sport program was a fraud. Prior to her appointment, informants reporting abuse used to be screened by Chuck Wielgus's secretary. All Woessner really did was serve as the new glorified and dedicated secretary for such complaints. Additionally, she was the pretty face of USA Swimming's representation at academic conferences and public forums contemplating the child abuse problem and the boogeyman in our midst. An example was her attendance at the 2013 "Safe to Compete" conference in Baltimore — organized by former baseball great Cal Ripken and hosted by the National Center for Missing and Exploited Children — while at the same time she said nothing about the emerging scandal of the alleged predation of a swimmer by famous Baltimore swimming coach Murray Stephens.[2]

Woessner and the others at the conference were most interested in promoting awareness of "stranger danger" in youth-serving programs. This approach gave short shrift to the actual dynamic of the specific phenomenon of swimming coach abuse. That was, most typically, perpetrated by a familiar figure — an athletic supervisor who might even be a family confidante — with profound day-to-day authority over the victim.

Whenever USA Swimming staged its own similar conferences, Woessner's sidekicks on panels would often be FBI agents — perhaps chasing the prospect of their own post-retirement gigs as trusted

2   Chapter 8 has more on the North Baltimore Aquatic Club.

investigators for the organization, in the footsteps of former agents like Paulette Brundage.

Records in lawsuits make abundantly clear the paucity of Woessner's substantive role. A year after she started, for example, she had this less-than-coherent breakdown of what she did every day in a deposition in the "Jane Doe" case involving the monster coach Andy King:

> [My work] does vary by what the substance of the complaint is about, because I — I get a wide range of things. What I generally try — it really does depend on what the complaint is. But I try to — I'm trying to best describe it — figure out if there's additional people I should talk to, if they're — it's kind of my job to — well, let me start over.
>
> I guess I try to figure out what the next step is, if that makes any sense, because there's several next steps possible. But ultimately if there does appear — I try to gather enough information to determine if there's been a violation of Code of Conduct or not. I — I let Chuck know, per our rulebook, the executive director is notified.
>
> And then if — if we have enough information to look like there needs to be an investigation or there are people to talk to relative to an investigation, we — we go forward with that process.

English translation: Both before and after there was a Safe Sport director, USA Swimming's chief executive, and the chief executive alone, decided whether a complaint rose to the level of being assigned to an investigator. And both before and after the appointment of the Safe Sport director, the chief executive, and the chief executive alone, decided whether that investigation would, in turn, get handed off to the National Board of Review for a disciplinary hearing and disposition.

Three days after Allard challenged USA Swimming on Woessner's ethics, she quit. Like Bill Clinton with Monica Lewinsky, Woessner went to pains to assure the public that she did not have sex with that man.

"While I normally consider my personal life to be private," her resignation letter read, "it is in the interest of full disclosure that I describe an incident from eleven years ago." Back in 2007, she admitted, "I engaged in kissing on a single occasion with then-coach, Sean Hutchison. I have never had sex with Sean Hutchison. I have never had a sexual or romantic relationship of any kind at any time with any USA Swimming coach, including Sean Hutchison."

For good measure in response to Allard's information on a range of USA Swimming figures, the organization threw in Pat Hogan's dismissal, too.

But the saga of swimming's rotten core was just diving in.

CHAPTER 3

SARAH EHEKIRCHER

She was a talented enough teen swimmer, specializing in breast-stroke, to earn an athletic scholarship at the University of Arkansas. Later she had a long career as a club coach, before the sport's politics and retaliation for her whistleblowing took a toll there, too.

Before all that, Sarah Ehekircher was a kid rendered homeless — thrown out on the street by the two adults in charge of raising her. Her coach leveraged his power over her when he moved her into his place, groomed her, and raped her. His abuse unfurled and reso-nated across seven years.

Sarah's personal story was bone-chilling enough. But what makes her biography especially valuable are the connections from it to almost every single motif of the corruption of the youth swim-ming system and the harm it inflicts on kids, especially girls. Her abusive coach, James Scott MacFarland, came out of the coaching staff and philosophy of Mark Schubert's Mission Viejo Nadadores in their heyday. Along the way, she knew dozens of coaches and swimmers in that orbit, and she witnessed a lot of the worst done to others, as well as to herself.

When USA Swimming chief Chuck Wielgus launched his bogus Safe Sport department in 2010, Sarah was one of the first to file a complaint. Swimming's subsequent National Board of Review hearing on the MacFarland allegations was a kangaroo court stacked against the accuser. At least one prominent coach, likely protecting his own business interests, stayed silent about the MacFarland-Ehekircher history he'd personally observed — through one period, at intimate range.

In 2018, after the start-up of the U.S. Center for Safe Sport, Sarah attempted to reopen the matter administratively and thereby find a belated measure of justice and accountability. She got stonewalled again. The processing of her information exposed both her case worker and the case worker's superior, the center's ill-defined "director of legal affairs," as irresponsible custodians of their putative mission, but more than that, as out-and-out con artists. Lying about its information on Sarah's age at the time MacFarland first had sex with her, Safe Sport also helped shut down a police department's statutory rape investigation.

To cap off her fiction-defying experiences, in and out of the water, Sarah even had a brief and disastrous stint working on the staff of swimming's defiant abuse apologist-in-chief, John Leonard, at the American Swimming Coaches Association in Florida.

If the saga of sex crimes and their cover-ups inside swimming were ever made into a movie, Sarah Ehekircher would be its Zelig. Or maybe its Forrest Gump.

≈

In a 2020 first-person article for Britain's *Guardian* newspaper, published to coincide with the filing of a lawsuit against USA Swimming (which, as of the writing of this book, remained ongoing), Sarah described growing up in Aurora, Colorado, a Denver suburb, and beginning to swim competitively in 1981, just before her 13th birthday. Early the next year her mother died of cancer, and "family life was turned upside down as my father's drinking became more than just a couple scotches each night, which was the beginning of the disconnect between the two of us. He barely noticed as I progressed rapidly through the levels of the team, putting me in the same group with swimmers who had been in the pool since they were five or six years old."

All young Sarah could think about was the Olympics. But when she was a high school junior, Mr. Ehekircher, by then remarried, tried to get her to cut back on swimming, with the edict that she needed to concentrate on schoolwork. That wasn't going to happen. One day he showed up at the pool and pulled her out of practice. He forbade her to go to the next morning's practice. Sarah went anyway. "I was more afraid of the swimming coach than I was of my father," she explained. When she got back to the house, she found that dad and stepmom had deposited all her things on the lawn and the door locks had been changed.

Sarah Ehekircher, age 17, had been kicked out of home.

For three weeks, she stayed with the family of a girlfriend. Then her coach, who was 34 years old, moved Sarah into his one-bedroom apartment.

The local team Scott MacFarland ran was called Mission Viejo Colorado. It had been launched by former executives of Schubert's club in California, who in a burst of sports entrepreneurism sought to export the Mission Viejo brand and model. (A similar nearby club in Highlands Ranch was coached by Matt Beck, who would land on USA Swimming's banned list.) Decades later, Sarah's lawsuit would name the Mission Viejo Nadadores as a co-defendant along with MacFarland and USA Swimming. The moral, if not rigorously legal, link was that MacFarland had learned to coach under Schubert, and did everything the Schubert and Mission Viejo way. Pointedly, this blueprint featured no policy or prohibition regarding coach sex with their young athletes.[1] For MacFarland, what might be most defining was that it never seemed an option for him simply to notify Child Protective Services that a juvenile he knew was having trouble at home.

In Sarah's own words in the *Guardian*:

> At first the arrangement was only emotionally abusive. He kept a scale in the kitchen and would have me weigh myself before I ate. He would put his hands around my arms to measure them and tell me how weak I was and would call me 'pooey.' After practice, he would then make me ride the stationary bike in the house for at least two hours.

The crossover from mere emotional abuse to the physical kind happened in July 1986, when a group from MacFarland's Colorado team flew to a 13-and-older meet in California. Sarah and a girl teammate shared a room at an Irvine motel. The other girl returned home a day early. Ostensibly to save money, MacFarland moved himself into Sarah's room for the last night. That's when, she said, he raped her the first time. This event carried special freight, since the age of consent, demarcating statutory rape, was 17 in Colorado but 18 in California; Sarah wouldn't turn 18 until December. Therefore, even if their sex had a smidgen of consent — which Sarah emphatically insisted was not the case — it was illegal.

The two went on to live together, on and off, in three states. After graduating high school, Sarah moved to California for the summer

---

1   The ambiguous (at best) practice of coaches driving swimmers to practice was an especially useful tip MacFarland had picked up in Mission Viejo. A legendary junior swimmer from the Nadadores who held a national age group record later read about Sarah Ehekircher's misfortunes with MacFarland, recalled her own time of being driven to practices by him, and "connected some dots," according to a coach who spoke with a close friend of the Mission Viejo star.

and competed for Swim San Diego's coach, Rick Shipherd, but she was soon back in Colorado. Since there would be nothing approaching a reckoning for the Irvine rape for many years, her first intensely conjoined crisis with MacFarland could be said to be her first pregnancy, which evidenced itself when she was a freshman at the University of Arkansas. During holiday training camp, the Arkansas coach sent Sarah home, and she got an abortion. The time off derailed her collegiate career. (She continued competing for clubs until she was 24.)

In May 1988, Sarah headed to the Fullerton Aquatic Swim Team under Bud McAlister, where she was a teammate of all-time great Janet Evans. Back in Colorado, MacFarland impregnated her again and there was a second abortion. In the fall of 1989, Sarah went off on her own again, this time to the Santa Barbara Swim Club of coach Larry Liebowitz. The next summer, during another California interlude, she started dating another swimmer. By early 1990 she was living with MacFarland yet again.

"Stockholm Syndrome," Sarah said, citing the term used to explain the self-destructive pattern of victims' attachments to their abusers.

Later in 1990, MacFarland sent Sarah off to his friends Bob and Kathy Gillette, who ran the Arizona Sports Ranch, a sprawling program including a youth swimming camp. Within a few months, Sarah landed a job at a restaurant and had her own apartment. The next year, when MacFarland got fired from his coaching post in Colorado, he relocated to Arizona himself to work under the Gillettes, and he and Sarah dwelled in the same rented house there, though they led mostly separate lives.

That fall MacFarland was hired by the Charlottesville YMCA Aquatic Club in Virginia. He got a trailer there and Sarah moved across the country with him. Also migrating to the Charlottesville staff from the Arizona Sports Ranch was a coach named Tim Bauer, and he moved into the trailer, too — MacFarland and Sarah in one bedroom, Bauer in the other. In subsequent investigations of MacFarland, Bauer would disclaim any knowledge of whether his trailermates lived together as a couple or had sex — as if there were no plausible standard of inference short of directly inspecting them in the act. Later a member of the USA Swimming board of directors, Bauer was only the most intimate of the many observers of Ehekircher-MacFarland scenarios who never helped Sarah in her complaints about MacFarland's abuse, because doing so might have harmed their business interests.

After an interlude in Colorado Springs, Sarah moved back into MacFarland's Charlottesville trailer. That was the year, 1993, she met and married another coach. Throughout that decade and the next, the abuse fallout rippled in suicide attempts, an ugly divorce, custody fights over their two children. Abuse survivors seldom pivot on a dime to healthy behavior. More often, they replicate and cycle the worst parts of what happened to them before.

≈

In April 2010, Sarah watched the investigative report on ABC's *20/20* about the widespread problem of swim coach abuse. "I said to myself, 'Thank God, someone is finally going to do something.' People were talking now. I felt it was safe for me to talk, as well."

She emailed Chuck Wielgus, USA Swimming's executive director, just as Wielgus (in response to the horrible publicity from *20/20*, which was worsened by his own halting and defensive interview denying the existence of a problem) was announcing the new Safe Sport program. To Sarah, Wielgus expressed concern, whether genuine or feigned. On April 22, 2010, he emailed her:

> Sarah - my gosh - your letter touches me in so many ways and while I [am] neither a lawyer or a counselor, I do think that you absolutely should be talking

with experienced professionals. I am currently out of the country, but am compelled to at the very least acknowledge that I have received your message and want to assure you that USA Swimming will [cooperate] and work with you in the most appropriate way possible. I am copying our legal counsel, Rich Young to make him aware of this and to help us determine what is the best way to move forward. I will be back in Colorado Springs on Monday and you should certainly feel free to call me.

On September 15, 2010, an evening during the national aquatics convention in Dallas, swimming's National Board of Review held a hearing on Sarah's complaint against MacFarland. It was a farce. MacFarland was "prosecuted" by one of USA Swimming's own lawyers, Jennifer Bielak. Sarah wasn't allowed to have a lawyer. The board chair was John Morse, a lawyer for the midwestern Drury Hotels chain. Young Indianapolis attorney Jon Little, the former Indiana University track athlete who was just getting started with a career largely focused on representing abuse survivors, was permitted to sit in as an observer but not to formally represent Sarah — by, for example, interjecting procedural objections. (At that point Little had determined that he couldn't file a court claim on Sarah's behalf since, under the California law of the time, the statute of limitations had expired on MacFarland's 1986 rape.)

Sarah: "I testified for five hours, with only one short break, from 5:00 until past 10:00 p.m. I felt totally revictimized, like I was the one on trial. They plowed through my credit reports, they turned old friends against me. Jennifer Bielak was antagonistic toward me; she didn't care about my interests."

The crux of the review board's decision not to find MacFarland guilty of code-of-conduct violations was their contention that they couldn't penetrate his denial of the 1986 Irvine incident. MacFarland conceded that he'd had sex with Sarah on multiple occasions, but insisted that not one of those times was in California. And until 2013, USA Swimming's code didn't altogether ban coach-athlete sex.[2] This rationalized an inability to nail MacFarland on anything other than a possible offense under the California criminal code.

The organization amassed hundreds of pages of documents in connection with the investigation but refused to release any of them, even to the complainant. Much later I'd acquire, from a USA Swimming source, an email from review board chair Morse in which he reflected on the MacFarland decision, which was issued on October 7, 2010. Morse wrote:

> The panel struggled with this matter for some time. We have tried our best to do the "right thing" by all parties involved (including Ms. Ehekircher). Because most of the events at issue here took place about 20 years ago and documentation that might otherwise be available in a case about conduct which happened a year ago, for example, has long ago become unavailable, several critical factual issues suffered. Given that the burden of proof in these matters falls on the Petitioner, this ultimately worked to Petitioner's (and the victim's) disadvantage. Although the conduct of Respondent in this matter left a lot to be desired and represented poor judgment at best (and no doubt caused Ms. Ehekircher pain and emotional damage), the Board could not find that Petitioner met its burden of proof to the preponderance of the evidence standard required.

---

2   Chapter 4 discusses the bad faith behind so much of the evolution of aquatics convention legislation to fill in this and other loopholes.

≈

In April 2018, with youth coach sexual abuse stories now au courant in major news media, Sarah Ehekircher finally found an outlet for hers at a place with greater circulation than my own website and the wide-ranging podcast of a dissident swimming coach, Chris DeSantis. At that time, MacFarland was still coaching, for the Magnolia Aquatic Club in Houston. On its website, the *Houston Chronicle* published an article with Sarah's story of MacFarland's abuse. Within hours after posting the story, the *Chronicle* pulled it, never to be seen again (except perhaps by some sleuth of the future at the Internet Archive's Wayback Machine who unearths ghost pages for history). I read the account during its blink-of-an-eye live cyber moment, and I challenged *Chronicle* editors on its takedown. Needless to add, the *Chronicle* print edition never published it.

Which is not to suggest that it didn't still get results. On April 16, the Magnolia club released a statement: "Coach MacFarland decided to retire from coaching and submitted his resignation. We accepted his letter of resignation and we wish Coach Scott well in this new chapter of his life."

Seeking an official banishment of MacFarland from the sport — as well as a correction of the hideous 2010 USA Swimming hearing, along with access to its transcript and other records — Sarah filed a complaint against him with the U.S. Center for Safe Sport. The investigator assigned to her case, Kathleen Smith, was later confirmed to be a lawyer. After receiving the details by email, Smith instructed Sarah to meet her for an intake interview — not at the center offices in Denver, but rather at another address in Denver. That turned out to be the office of the Zonies law firm, which counseled the Olympic Committee and its entities on various matters.

The center's deception got worse. In the email to Sarah, Smith also wrote, "I just wanted to let you know that another member of the Response and Resolution team, Michael Henry, will be joining our meeting tomorrow. We try to have a second person whenever possible to help with note-taking and any miscellaneous things that may need to be done."

Later it would be easy to determine that Michael Henry, Smith's supposed gopher or man Friday for the intake interview, was actually the head of the U.S. Center for Safe Sport investigations division. Indeed, Henry was the center's highest-paid employee, according to its Internal Revenue Service nonprofit filings; in 2019 he enjoyed a salary of $148,938, supplemented by "bonus & incentive compensation" of $69,985. When convenient, Henry called himself "Director, Investigations & Outcomes." From time to time, his email signature upgraded that to "Director of Legal Affairs," though the center would deny that he ever held that title. (This director of legal affairs — or not — completed law school but never passed a state bar law exam or obtained a license to practice law.)

The interview of Sarah was something of a "bad cop / bad cop" routine. Sarah said Henry and Smith sandbagged and double-teamed her. She didn't have her own lawyer present, only a sympathetic coach from the area who was there to offer some moral support. The coach was utterly ineffective in keeping Henry and Smith in line. In violation of every best practice handbook for agencies said to exist to support the claims of abuse survivors, the two Safe Sport investigators aggressively cross-examined Sarah about every aspect of her personal life, before, during, and after MacFarland's alleged misconduct. They also audio-recorded the interview and refused to give Sarah a copy — or any records from USA Swimming's National Board of Review.

In the end, the U.S. Center for Safe Sport simply rubber-stamped the findings eight years earlier of USA Swimming's review board. Scott MacFarland wasn't sanctioned.

Michael Henry went on to get pushed out of Safe Sport after a scandal broke in 2019 of a cyber hack of the center's complaint database. Little wonder there was a problem with information security, since the computer server was housed in the office kitchen, where all employees moved in and out, fetching lunch from the refrigerator. This incident was typical of the Safe Sport center's embarrassingly unprofessional operation.

The next year, Henry was shown the door and he fell upward. Today he's chief of the federal courts' Office of Judicial Integrity.

≈

By 2020, despite lobbying by both USA Swimming and the Catholic Church, new legislation in California had opened a window for abuse survivors to enter civil claims that were earlier barred under the statute of limitations. Represented by Jon Little, Sarah filed her lawsuit, in the same California court as Ariana Kukors's and alleging the same counts of sexual abuse of a minor, negligence, and intentional infliction of emotional distress. A footnote of the complaint stated: "Plaintiff is not asserting that Mark Schubert molested any underage swimmers; just that he actively participated in the cover-up of several sexual abuse allegations of other coaches and swimmers."

By then, Sarah's own coaching career was in ruins, thanks to the trolling and smears of a Colorado woman, Tanya Birch, who'd also swum under MacFarland many years earlier. As we'll see, Birch's family ties in swimming were, to put it charitably, less than pure as the driven Rocky Mountain snow.

In 2018 I got an email from a camouflage "burner" account, "subrown@usa.com." The sender called herself Susan Brown. She said she was a Colorado swim parent who was disgusted by my championing of Sarah Ehekircher's story. With shaky literacy, Susan Brown's message asserted that "there isn't many in USA Swimming that feels any sympathy for . . . a middle aged woman now 30 yrs later acting like a scorned woman intent on destroying her former coach. If you ask around USA swimming, Ehekircher doesn't have many friends or even people who respect her. You will find many people who have seen how evil and vicious [*sic*]."

I soon figured out that "Susan Brown" was Tanya Birch. She didn't respond when I confronted her with this finding, in messages sent to both her and her brother through normal email addresses.

Brown/Birch's poison pen further advised me to direct my attention to Sarah's own alleged abusive coaching behavior at the Rocky Mountain Thunder club in the Denver suburb of Lakewood. Birch's relentless smear campaign in the local swimming community decimated the membership ranks of the team, which collapsed. This was Sarah's last job in the industry.

Birch's brother, meanwhile, was a coach in Florida — Todd Hoffmeier, owner of the Greater Tampa Swim Association. Here's where, as with all the tentacles of Sarah Ehekircher's sad tale, the scandals gain viscosity. In July 2019, Hoffmeier hired for his staff Linck Bergen, son of Hall of Fame coach Paul Bergen, whose molestation of eventual gold medalist Deena Deardurff was featured in the 2010 report on ABC's *20/20*.[3] Linck Bergen had recently been fired by the Tualatin Hills club in Oregon, without public explanation; the backstory was that he'd been smuggling drugs from Norway. Barely a month after he started in Tampa, both Bergen and his wife Michelle were arrested on charges of possession of methamphetamines and drug paraphernalia. The drug charge being a high-end Class 3 felony in that jurisdiction, Hoffmeier fired Bergen. In the aftermath, another coach, Ryan Gober, left for another team, and Hoffmeier sued Gober for allegedly violating a non-compete clause in their agreement. Bitter business litigation ensued.

---

3   Paul Bergen appears throughout the book, including Chapter 11, which is dedicated to his history.

Gober also coached at the University of Tampa. The university started receiving email complaints about Gober's conduct. His lawyer, Nathan McCoy, shared the emails with me.

The sender of some of them was "subrown@usa.com" — Todd Hoffmeier's sister and Sarah Ehekircher's poison-pen tormentor.

≈

"In the swimming community, especially in those days, everyone talked about which coach was sleeping with which swimmer," Sarah recalled. "These were open secrets. Where there was abuse involved, it was obvious in retrospect that the coaches doing the abuse knew where to spot vulnerability in their victims."

In California and throughout the country, dozens of lawsuits put swimming abuse in the headlines. In an attempt to forestall or mitigate litigation, USA Swimming set up a program (half-heartedly publicized, at best) called Swim Assist, which was designed to help underwrite therapy and treatment for ex-athletes claiming to be coach abuse survivors. Though Swim Assist's literature advertised that pay-outs to individuals were capped at $9,000, USA Swimming discreetly sent Sarah to two separate treatment programs, one in Texas and one in Arizona, at a total cost of more than $100,000. (In Arizona, Sarah had another nightmarish experience of what she described as *abuse at the treatment clinic* — that's a whole other story.)

No chronicle of Sarah Ehekircher's extraordinary times in and out of the water — both as a victim of swimming's crimes and as a bystander on life's pool deck of outrages — would be complete without covering an episode more than a decade after she'd finally wrenched herself free of Scott MacFarland.

In 2003, Sarah, by now an accomplished coach, was encouraged to apply for a position as director of SwimAmerica, the nation-ally marketed learn-to-swim program of the American Swimming

Coaches Association. The ASCA boss, John Leonard, was introduced in the previous chapter; there will be a lot more to say about him throughout this book. Though USA Swimming has been negligent for decades in its protection of youth athletes, it was Leonard, of the coaches' trade group, who earned the undisputed gold medal for being the most pernicious voice of authority in discussions of the abuse issue.

More than anyone, both while serving on swimming industry task forces and in public statements, Leonard downplayed the idea that any sort of extra-administrative discretion should be applied to the standards of a youth-serving organization. Leonard advocated only criminal "beyond a reasonable doubt" criteria for whether coaches accused of abuse should be blocked from certification or, at a later point, considered for expulsion. Preferably, there had to be actual criminal charges and convictions — and even then, through Leonard's patronage, there might still be customized paths for remaining active in the sport. When some coaches did get banned or shadow-banned by USA Swimming, Leonard kept several prominent ones in gainful employment, through ASCA consultancies, via troubleshooting to facilitate coaching positions abroad, and the like.

In 2012, Leonard emailed me:

> ASCA is a **voluntary** membership organization.
>
> We have no investigatory powers, funds, or responsibility.
>
> USA-Swimming is required membership for anyone who coaches a USA-Swimming team.
>
> They have "control power" over who can coach in their organization.
>
> We do not have an organization that deals directly with children, nor is that part of our purpose in any

way, shape or form, according to our formative documents from 1958 and thereafter.

Casual observers could be excused for wondering where USA Swimming ended and ASCA began. Confusion as to the ways ASCA was relied on for vetting coaches compelled the issuance of a "frequently asked questions" document circulated to USA Swimming board members. Question No. 12 riddled: "Why does coaches' education certification channel through ASCA?" The answer was: "USA Swimming has established certain requirements for coach members. These requirements include maintaining current safety certifications, passing regular background checks and Safe Sport training, and meeting a minimum education requirement. The required 'Foundations of Coaching' basic education course has been jointly developed by USA Swimming and ASCA. Similarly, we have partnered with outside experts like the American Red Cross and Praesidium to deliver appropriate safety certification and athlete protection programs. ASCA provides numerous coach education opportunities and a voluntary coach's certification program which compliment [*sic*] USA Swimming resources. We encourage coaches to take advantage of multiple educational avenues."

Not surprisingly, Sarah Ehekircher's experience illustrated that Leonard's own office practices included creepiness parallel to his disclaimers of responsibility for sexual misconduct.

"The way he latched onto me during the job application process for SwimAmerica was absolutely chilling and disturbing," she said. "I honestly had the impression that he thought he was doing more than hiring a staffer. He was 'hiring' a new wife."

Sarah met Leonard at a clinic in California and he invited her out for drinks. Throughout the months they spent time together, both before and during her ASCA employment, she said he "told strange, dark anecdotes of his exploits in Vietnam. He said he'd been a sniper with over 100 kills. How I came to process this was that it was his way of impressing and intimidating."

(In 2012 Leonard was deposed during Jancy Thompson's lawsuit against USA Swimming over her abuse by coach Norm Havercroft. There, Leonard admitted that he served in the Army Reserve, never set foot in Vietnam, and was never a sniper.)

Sarah brought up to Leonard her grooming and abuse at the hands of MacFarland. Leonard was unsympathetic; he betrayed no inkling of a sentiment that the events she described were anything out of the norm. "He said, 'You need to get over it, Sarah. Get on with your life. It happens all the time.'"

Leonard flew Sarah from Colorado to Florida for a job interview. She said her "interview" lasted three days and included such interactions as an outing on his boat. *Who does that?* she wondered.

Still, she needed work and SwimAmerica was a prestigious position, so when the offer beckoned, she accepted it. Working for ASCA was when the real misery started.

"Leonard took me out to lunch every day," Sarah told me. "I mean *every single day.* Here was the supervisor parading his underling through the office and past the staff and out the door, ostentatiously, at the break hour, without fail. It was humiliating. The dynamic was that he was 'secretly' dating me, and I had no choice other than to go along with the boss. I was afraid to do anything to piss him off. I lived four blocks from the office and he'd drive by every day. He'd assign me to pick him up at 3 a.m. at the airport. I thought he'd kill me if I didn't."

Sarah's predicament wound down the hard way when, only weeks into her employment, her appendix ruptured and attached to her intestine. She underwent life-threatening abdominal surgery, which hospitalized her for two weeks. Sarah said that when she returned home, still unable to stand straight thanks to a healing seven-inch scar, Leonard refused to send lunch over to her, with the explanation, "You can't expect anyone to care about you when you've only worked here for a month."

The boss also forced her back to work prematurely and docked her pay for the cost of an unused plane ticket for a business trip she was no longer in condition to take.

After fighting her way through the direction of a SwimAmerica training class, weeks earlier than her doctors had advised a return to full activities, Sarah asked for a Friday off to fulfill a long-standing commitment as a bridesmaid at a friend's wedding. Leonard denied the request. Ehekircher thereupon walked out of the office and never returned. "I emailed my resignation and told Leonard off. He started sending me nasty emails, but after I began raising the subject of sexual harassment, his tone changed."

Leonard didn't directly respond to my account of Sarah's time with him and ASCA. Instead, he had a surrogate, a British guy named Craig Lord who wrote and edited for swimming publications, query me as to who was paying me to report all these terrible things.

Lord never published my one-word answer on the record: nobody.

CHAPTER 4

BACKGROUND OF
THE BACKGROUND CHECKS

Ariana Kukors and Sarah Ehekircher endured classic coach-choreographed rape. Swimming also has had challenges less moral and legal on their face, and more in the realm of the general ethical underpinnings of contemporary office policies and rules. While one of the sport's common patterns was indeed years of grooming followed by the coach's deceptive assertion of a consensual adult-age relationship, there were many additional examples of couplings not quite as fraught. Their origin stories — for lack of a better term — still raised, at minimum, questions about the implications of a coach exerting corrupt power, even years later, over the career of a swimmer or even ex-swimmer, regardless of age.

Leaving aside possible root impropriety, the area of office entanglements is an altogether more complicated one for defining boundaries to apply to all professional contexts in all industries. Sports, of course, serve up a unique dimension: athletic competition plays out measurably and in public, putting the potential problem and its stakes in starker view.

For some women sports advocates, whose constituency was overwhelmingly elite athletes, it became a mission to ban *all* coach-athlete cohabitation or romantic (or romantic-esque) relationships. Their goals of shrinking the space for exploitation and of leveling competitive conditions were rational and noble. In 2013, the relevant aquatics convention legislation finally passed. This failed to close larger questions, however. Pushing the paradigm that the pool was a setting of "workplace" rules, with a hint of "labor-management negotiations" to define boundaries, came at a cost to the values of youth sports, which always wind up getting commingled with those of professionalized sports.

In my view, age-group clubs are *not* job sites; they are, rather, places where the super-majority of participants simply immerse themselves in an extracurricular activity, and from which a tiny subset go on to compete in big-time sports. Only the economic interests of the Olympic movement, with its appeals to the fantasies of both groups, justify elevating the workplace model over that of an educational platform. The consequence is a brutal breakdown of restraint and safety. Like almost everything else in the youth sports system, the supremacy of the workplace model has the effect of deferring to the sport's high-revenue upper tiers.

Once you grasp as much, you begin to clarify that the principal corrective enforcement building block for curbing abuse is not actually legislation or policy. It's something considerably more elusive: a healthy culture. Under the brand of USA Swimming, the Olympic regime has shown a consistent capacity for lying or covering up in service of selective enforcement toward good ends. The operative word here is "norms." The last decades of national life have brought home, across the board, the importance of norms. Swimming's are horrible.

A good illustration of what is often the futility of the process of tinkering with the conduct code for coaches was a debate at aquatics conventions, hashed out across years, over whether to pass a provision specifically prohibiting coaches from imbibing alcohol in the presence of underage athletes. This measure, well-intentioned, was also far from dispositive; it had a feel of shopping for language that would cover micro-violations with a virtue signal. As in the joke of the title of the old movie *Please Don't Eat the Daisies*, there was a suggestion of listing exhaustively the small things one shouldn't do, while big-picture comprehension remained fuzzy. Could coaches stage orgies with underage athletes so long as no liquor was present? But incrementalism is better than nothing, so 12-ounce beer can curls in front of the kids were officially frowned upon in legislative black and white.

Swimming insiders called this the "Mary Jo Swalley rule," after a long-time coach who was notorious for knocking them down in public. An executive director of Southern California Swimming who ran for USA Swimming board president, Swalley catalyzed the passing of this indispensable new edict after being observed having a public beer-chugging contest with an athlete. One of her drinking buddies over the years was Bill Jewell, the Mark Schubert assistant who, in Fullerton, hired the private eye who spied on Sean Hutchison and Ariana Kukors.

≈

The grand example of scrambling to backfill the gap between the real and the ideal, when it came to absence of efficacy or even good faith on the part of USA Swimming executives, involved coach background checks. A system of vetting coaches began in 2006, but it proved to be the proverbial chicken coop guarded by foxes. The Kukors lawsuit, for example, would allege that higher-ups had conspired to rig Sean Hutchison's clearance. Chuck Wielgus's lie about his lack of knowledge of — or perhaps it was befuddlement over — the status and movements of the monster Andy King was another serious tell. In swimming, the solemn task of background checks has always wallowed in low comedy. It's much easier to brag about "progress" on the technicalities than to practice common season and project basic intellectual honesty in efforts to keep bad actors off pool decks.

One of USA Swimming's consultants on background checks, from 2010 until at least 2013, was Barry Nadell, owner-operator of a Southern California private investigation company. In 2012, Nadell also registered with the Los Angeles County clerk's office the fictitious business names "Hooking Up With Tawnie Lynn," "Hookin Up With Tawnie Lynn," "Nadell Media," and "Nadell Productions." It turned out these were all in support of the then 62-year-old Nadell's development of a television show to be called *Hooking Up with Tawnie Lynn* and an associated website, hookingupwithtawnielynn.com.

When confronted, Nadell denied that this side hustle raised propriety issues or cast such an appearance. "There is nothing to talk about," he told me. "It's personal. The [business registrations] are just catchy names." Was it reasonable to speculate, I asked, that Nadell contemplated the launch of a pornography site or, less salaciously, an online dating service? "They do not have to do with pornography. They do not have to do with a dating service." Had he disclosed this outside venture to USA Swimming? "No."

"I have a number of investments," expounded this expert contractor for swimming's background check system. "I also own a Starbucks and property in Atlanta. I'm a wealthy man."

Two days after our conversation, Nadell called me back. He said he'd been caught off guard and he wanted to offer a fuller explanation, which was this: "Basically I met with some people and decided last year to be a financier and producer of what we're going to do as an online talk show. It's been in development for a long time. The way these things work, I don't even know if we're going to end up doing it."

Should the show have indeed made it to a mobile device near you, the hostess was expected to be the Los Angeles model and actress Tawnie Lynn — hence the name registration. At the time, you could see her at tawnielynn.com. You could see a lot of her, in fact.

"Tawnie Lynn is somebody I met," Nadell continued. "The show would be about the ups and downs of dating. I'm not in the pornography business. I don't go to strip clubs. I'm just someone who has been an investor in different things, and dating is a hot subject."

Asked to elaborate on his work for USA Swimming, Nadell said, "We [talked about the background check] program they currently had and whether it needed some revisions. The changes took a lot of time to implement, through conversations and board approval. They asked me to help them find a new vendor. They wound up choosing a company called Axiom Screening Solutions. I was the go-between. Honestly, I don't remember a lot of it. I know we instituted a program for continual updates of criminal checks. In the past they used to do a single check and that was the end of it. We also instituted broader criminal checks, going to counties and residences that people lived in, where they lived in the past, and so forth."

Nadell said he knew nothing about two coaches named Charles Baechler and James Pantera. But by that time, a lot of other people did.

≈

Charles Baechler's role as head coach of the Mitchell Aquatic Club and Watertown Area Swim Club in South Dakota, and later briefly of the Woodmoor Waves in Colorado, was part of a second career. He was also an official of the South Dakota local swimming committee or LSC, USA Swimming's regional affiliate.

Baechler's first career was the law. It ended badly. He rose to district court judge in Washington State's Pend Oreille County but had to step down from the bench in scandal, and eventually was criminally sentenced on charges that he raped a woman who'd appeared in his court. The incident took place in 1998. The woman was facing drunk-driving charges. In the course of hearing them, Baechler also handed her divorce papers, which had been served by the woman's husband. At the conclusion of court business, the judge offered the woman the keys to his lake house. It was there, five days later, that she said he sexually assaulted her.

Baechler was brought before a judicial misconduct commission. At the behest of the state attorney general, on referral from the county district attorney, he was investigated by the Washington State Patrol and charged with fourth-degree assault. He was sentenced to two years' probation and 30 days of electronic home monitoring.

But under USA Swimming's crack background-check system, whatever had disqualified Baechler from continuing to preside over a court of law didn't impede his qualification to preside over a swimming team in another state, supervising an activity for half-dressed kids. Moving to South Dakota, Baechler coached first in Mitchell and then about 100 miles north in Watertown, and held multiple leadership posts in regional governance. In 2011 he was hired to coach the Woodmoor Waves, whose pool in Monument, Colorado, was in the veritable backyard of national swimming headquarters.

Baechler's own account to me was transparent enough to warrant extended reproduction. He called the Washington event "a very painful period of my life, a period that has had far-reaching effects on me personally and professionally, but it is not something that I hide from, nor that I've hidden from the teams that have employed me or from the organization that has certified me." He continued:

> The assertions that you have relayed are correct to the extent that the nature of the allegation that was made against me in 1998, at the beginning of my second term as District Court Judge of Pend Oreille County, was that of a felony level sexual assault. Once the allegation was made, there was an exhausting thirteen month investigation involving the Washington State Patrol

Detective's division, the Washington State Attorney General's office, and the Washington State Judicial Conduct Commission. I fully cooperated with those investigations, and a plea was entered to the misdemeanor charge of Fourth Degree Simple Assault. That plea has been legally expunged after successful completion of probation and by operation of law pursuant to statutory authority granted to the Courts of the State of Washington.

It is important to note that examination of court records will demonstrate that the plea which was entered was in no way an admission to the accuracy of the allegations that were made against me. The plea was an Alford Plea, a mechanism which exists under Washington State law that enables someone accused of a criminal offense to enter a plea in order to complete a plea agreement while still contesting the allegation before the court. As an experienced journalist I know that you understand that if the State believed that there were credible facts that demonstrated that a felony had been committed by a sitting judge, the State would have vigorously proceeded to prosecute that case. It was only after the conclusion of the various investigations, examination of the evidence that I had provided, and discovery of significant disparities in various versions of the allegations made against me that the Attorney General approached my attorney and offered to resolve the case by a plea to a misdemeanor offense. The terms of the plea stipulated that this offense was not categorized as a sexual assault for purposes of the sexual offender registry, that there was a recommendation of no jail time, and that the state recommended that I be granted the ability to expunge the conviction after successful completion of two years probation. My attorney rightfully urged me to accept the state's offer which provided a guaranteed result rather than risk an adverse jury verdict, no matter how unlikely. I followed my attorney's advice.

Baechler went on to reflect on "whether my employment as a coach, who has been certified by USA Swimming, demonstrates flaws in that organization's background checks or screening procedures. Obviously, USA Swimming takes the matter of athlete safety very seriously, as a coach I can tell you that it is our first and most serious responsibility."

I can only respond to your concerns as follows. I personally informed Board members of the two teams who have employed me as their head coach of the circumstances referenced above prior to actually having been hired by those teams. I have completed all background check requirements of USA Swimming in a timely and accurate manner, including this incident, although by operation of law I could have truthfully said that this conviction did not exist at the time those background checks were completed. I am under no legal restraint relating to contact with the athletes that I coach, nor am I under any obligation to register or report a conviction that was expunged almost thirteen years ago to any legal authority or law enforcement agency. I fully comply with and support all rules relating to the regulation of appropriate contact between coaches and athletes that are in place as the result of USA Swimming's concern for it's athletes. I have never been the subject of inquiry or complaint, formal or informal, regarding any contact with my athletes.

This has been a devastating episode in my life. I still deal with the resulting depression and sense of loss on almost a daily basis; not always successfully. However, despite efforts by people who have used this episode over the years to discredit my reputation, I believe that all things happen for a reason and I'm very proud to be part of this great sport. It would be tragic to try to depict USA Swimming as anything other than an exemplary organization when it comes to monitoring our athlete's safety and their environments.

Unfortunately for Baechler and everyone in his path, a neutral reading of USA Swimming's code Section 304.3.6 is that an Alford plea to a sex offense charge in no way should have shielded him from a red flag in job screening. This provision covers "[c]onviction of, imposition of a deferred sentence for, or any plea of guilty or no contest at any time, past or present, or the existence of any pending charges, for (i) any felony, (ii) any offense involving use, possession, distribution or intent to distribute illegal drugs or substances, (iii) any crime involving sexual misconduct, or (iv) any criminal offense against a minor."

Now for more of Baechler's Moot Court defense:

Please note that for purposes of applying a rule or statute such as section 304.3.6 referenced below, the controlling factor is the statute supporting the conviction, not the nature of the allegation. The conviction was for Fourth Degree Assault which is not a felony, not an offense involving the use, possession, distribution or intent to distribute illegal drugs or substances, nor is it a crime involving sexual misconduct. The language of the actual statute defines whether a conviction would fall into one of these categories. There are crimes which exist under the Washington criminal code which address those areas, they were not charged, and I was not convicted of any of those crimes.

USA Swimming's director of Safe Sport, Susan Woessner, and other officials were invited to chime in on Baechler's explanation, which seemed more creative than persuasive. Yes, the defrocked judge's Alford plea did seem to succeed in keeping his mug shot off some internet sex registry sites — but was that good enough for a responsible third party to hire him to supervise kids? Did someone with a past so checkered have an *affirmative right* to carry on with his life via the specific job of age-group swimming coach? Or should his criminal record, appropriately, have limited his future employment options?

More broadly, there's the question of whether the standard for a swimming coach facing down sex crime allegations should be "beyond a reasonable doubt" or "preponderance of the evidence." Simply and commonsensically, is the discretion of the hiring entity not allowed — indeed expected — to weigh youth safety first, last, and everything in between?

In November 2012, no one from Colorado Springs responded to these questions. Two months later, USA Swimming did announce a formal investigation of Baechler (with Woessner claiming it had been opened in December). In addition to a complaint about his coaching credentials, the organization had received a complaint from Colorado about the failure of the Woodmoor Waves and a team official there, Brian Donahue, to report newly uncovered information about Baechler. This information had caused Baechler's dismissal from his hire there the year before.

Woessner refused to undertake a direct investigation of the Woodmoor club. Providing what she called "some perspective that may help" alleviate concerns in that regard, she said her "present understanding" was that Woodmoor "was not involved in Mr. Baechler's commission and/or concealment of a crime." Similarly, Woodmoor was not involved in the 9/11 attacks or the January 6 insurrection at the Capitol, but that didn't mean it would have been justified in hiring Osama bin Laden or Oath Keepers leader Stewart Rhodes.

As to the embattled coach himself, Woessner said, "In mid-2011, Mr. Baechler had successfully passed a criminal background check," and under the terms of his Washington no-contest plea, his conviction had been expunged following a period of good behavior, "making it irretrievable by a criminal background check."

Experts on background checks disputed that a professionally executed check truly would have been vulnerable to such a loophole. And in fact, Woodmoor had terminated its announced hire of Baechler precisely *because* it learned of his guilty plea "stemming from allegations of sexual misconduct." At that point, the club was also compelled by the USA Swimming code to report its information — yet failed to do so.

Further, Baechler's record, when he was introduced to the families of the Woodmoor Waves as its next head coach, by then included two drunk-driving strikes, as well. Nor were ankle-bracelet tracking or extraordinary investigative measures required to learn the circumstances under which he'd left the club in Mitchell for the one in Watertown. That was because of another incident in which he was charged with simple assault, disorderly conduct, and obstructing a police officer.

The date of the newest incident was October 16, 2011. Returning to Mitchell months after the debacle of his brief tenure at Woodmoor, Baechler picked up a *third* citation for driving under the influence. The local *Daily Republic* newspaper reported: "The right side of the vehicle was in the ditch. Baechler performed poorly on field sobriety tests, and a blow test showed a 0.162 blood alcohol level. The legal driving limit in South Dakota is 0.08. A third DUI within a 10-year period is a felony charge with a maximum sentence of two years in prison, a $2,000 fine or both."

Baechler apparently persuaded the sentencing judge into finding that this was his second, rather than third, DUI strike. As a result, he got a 180-day jail sentence with 90 days suspended, and one year on probation and without driving privileges. The capper of the newspaper account was that Baechler was being allowed "to serve his jail time in 30-day periods in December, March and August to accommodate his work schedule as head coach of USA Swimming in Watertown."

Woessner let the Woodmoor Waves off the hook not on the basis of its reporting or failure to report seriously compromising information on Baechler. Rather, she decreed that his hire could be interpreted as having been "provisional." And no permanent head coach meant no harm, no foul. Once again, Woessner was protecting the reputation of an institution rather than the safety of the kids it served. Woessner elided the way Baechler's hire at Woodmoor, now retroactively labeled non-permanent, had come undone after a board member there, Terri-Ann Snediker, got wind of the Washington State sex conviction and informed club president Donahue.

≈

The Charles Baechler story exposed more than just a possible frayed safety net of background check procedures in that period; it also revealed USA Swimming's flat-out cherry-picking of standards. The case of James Pantera, a multi-alias con man who started his own sanctioned club in San Diego, reoriented the low comedy, sinking it to new depths of depravity. In order to get the goods here, you didn't even need to subscribe to a background check service. All you needed was an internet connection and five minutes of searching via Google.

The problem with Pantera, as identified by Mike Saltzstein, a dissident former USA Swimming vice president, was that there was no reference check whatsoever for a coach starting a new team. There was only scrutiny, such as it was, for someone applying for association with an *existing* team.

The top line of the Google search showed that one James S. Pantera — alias James D. Land, alias James Sabre Panter Jr., among as many as ten other AKAs — had been convicted a dozen years earlier, in federal court in Wisconsin, for (a) false statements in application for or use of a passport; (b) unlawful transport of firearms; and (c) embezzlement, stealing, fraud, false statements, and forgery. Armed with three distinct dates of birth and multiple Social Security numbers, he was pointed to by the FBI as a prototype for his skill at crafting fake identities, and featured in an article about his crimes on the front page of a newspaper.

Early in 2013, Saltzstein was tipped to look up Pantera's background online. In February, Saltzstein compiled and sent to USA Swimming a 103-page collection of documents. One of the open questions of this matter was what exactly Pantera had intended to get out of his fraudulent access to USA Swimming and its young athletes when he completed his paperwork the previous fall to form a club at the Claremont Recreation Center, a facility of the San Diego City Parks and Recreation Department. Pantera's bizarre personal claims included that he had American Swimming Coaches Association Level 5 certification (no such record could be found on the ASCA website database). Along the way, he made scattered representations that some of his relatives had perished in a plane crash on Super Bowl Sunday, while others were killed in a terrorist attack in Israel whose news coverage was suppressed. According to the Saltzstein material, he enlisted in the American military on two separate occasions, for the purpose of collecting signing bonuses.

Bruce Stratton, USA Swimming's board president, wrote back to Saltzstein that "appropriate action" would be taken.

Pantera simultaneously conned the San Diego Unified School District, where he was listed as swimming coach at Serra High School; his own website called him the head coach there, and the Serra athletics site had him as the team's one and only coach. At first, a spokesperson for the district tried to maintain it was awaiting "results of background checks and a tuberculosis test required under the California Education Code. When those results are back, his application will be reviewed for eligibility" to become an "assistant" coach. After follow-up inquiries, the district quickly updated this to: "Mr. Pantera has not met the requirements under the Education Code for employment by our district. He will not be hired, nor will he be allowed to volunteer his time."

Later in February, Saltzstein sent USA Swimming executives an even more exhaustive rendering of Pantera's past. This one, 121 pages in length, additionally chronicled Pantera's movements in embedding himself in the local swimming community:

> Pantera appears to have engaged in a series of "grooming" behaviors through gifts, stories of access, a tragic history, "philanthropic" activities and promises. Pantera has followed a systematic process of finding (aka grooming) key parents and community members to help his stories and misrepresent their actions. This cover now has risen to public attacks on those who question his history, or have access to the data that will discredit his versions of the truth. The author of this report has been warned by two sets of court officers that I should

protect my physical safety should any action be taken on Pantera's membership.

On October 14, 2013, James Pantera was added to USA Swimming's banned list. A footnote clarified that "James Sabre Pantera," "Robert Michael Binkin," "James David Land," and "James Wallace" were similarly unwelcome. He, or they, had been found to have engaged in what the banned list categorized as "other misconduct," running afoul of:

- Section 304.3.6, "Conviction of, imposition of a deferred sentence for, or any plea of guilty or no contest at any time, past or present . . . for any felony . . ."
- Section 304.3.14, "Any act of fraud, deception or dishonesty in connection with any USA Swimming-related activity."
- Section 304.3.18, "Any other material and intentional act, conduct or omission not provided for above, which is detrimental to the image or reputation of USA Swimming, a LSC or the sport of swimming."

You couldn't help but conclude that, in USA Swimming's eyes, it was the last offense that was the worst.

CHAPTER 5

DEATH BECOMES THEM

It was the afternoon of June 29, 2010, when a pretty 16-year-old girl drove her car to the intersection of State Highways 116 and 117 in rural central Illinois. Calmly, she parked. With equal resolution, she walked straight into the path of an oncoming tractor-trailer, taking her own life.

Sarah Burt had made the National Honor Society at Metamora Township High School; she'd been looking forward to pharmacy school. She worked as a lifeguard for the local park district. She loved giving swimming lessons to little kids.

What brought Sarah to this pass was something few others knew: her swim coach had groomed her for years, in a "relationship" that was, unquestionably, morally repugnant, and in many jurisdictions was defined as statutory rape. Yet neither the justice system nor USA Swimming, the sport's national governing body, would ever discipline this coach.

Sarah Burt's tragedy doesn't necessarily mean that abuse inevitably leads to the worst possible outcomes. t's true that Sarah Ehekircher and many other young victims of swimming coaches have also made one or more attempts — purposeful or performative — to take their own lives. In Ireland, Olympic swimming head coach George Gibney, whom we'll meet in Chapter 13, left one known suicide casualty and a possible undocumented trail of others. Still, the ability to predict outcomes from what is actually a continuum of soul-searing experiences is not so glib. In Stieg Larsson's novels, beginning with *The Girl with the Dragon Tattoo*, the protagonist Lisbeth Salander, who endured serial heinous mistreatment under a corrupt foster care system, springs back to transform herself into a kind of ninja vigilante. In other cases, fictional and real-life, girls or young women who were harassed or inappropriately touched, in small or large ways, either subsequently thrive despite the experience or are ruined for life because of what an outsider might consider the most trivial offense. Or, in various measures, both.

Sarah Burt, a name lost to the underground history of swimming, shouldn't be held up as a prototype of anyone except herself. Her world and her life collapsed uniquely under a unique set of facts. But she's a reminder, in case we needed one, that abuse is unacceptable; that the categories of consequences most definitely can include the worst; and that the sport of swimming's history is dotted, disproportionately, with similar examples.

≈

A values-based analysis of swimming's dark side turns to a damning death narrative having nothing whatsoever to do with sexual abuse — and everything to do with the profoundly interlocking institutional bankruptcies in which abuse flourishes.

The deceased swimmer was Fran Crippen, a 27-year-old male. Crippen died at the 2010 FINA Open Water Championships in Dubai, on the coast of the United Arab Emirates. The event was in that somewhat counterintuitive locale because of the global power-brokering of an Indiana businessman, Dale Neuburger. A long-standing USA Swimming leader, Neuburger was also a lord of the rings at FINA, the world swimming governance group, headquartered in Switzerland. He combined his FINA vice presidency with his interests as a partner of an Indianapolis company, TSE Consulting (today known as Burson Cohn & Wolfe Sports).

At Princeton University in the late 1960s and early '70s, Neuburger was a contemporary of Ross Wales, who through that period competed with Mitch Ivey at Stanford University and Cal State University–Long Beach.[1] A medalist at both the 1968 and 1972 Olympics, Ivey went on to become one of the world's most famous swim coaches when he succeeded the legendary George Haines at the Santa Clara Swim Club. Ivey also was one of the most infamous coach abusers, culminating in his dismissal from the University of Florida in 1993 following an ESPN report on allegations of sexual harassment and sleeping with his swimmers. (Random factoid: the second of his three wives was an 18-year-old swimmer when he married her.) By the time of the ESPN exposé of Ivey, Neuburger was in the fourth of his 28 years on the USA Swimming board of directors, which he also served as president from 1998 to 2002.

It would take another 20 years after ESPN for USA Swimming to get around to adding Ivey to its banned list. In the interim, in 2011, Neuburger was deposed in a lawsuit against the organization by an abuse victim. Here's how part of the deposition went:

Q. Do you know Mitch Ivey?

A. I don't know him.

Q. Do you know who he is?

A. I know the name.

---

1   Like Neuburger, Wales would become a USA Swimming board president. Unlike Neuburger, Wales would occasionally say something open and honest, which is why Neuburger moved up in the sport's hierarchy and Wales did not.

Q. Have you ever seen him on television?

A. No, not to my knowledge.

Q. Were you on the USA Swimming board of directors in 1993?

A. Yes.

Q. Do you recall any discussions about Mitch Ivey in 1993?

A. No.

Q. So is it your recollection that there were no discussions of Mitch Ivey after he was on ESPN Outside The Lines in 1993?

A. If Mr. Ivey was part of a television broadcast, I'm not aware of it.

Q. You've never seen it?

A. I've not seen the broadcast that you refer to.

Q. Do you know if he was the coach at the University of Florida?

A. I think that is correct. I can't give his coaching affiliations, but I believe at one time he coached at the University of Florida.

Q. Do you know if he was fired from the University of Florida?

A. I do not. . . . I know nothing about Mr. Ivey. I've never — to my knowledge I don't believe I've ever met him . . . and therefore I wouldn't know any of his business arrangements.

What Neuburger did seem to know quite a lot about, across decades, was how to turn a profit from swimming. At TSE Consulting, he helped set up foreign coaching jobs and consultancies for people like Bob Bowman, Michael Phelps's coach. These arrangements were mildly controversial inside American swimming, since they spread national know-how to other countries, which conceivably could go on to use it in challenging U.S. hegemony at the Olympics. Can't have that.

Neuburger's biggest coup was manipulating the awarding of events to various municipalities and nations. When there was bidding to host major aquatics events, TSE often landed consulting contracts for top-tier bidders. According to Neuburger's critics, he then exploited his FINA board position to put his thumb on the scale in favor of his clients. That's how the 2010 Open Water Championships wound up in Dubai. The temperature in the Persian Gulf waters off Fujairah the day of the event was 85 degrees Fahrenheit, far too warm for competitive swimming. Fran Crippen succumbed either to heatstroke or to drowning after cardiac arrhythmia.[2]

For the next year's open water championships, FINA proved that this was a lesson unlearned when it chose to stage the event in the even more dangerous venue of Shanghai. On race day, the

---

2   Crippen came out of the Germantown Academy program in Pennsylvania run by Dick Shoulberg – about whom there's more in Chapter 7.

Yellow Sea waters off Shanghai measured as high as 87 degrees. Three swimmers — including the reigning world champions, Alex Meyer of the U.S. and Linsy Heister of the Netherlands — refused even to get in the water. More than half the field was pulled out or hospitalized. The race had been moved to the early morning hours to mitigate the midday heat, but even the eventual winner, Bulgaria's Petar Stoychev, expressed dismay that it had been allowed to go forward at all.

A prominent voice among the swimming authorities dismissing the naysayers was Flavio Bomio, an influential Swiss Olympic coach. Bomio himself spent much of the six-hour competition inside an air-conditioned tent.

Later that year, Bomio would be imprisoned in Switzerland. For sexual abuse — of course. Across the previous three decades, he'd molested at least 30 boys between the ages of 12 and 16.

You can take the sexual abuse out of the deaths in swimming. What you can't remove from the sport is its overall low regard for the well-being of young athletes.

CHAPTER 6

WELCOME TO THE "UNITED STATES SPORTS INSURANCE COMPANY"... IN SUNNY BARBADOS

You may have noticed the city of Indianapolis turning up quite a bit in the business histories of swimming and other amateur sports. The corporate office of the National Collegiate Athletic Association is in that city. Indianapolis is also the headquarters of USA Gymnastics, and housed USA Canoe and Kayak under Chuck Wielgus, before Wielgus moved up the chain of apparatchiks to head USA Swimming. In the newfangled world of lawyers and MBA types specializing in the business of sports, the Hoosier State is a capital.

Another figure of note was Jack Swarbrick, who was board chair of the Indiana Sports Corp, the nation's first civic sports commission, which started in 1979 with the focus of attracting marquee events. There, he rubbed shoulders with Dale Neuburger, of TSE Consulting and national and global swimming governance. Swarbrick went on to serve 18 years as the athletic director of the University of Notre Dame, one of the nation's iconic sports brands. At Notre Dame, Swarbrick had to learn a thing or two about how to handle sex scandals, mostly in relation to campus rape allegations involving Fighting Irish football players. Before that, he was general counsel for USA Gymnastics. At the Indianapolis law firm Baker & Daniels, he also advised USA Swimming. Swarbrick was part of a circle of attorneys who networked professionally from their alumni associations with

Stanford Law School. The leader of that group was Richard Young of the Denver office of Holme Roberts & Owen (a firm since absorbed by Bryan Cave Leighton Paisner), which handled the bulk of swimming's legal matters.

Most insiders credit Jack Swarbrick — at a USA Swimming aquatics convention in the late '90s — with being the first significant voice to warn the leaders of the sport that, like it or not, times were changing and they had better start preparing themselves for the emerging issue of sexual abuse. Critics such as lawyer and former swimming gold medalist Nancy Hogshead-Makar, who now heads the advocacy group Champion Women, have described the general problem as a culture that has always seemed to take for granted that competitive youth swimming would be an unsafe and overly sexualized platform. Hogshead-Makar's go-to rap on this subject is: "Not every coach is a pedophile, but every pedophile wants to be a coach. Why? Because you get to spend hour after hour in an authority position over athletes, unsupervised, with almost no oversight or consequences to really horrible behavior."

Swarbrick's convention observations on the legal ramifications of sexual abuse would come to light, more than a decade later, in Jancy Thompson's lawsuit against USA Swimming over her abuse by coach Norm Havercroft. In a deposition in that case, American Swimming Coaches Association executive director John Leonard recalled the remarks. He also testified as to his own characteristically disdainful reaction.

"Show me the numbers," Leonard said he told Swarbrick. "Show me where this [abuse] is an issue that is large."

On the basis of Swarbrick's advice, and overcoming Leonard's hard-core skepticism, USA Swimming established its first code of conduct for coaches in 1999. Four years later the organization set up its first task force to study sexual abuse after former Olympic gold medalist David Berkoff spoke out about rumored instances of top coaches having sex with their swimmers, many of them underage.[1] As leader of the professional coaches' trade association, Leonard would always be the most truculent voice within such study groups, and the most resistant to whatever ambitious reforms sprang from them. But by 2006, at least those dubiously effective background checks were in place. Swimming was starting to make a show of it, which might well have been the thrust and extent of Swarbrick's urgings.

The ASCA coaches' lobby wasn't the only barrier to consistent ameliorative measures. Coaches are employed by thousands of individual age-group clubs of all sizes and shapes and with various business models. Some teams are owned by their coaches; others are run by self-perpetuating nonprofit boards consisting of parents. What nearly all have in common is rental of public facilities, such as park district pools or high school or community college aquatic centers, at subsidized rates. While a few had sufficient resources to own and control their own pools, almost all leveraged their stations in their communities through not financial might, but the capital of national pride and the Olympic image.

This patchwork of local clubs, operating on shoestrings, parent volunteers, and revenue from bake sales and swim-a-thon fundraisers, contrasted with the vast USA Swimming revenue streams at the top. Nonprofit Form 990 filings with the Internal Revenue Service show the book value of the organization's assets hovering in the neighborhood of $50 million. At the time of his death in 2017, Wielgus drew annual compensation of more than $1.2 million. In 2021, his successor Timothy Hinchey made $1,037,208. The staff in Colorado Springs exceeds 100, with more than a dozen executives averaging annual salaries of more than $300,000. The public relations and marketing budgets of USA Swimming alone very well might exceed the combined expenditures for everything in

---

1 Berkoff and his work are covered in the next chapter.

all Olympic sports in a number of Third World countries. The St. Louis-based Bryan Cave law firm's three Colorado offices, and more recently Atlanta's King & Spalding LLP, annually log millions of dollars' worth of billable hours.

≈

Belying their homegrown image, youth sports are big business. So is organization insurance for youth sports. Swimming's insurance structure, as well as the volume of underlying sexual abuse claims, gave rise to the sport's liability crisis. The two went hand in hand.

Around the same time Jack Swarbrick was issuing his warning, internal documents show, the parent U.S. Olympic Committee was briefly telling USA Swimming that it could no longer use the Olympic Training Center facilities in Colorado Springs. The reason was insurance: USA Swimming was the only sport body without what the Olympic overseers considered sufficient coverage; at the time, its general liability policy contained a clause excluding coverage for claims of abuse or molestation. USOC's risk manager explained all this bluntly, in writing, to USA Swimming's consultant, Risk Management Services. In turn, on May 3, 1999, the senior vice president of RMS, Sandi Blumit, submitted notes to swimming executives detailing the problem.

"[The Olympic Committee] mandates innocents should be protected by their [national governing body]. Therefore, can't delete abuse and molestation," Blumit wrote, adding that as a consequence the committee "would not allow any local members' clubs, volunteers or members on premises (training center)."

This impasse was resolved two days later when USA Swimming advised USOC that it would amend its insurance coverage to include claims of abuse and molestation. Swimmers and their coaches were allowed back to the training center.

What appears most significant about this from a distance of more than two decades is that Blumit's presentation of the controversy was made not to USA Swimming's board but to its wholly owned subsidiary, United States Sports Insurance Company, Inc. The story of USSIC embodies some of the financial maneuvers of corporate insurance practices that would become a focus of a federal grand jury investigation.

USSIC had been incorporated in 1988. That was because USA Swimming's main insurance carrier, AIG, was complaining that premiums were too low in multiple areas of liability, including abuse. Given the level of exposure, AIG would only discuss annual premiums in the range of $1 million. (Previously, they'd been closer to $200,000.) As Ronnie Lee Van Pool, USA Swimming's board president from 2002 to 2006, put it in a 2010 deposition in an abuse lawsuit: "We would have to pay a million dollars to get a million dollars of coverage."

During that period, both for-profit and nonprofit entities faced the same problem of steeply rising liability premiums. Their collective response was a new industry wrinkle concocted by lawyers and actuarial specialists. It was called "captive reinsurance." In a nutshell, with smart exploitation of tax breaks and regulatory gimmicks, corporations could save money through a combination of insuring themselves, managing claims themselves, and underwriting the risks of their third-party commercial carriers. (Famously, the Catholic Church has a captive, National Catholic Risk Retention Group, Inc.)

By the time USA Swimming got around to forming USSIC, the parent Olympic Committee already had its own captive, Panol Insurance. But foreshadowing the dispute over access to the training center a decade later, Panol was just as reluctant to underwrite USA Swimming's risks at the established premiums as AIG had been. While other sport bodies saw their premiums reduced or coverages remaining stable, underwriters for swimming considered it uniquely beset with both greater risks and poor risk management.

Needing a captive reinsurer of its own, USA Swimming had to figure out where to locate it. In the late 1980s, Caribbean countries were jostling to be the preferred home of captives. Barbados won the competition for USSIC. This island nation offered many years of tax abatement, as well as a structure so loose that all the operation really required was a dummy bank account and a set of books domiciled on the island. The clincher may have been the absence of a tax treaty between Barbados and the U.S. After all, the less exposure to American laws and their pesky inspectors and enforcers, the better.

USSIC set up shop on White Town Road in Bridgetown, the Barbadian capital. Local law mandated an annual board of directors meeting on site. In practice, this became a pretext for staging a beachfront bacchanal, below the radar of dues-paying USA Swimming families and their swimmers. It was a favorite perk for officials in the know.

Jay Adkisson, an attorney who is an expert on captive reinsurance, told me, "Offshore jurisdictions inevitably have the lingering odor of offshore tax evasion and sleaze."

The phenomenon of locating captives offshore has receded. Several U.S. states, notably Delaware, have tweaked local laws to escalate their own inducements to become insurance regulatory havens. As the image of swimming suffered during the publicity of abuse scandals, officials also realized that a foreign subsidiary, even if legal, was borderline and also a bad look for an organization marketing patriotism as much as athletics. It was one thing to endure ridicule over American flag pins and other merchandise made in the factories of China and other far-flung locales; what about an entity actually owned by national Olympic interests that had incorporation and paperwork abroad, all harboring the nasty truths and secrets of mitigating the financial fallout from coach abuse? In 2013, USSIC was brought onshore and put into what the money types know as "runoff mode." Three years later, London's Randall & Quilter Investment Holdings Ltd. purchased USSIC's assets for $2.1 million, and swimming was officially out of the captive business.

≈

In its heyday, the United States Sports Insurance Company featured an unorthodox feature in swimming's insurance structure, which would become a focus of the federal grand jury investigation. This was called the "wasting" provision. More on that in a moment.

USA Swimming also found a way to work around the Olympic Committee mandate to include specific abuse coverage in its umbrella liability coverage. The trick was not to extend that coverage to the country's 2,000 member clubs across the country. Instead, the clubs were given USSIC-underwritten coverage to cover claims of abuse or molestation by coaches. And that coverage was capped at $100,000 per claim.

As for the wasting clause in insurance policies, that acted like the ultimate deductible: every dollar spent on defending a claim was correspondingly reduced from the coverage. Thus, if investigators and defense lawyers for USA Swimming ran up a tab of $100,000 in a particular case, a victim-claimant stood to collect a maximum of $100,000 minus $100,000. A net of zero dollars. In such a case, the club being sued would also have zero dollars remaining to defend itself, its coaches, and its board of directors. Furthermore, the coverage limited member clubs to two claims a year.

The concept at work here was that an individual club could be thrown under the bus, with its coaches forced into bankruptcy and any parent board left holding the bag. The larger goals were twofold: protecting USA Swimming from claims made against its member clubs, and denying large settlements to victims. But plaintiffs in many cases required, in order to cover their injuries and therapy, more robust financial recoveries than this system.

The only way plaintiffs could find substantial relief, justifying the costs of long and complex litigation, was to get past the member clubs' coverage and reach all the way to USA Swimming's general liability coverage. Strategies meant to pierce the national organization's financial veil are largely what have driven the lawsuits of recent years. In addition, swimming's whole defensive and misleading infrastructure started getting scrutinized by federal prosecutors.

In 2022 this line of attack was emboldened when the California Supreme Court ruled that USA Taekwondo — and not just an individual predator, its convicted coach Marc Gitelman — was liable under the principle of "duty of care" in the case of Yasmin Brown, Kendra Gatt, and Brianna Bordon, who'd won a theoretical $60 million in a lawsuit against Gitelman. That decision potentially meant that abuse survivors could go after the deeper pockets of national sport governing bodies. (The U.S. Olympic and Paralympic Committee remained excluded from liability under this court ruling, however.)

≈

Swimming's insurance practices did more than just protect the people at the top. They also generated paper profits. In return for tamping down victims' claims, USSIC formulated a "safety rebate," reflecting successful years when premiums and underwriting costs were exceeded by savings. As these rebates flourished, USSIC's assets ballooned to as much as $27 million, according to IRS filings. In 2008 the company held a portfolio of U.S. government bonds totaling more than $12 million. Two years later, the value of corporate bond holdings and other fixed income approached $15 million.

There was money to be saved in swimming's creative insurance defenses. Plus money to be made. And to ease the stress for all, you had those annual parties on remote stretches of white sand.

CHAPTER 7

DAVID BERKOFF BLASTS OFF.
HIS COACHES FADE AWAY.

In the wake of ABC's *20/20* report in 2010, a Minnesota man named Jeff Chida was campaigning for a ban of John Sfire, for the previous 18 years the coach of the Rochester Swim Club, whose athletes had included Chida's son. Amidst the surrounding publicity, Sfire left the team. Chida said he'd corresponded with USA Swimming boss Chuck Wielgus about Sfire over the previous decade, and the coach had been hit twice with sanctions for mis-recording swimmers' times and other technical violations. But it would be 2017 by the time Sfire got added to the permanent banned list for sexual misconduct.

Except for one factor, Sfire would have been just another example from swimming's vast abuse history — one of the many mentioned in the massive collection of internal documents subpoenaed by that FBI field office following the 2012 California Supreme Court's termination of USA Swimming's contempt of discovery orders. But that one factor resonated — for among the people Chida contacted during his campaign to bring Sfire to account was the prominent swimming figure David Berkoff. A Hall of Famer in the water, Berkoff had become a sporadic anti-abuse activist from Missoula, Montana, where he practiced law and coached.

In a wide-ranging email reply to Chida, Berkoff pulled no punches. He dropped names, details of long-gossiped coach-swimmer anecdotes, and USA Swimming governance watersheds — all of which readers of his email proceeded to decode.

Here's part of what Berkoff wrote on July 26, 2010:

> [USA Swimming] [d]enying knowledge of Rick Curl, Mitch Ivey and others banging their swimmers! It's a flat out lie. They knew about it because we (coaches and athletes) were all talking about it in late 1980's and early 1990's. I was told by several of Mitch Ivey's swimmers that he was sleeping with Lisa Dorman in 1988. I heard the whole Suzette Moran story from Pablo Morales over a handful of beers and nearly threw up. I was told Rick Curl was molesting Kelley Davies for years starting when she was 12 by some of the Texas guys. That was the entire reason I formed the abuse subcommittee. I was sick and tired of this crap. No one was standing up. No one was willing to take on these perverts.

At the time, Berkoff was running for the USA Swimming board as a reform candidate, in the fallout of the *20/20* report's disruptions, which had motivated Wielgus to launch Safe Sport. Berkoff won his election. Over the next two years, he served as technical vice president.

In the email to Chida, Berkoff went on to name-check the boss of the coaches' association as a central villain of the abuse story. John Leonard, Berkoff said, had blocked his work in setting up, or at least trying to set up, a subcommittee to study the issue, back when Berkoff was an athlete representative on the swimming board. According to Berkoff, Leonard "told me he was opposed to an all-out ban on swimmer-coach relationships because he had married one of his former swimmers. I finally threw in the towel out of frustration because no one wanted to stand up for background checks or banning coach-swimmer relationships."

In his encore on the board in 2010–12, David Berkoff's performance was, to put it charitably, convoluted and of mixed effectiveness. Zig-zagging rhetoric betrayed a softness behind the harshness of the headline buzz. The package from newly minted vice president Berkoff was neither intuitive, from what had seemed to have been his campaign platform, nor especially persuasive as clever tactical pressure. On the inside, he didn't really enlarge the space for confronting the evil at swimming's coaching and leadership core; he played a kind of rope-a-dope with it.

Still, the full record of Berkoff's lifelong devotion to the sport makes his shortcomings poignant. They seemed to come from a place more complicated than sheer hypocrisy, and in at least one area — the daylighting of what was probably a version of USA Swimming's controversial "flagged list" of bad actors — they weren't a complete failure.

Any assessment of Berkoff has to begin by recognizing that, inside the pool, he belongs on the list of the game-changers of swimming history. This was thanks to an insight immortalized as the "Berkoff Blastoff." Noticing that backstrokers could attain faster starts by plowing underwater when they pushed off the wall, rather than staying on the surface, he used that technique to propel himself to becoming one of the world's best in those events. Indeed, in direct response to the Berkoff Blastoff, the international competitive rules had to be tweaked to mandate that backstrokers must return to the surface within 15 meters of their underwater starts, lest their races devolve into deep-depth gamesmanship marathons, in substitution for fair tests of speed in the essential surface skill of the backstroke itself. In 1968 high jumper Dick Fosbury revolutionized his event by demonstrating in Mexico City, where he won the gold medal, that the physics of his backward reverse-limbo leap offered an advantage over the then-favored forward lunge up and over the bar; today the "Fosbury Flop" is universal. The Berkoff Blastoff similarly changed swimming backstroke practice.

Besides being an athletic innovator, Berkoff (who got both his undergraduate and law degrees at Harvard University, where he swam collegiately) was, as he advertised, moved to outrage over the breadth and persistence of coach abuse. He seemed determined to stamp it out — though, as we'll see, he suffered from blind spots in his direct experiences. Later, curiously, he validated official excuses behind some of USA Swimming's inept public explanations. These highlighted chief Wielgus's lack of sophistication and clarity in formulating media sound bites, and pleaded for patience — thereby granting a pass for his basic cravenness in carrying out executive responsibilities and ensuring that abusive coaches would get driven out.

In the 2010s, Berkoff displayed no ability, nor perhaps will, to take the anti-abuse cause into swimming's inner councils in concrete and meaningful ways; and when called out for this lapse, he pleaded, less than convincingly, that he somehow was maximizing his moral authority as an earnest insider more shrewdly than others could possibly understand, and was simply choosing not to bow to the unreasonable demands of the woke mob. Perhaps most bizarrely for someone who enjoyed an official platform from which to make his case — USA Swimming board meetings and committees — he took arguments with critics to obscure internet discussion sites, where he was often trolled and flamed. Sometimes he flamed back. Whatever else you could say about David Berkoff, the word "gravitas" didn't attach. Once, on the online comment board of *Swimming World* magazine, he wondered if the naysayers there were "just interested in castrating all the men around here."

In his one and only live conversation with me, by phone in April 2012, Berkoff said this: "As a board member, I have to be careful of what I say. I think the 2010 changes in the conduct code and publication of banned coaches were a huge step, and a lot more is being implemented behind the scenes. There isn't a doubt in my mind that Chuck wants to do the right thing and root out any coach who ever violated an athlete. But these things take time, and the bulk of the problem actually predates Chuck."

The formula came down to bluster outside the corridors of power, which was dutifully walked back once on the inside. It added up to weak tea for solving abuse. Berkoff's approach was typified by the way he handled the Rick Curl controversy, which he'd so vociferously articulated to Jeff Chida, when it burst out into the open.

≈

Curl was a top coach in the Washington, D.C., area. One of his swimmers, Tom Dolan, won medals at two Olympics, and Curl's company, the Curl-Burke Swim Club, grew into a sprawling entity with nearly a thousand swimmers at ten locations.

Meanwhile, as Berkoff's email to Chida noted, it was a long-open secret in the swimming world that things had turned dreadful for one of Curl's stars, Kelley Davies; also that the reason was Curl's years-long molestations of her, beginning in 1983 when she was 13 and he was 33. Davies went on to win the 200-meter butterfly gold at the 1987 Pan Pacifics in Australia. Later that year, early in her time at the University of Texas, she told details of her experiences with Curl to a well-attended Fellowship of Christian Athletes gathering. Along the way, her personal life cratered, with a nervous breakdown and an eating disorder, and she failed to qualify for the 1988 Olympics. Many people knew this background. Specifically, Davies told Richard Quick, the Texas women's swimming head coach. (Quick was not at the Fellowship of Christian Athletes event, but others there said that Eddie Reese, head of the entire university intercollegiate swimming program, was.) According to her, Quick "just said, 'I'm sorry.'"

In 1989 Davies's parents in Maryland reached a $150,000 settlement of a civil lawsuit against Curl, after receiving advice that the coach probably couldn't be criminally prosecuted to their satisfaction. The settlement was accompanied by both Curl's signature on a confession and those of Davies's mother and father on a non-disclosure agreement. In the usual quiet way, Curl was removed from his job as swim coach at the University of Maryland. He emigrated to Australia, where he set up shop with the famous Carlile Swim School.

By then, Texas women's coach Quick had left that university for Stanford. His successor in Austin? Mark Schubert.[1]

But two decades later, with the coast clear, Curl was back in the U.S. Kelley Davies, now Kelley Currin, spotted him in televised coverage of the 2012 Olympic Trials in Omaha, Nebraska, and she was furious. She decided to tell her story to the *Washington Post*.

In a matter of months, Curl was brought before USA Swimming's National Board of Review, then criminally investigated by Maryland law enforcement. At an "emergency hearing" four weeks after the Olympic Trials and one week after publication of the *Post* article, he was "provisionally suspended." (USA Swimming claimed that its investigator, one of those ace retired FBI agents, had been searching for Kelley Davies Currin for a year. There's no evidence that she was living incognito in Texas, her state of residence of more than 20 years.)

---

1   Schubert – later instrumental in having a private investigator follow around Sean Hutchison and Ariana Kukors, as chronicled in Chapter 1 – clearly had a thing for deploying detectives to acquire dirt on his coaching rivals. In 2012 he told Scott Reid of the *Orange County Register* that in 2003 he'd hired an investigator "to try to determine if Curl was continuing to sexually abuse young swimmers but found no evidence of misconduct," the newspaper account said. Schubert added that when Curl got elected to the presidency of the American Swimming Coaches Association in the mid-2000s, he and Quick "took steps behind the scenes to ensure Curl was not allowed to take office. '[We] went to John Leonard and said "This shall not happen" and we told him why.'"

The permanent ban of the coach became effective on September 18, 2012. The same day, the Curl-Burke Swim Club rebranded: henceforth it would be known as Nation's Capital Swim Club. A month later, the team's erstwhile eponym was arrested. The following February, his lawyers committed to paper his agreement to plead guilty to child sexual abuse.

At the ultimate May 22, 2013, hearing in Rockville, Maryland, Kelley Currin recounted the whole story in a victim impact address to the Montgomery County Circuit Court judge, who proceeded to sentence Curl to seven years in state prison. (Curl would be paroled after serving less than three years.) In remarks to the media outside on the courthouse steps, Currin picked up where she left off, taking aim at all the USA Swimming leaders who dodged accountability. She saved her most blistering remarks for David Berkoff, who, after winning election to the USA Swimming board, waved away the implications of his dramatic 2010 email to Chida.[2] Davies Currin said:

> Now that justice has been levied against Rick Curl, it is time to hold accountable USA Swimming Executive Director Chuck Wielgus and Vice President David Berkoff, as well as former USA Swimming National Team Director and Hall of Fame coach Mark Schubert, for their actions in helping create a culture that protects predator coaches and vilifies young victims who have the courage to come forward. . . .

2 Pablo Morales, cited by Berkoff as a source of his information, won three Olympic gold medals in the '80s and '90s, and held the world record in the 200-meter butterfly. To me, he denied Berkoff's ever having had any such conversation with him about abuse of Kelley Davies and many others. Berkoff, however, convincingly doubled down on the account of his email to Chida, detailing the year, city and type of restaurant, and circumstances of the alleged conversation with Morales. All this even as Berkoff, in subsequent public statements, was also strategically watering down whether the substance of the Curl story constituted actionable fact.

Perhaps the most glaring example of ineptitude is the story of former Olympic gold medalist and current Vice President David Berkoff. Back in the late 1980's and early 1990's, Mr. Berkoff was part of a group of swimmers which was discussing "over a handful of beers" that Rick Curl was "banging" me and that Mitch Ivey was sleeping with one of his swimmers (see attached email). . . .

When it came time to testify under penalty of perjury in a deposition in January of 2012, however, Mr. Berkoff significantly "backed off" from that comment and generally did not remember anything about this process. "Just an idea that was kicked around without anything formalized" is essentially how Mr. Berkoff described it in deposition."

Davies Currin concluded: "I have no confidence whatsoever that USA Swimming will protect swimmers from sex abuse. . . . I urge Congressional intervention. USA Swimming is a creation of Congress and therefore Congress needs to intervene and address this crisis."

In an editorial, the *Washington Post* agreed. "Ms. Currin is exactly right in calling on Congress, which created USA Swimming in 1979, to start asking questions and providing the oversight that seems to have been sorely lacking," the newspaper opined.

Since the *Post* is the voice of a company town of the federal government, it's not surprising that its call was heeded. Congressman George Miller carried the flag.[3]

David Berkoff's takeaway from the Rick Curl affair was peculiar and, by now, familiar. Below a headline calling the swimming vice

---

3   Chapter 15 covers the sadly ineffective fate of Congressman Miller's work.

president "mired in national sex abuse case," his hometown news-paper, the *Missoula Independent*, published an interview in which Berkoff said he'd had no idea that Curl was coaching on deck at the Olympic Trials. As for what happened between the coach and his swimmer a quarter of a century earlier: "I don't know. I heard rumors."

≈

In the spring of 2013, Berkoff added to the misgivings about him by playing a dishonorable hand in USA Swimming's attempt to quash reporting on the documents it had been forced to release under the previous year's California court's discovery order, ultimately rati-fied by the state supreme court. In a USA Swimming filing in Santa Clara County Superior Court, Berkoff signed a declaration seeking to portray that something nefarious had occurred in the subsequent acquisition of many of these documents by my reporting partner Tim Joyce and myself, and to support a motion to compel the return of the documents, which had been subpoenaed and acquired by the FBI.

"When I visited the Muchnick blog somewhere between 9:00 a.m. and 10:00 a.m. Mountain Time on February 21, 2013," the Berkoff declaration said. "I found that the blog contained a link to a pdf formatted document of a subpoena issued by the FBI to the law firm of Corsiglia McMahon & Allard. LLP ('Allard firm'). I accessed the link and read the FBI subpoena."

Berkoff continued by noting that the subpoena "clearly stated in bold capitalized letters that the Allard firm, as the respondent, should not disseminate the subpoena or tell anyone that the subpoena had been issued because it could affect a criminal investigation."

No one offered evidence that Bob Allard's firm had been Joyce's and my source for the underlying documents. (And it wasn't.) On legal advice, I took down the online posting of the FBI subpoena, but Joyce and I continued to utilize the documents themselves, which had been leaked by an FBI source, for support of scores of articles about banned, shadow-banned, and never-disciplined coaches who, over the course of many years, were credibly accused of abusing youth swimmers in their charge.

USA Swimming's gambit of so weaponizing the purportedly reform-minded Berkoff amounted to an effort to suppress information it had already been ordered to liberate. The desired effect would have been to couch its own failures to curb abuse in the strictures allegedly imposed on the information in court filings. The effect would not have been to avoid compromising criminal investigations

≈

Weaselly though he could be throughout his tenure on the USA Swimming board, Berkoff did perform one unquestionably valuable public service there. The organization was known to maintain a mysterious "flagged" list, as a supplement to (and for many years likely larger than) the official and eventually published banned list. In a declaration, Chuck Wielgus admitted that the flagged list existed. But its contents remained secret. What this meant was that certain prominent coaches with the baggage of lurid and verifiable allegations (Paul Bergen and Murray Stephens were two examples, and Mitch Ivey was another before his belated ban in 2013) could pull off vague, unannounced separations from their famous positions in the sport — while continuing to remain involved through consultancies, off-the-books assistant posts, or jobs outside the U.S. or with entities not under the jurisdiction of USA Swimming.

Admirably, David Berkoff helped peel back this curtain with a 69-page research memorandum he circulated to fellow board members. The memo became public record in court filings. Readers of this book can view it at muchnick.net/berkofflist.pdf.

Berkoff called it "The List," and explained its five parts:

(1) persons listed on the current version of the USA Swimming "Banned List" as a result of sexual misconduct in any form.

(2) persons listed on the current version of the USA Swimming "Banned List" as a result of other misconduct.

(3) US residents associated with swimming not listed on the current version of the old USA Swimming "Banned List" but who have been arrested for or who are accused by a police body of sexual misconduct in any form;

(4) international swimming coaches that have been banned by their NGB or who have been convicted of serious crimes; and

(5) persons who have been publicly accused (by way of published media and by an identifiable accuser) of sexual abuse or misconduct.

In a disclaimer, Berkoff said he couldn't affirm or deny the truth of accusations in part 5 "where there has been no criminal, civil, or administrative decision regarding the claim."

The list contained technical mistakes — for example, Berkoff called the Irish coach George Gibney "British." But parts of it were probably a decent approximation of the flagged list. In other words, unlike some other things Berkoff said and did, here he opened up, and didn't impede, public understanding of the range of covered-up cases.

More than a decade later, in 2022, Berkoff was a plaintiff's witness in a North Carolina civil action brought by a woman, who was suing USA Swimming for damages over the sexual abuse by her criminally convicted former coach, Nathan Weddle. Berkoff's testimony was considered important and helpful to the woman's attempt to pierce the national organization's shield from liability for misconduct by member coaches and clubs (though that effort failed in this case, as it has in many others). In the course of recounting his long history with swimming and this issue, Berkoff noted that his own former Harvard coach, Joe Bernal, was on the banned list, and also discussed the flagged list.

Unfortunately, Joe Bernal wasn't the only shady figure among key career mentors of Berkoff who would be exposed for being less benignly fatherly and more pernicious than their managed images had projected. This double-helix irony was a feature, not a bug, of the swimming world's bottomless pit of incest. The anecdotal flaws of once-revered coaches, even Berkoff's, accrued into a systemic DNA. Once exposed, they turned back on some of the sport's guiding lights, and they turned the lights out on them.

≈

Before Harvard, Berkoff swam at the Germantown Academy, a prep school in Fort Washington, Pennsylvania. It was the same program, under coach Dick Shoulberg, that produced Fran Crippen, the open-water swimmer who died in the Persian Gulf. Shoulberg's coaching technique was numbingly unsophisticated, his critics said: he simply ordered laps, laps, and more laps. He wasn't much for teaching technique; it was all about grinding into condition with long distances and hours in the water, and never quitting. After Crippen perished, Germantown observers wondered if he might still be alive — even with the championships having been set in unsafely warm waters, per Dale Neuburger's business interests — had Crippen ever been trained that there was a point at which it was OK to stop.

Shoulberg was revered in his bubble in the suburbs north of Philadelphia, until he was reviled. As the public assumed the best about his values and ethics, few scrutinized the school's relationship with John du Pont, the industrial scion and delusional sports benefactor, whose murder of Dave Schultz, an amateur wrestler with whom he was obsessed, would be the subject of the movie *Foxcatcher*. (Steve Carell was nominated for an Academy Award for his portrayal of du Pont.) Fancying himself a potentate of, in addition to wrestling, the modern pentathlon (whose bewildering array of events consists of swimming, fencing, equestrian show jumping, pistol shooting, and distance running), du Pont invited Shoulberg to train his athletes some summers at Foxcatcher Farm, the du Pont estate.[4]

≈

In 2003 Shoulberg was part of the USA Swimming committee tasked with the latest assessment of abuse issues and proposed solutions. He gave off the vibe of someone with strongly principled views.

Shoulberg wrote in one memo, "[S]omewhere I think our athletes need to be reminded of the seriousness of statutory rape and that it is looked upon as a felony. Unfortunately I know of instances (after the fact) on national trips that I have been on that these acts have taken place. In some cases, I was informed years later. My concern is if we are trying to protect the athletes and our organization, we must provide as much information as possible to all

---

4 Irish coach George Gibney, of the horrors of Chapters 13 and 14, was also graced with a visit by du Pont to Gibney's swimming program at Newpark Comprehensive School outside Dublin.

members of U.S. Swimming to protect first themselves and second the organization."

(Perhaps significantly, as history would reveal, it was unclear if the perpetrators to whom he was referring in this passage were coaches or swimmers.)

Later, seeming to object to the small punch of the committee's final report, Shoulberg emailed: "I am disappointed on the outcome of the Board. I feel that there are too many coaches still coaching who have destroyed kids' lives and there will be more coaches in the future who will destroy kids' lives."

Most impressive of all was Shoulberg's withering analogy about the failure to adopt a true "zero tolerance" policy: "I would hate to see our organization ever in the predicament of the current Roman Catholic Church — protecting child molestors!"

Yet Shoulberg's Germantown program did just that. In 1994 the school dismissed an assistant coach, Joe Weber, then in his late 20s, upon his arrest for having had oral sex with a 14-year-old swimmer. Weber spent five years in prison. In 2012 Weber was back coaching for the YMCA and USA Swimming clubs in Somerset, New Jersey, when a more complete background check of him surfaced. The Y fired him. But why had Shoulberg and Germantown done nothing to publicize the sex-crime conviction of an employee who, absent such publicity, was much likelier to find a job that would allow him to prey on the kids of another community? This was not "like" the Catholic Church's culpability in steering abusive priests from one parish to another. This was *exactly that*. (Weber got added to the USA Swimming banned list 18 years after his bust at Germantown and six months after the Somerset Y canned him.)

Over the years, the Germantown culture suffered from, at minimum, porous behavioral boundaries. Male athlete-on-athlete hazing and worse were rife cruelties, redolent of a *Lord of the Flies* atmosphere.

They got reported to Shoulberg and to school administrators, who did nothing to stem the misconduct.

The episode of assistant coach Marie Labosky told another dimension. Labosky had swum at Germantown and then the University of Notre Dame, and her parents owned a swimsuit and apparel shop. On Facebook, she posted videos of male teens pole-dancing and simulating sex acts at a sophomoric pool party she supervised. Labosky was shunted off to the Parkland Swim Club up the road in Allentown, Pennsylvania — until Parkland parents learned of the Germantown incident and took up the matter with USA Swimming. A no-publicity separation from the coaching profession was arranged. Labosky found employment with major swimming sponsor Speedo — perhaps through her family's commercial connections with the company or with the help of USA Swimming fixers.[5]

In scenarios falling short of sexual abuse but going well beyond what should have been tolerated, much less routinized, several Germantown female alumnae told me of traumatizing experiences when they were girl swimmers there. One woman left the sport and said she was able to reconstruct her adult life only after many years of therapy.[6] A good student as well as a precocious swimming talent, this woman came to regret deeply her family's decision to allow Germantown to recruit her for seventh grade enrollment at age 13. She was thrown immediately into the varsity team regimen, with practices at 6 a.m. and 3 p.m. every weekday, 7 a.m. every Saturday, and 9 a.m. every Sunday.

"I felt like I was a prisoner," the woman told me. "I used to love swimming. I had the passion and the drive. But at Germantown it

---

5 Labosky's head coach at Parkland was Erik Posegay. He went from there to Michael Phelps's North Baltimore Aquatic Club – subject of Chapter 8 – and now coaches in the NCAA ranks.

6 A portion of the therapy fees was subsidized by USA Swimming's underpublicized "Swim Assist" program, which also funded the treatment for Sarah Ehekircher mentioned in Chapter 3.

was just dread and depression. They took the joy out of everything. You couldn't have a birthday. You couldn't eat a cookie."

This swimmer said an assistant coach humiliated her when she got her period. The meanness of coaches was a general theme. Shoulberg himself slapped her and made derogatory remarks about her body. Once a month the girls' weight and body fat were measured in front of everyone. One of Shoulberg's favorite words was "cancer." As in, when there was a complaint about the workload, "Do you have cancer or something?" Or, "You're a cancer on the team."

At the end of eighth grade, when the girl was 14, she tried to kill herself with an overdose of Advils. Another time she blacked out in the pool, an ambulance was summoned, and her stomach was pumped. She'd find herself falling asleep in class. She lived more than a half hour from the pool, and after she got her driver's license, she sometimes drove herself; once, in a stupor, she crashed on the way.

With all that, she swam well enough in high school to attract a college scholarship. A dislocated shoulder during her freshman year prompted a decision to retire from competitive swimming rather than aggressively rehab.

Across decades, the Germantown administration turned deaf ears to complaints about Shoulberg. Finally a lawsuit by an ex-swimmer — at least the second fielded by the school over the program — made Shoulberg's continued dominance untenable, especially when the *Philadelphia Inquirer* subsequently reported on a police investigation of a swimmer-on-swimmer assault. In the fall of 2013, the school put the long-time coach, now 73, on administrative leave.

The bad press soon passed, however, and his supporters rallied, pressuring Germantown to restore Shoulberg to a position called "coach emeritus," through 2014–15, after which he voluntarily retired. Katrina Radke, in an opinion piece at the online SwimSwam news site, wrote, "Obviously there was a lot more controversy around [Shoulberg's reinstatement at Germantown] than is said in the official letter. Yet, when people rally to support a man who has a huge heart and great intentions, truth and a more proper outcome prevails, as it did in this case. We should all be encouraged to follow his example to speak up for what we believe in." The author didn't specify whatever it was that Shoulberg believed in — at least, as reflected in the record of his actions and inactions.

USA Swimming contributed to Shoulberg's soft landing by naming him the official "camp observer" on the staff of the USA Swimming National Junior Team Camp in Colorado Springs.

≈

Dick Shoulberg was the paterfamilias with a dark side. David Berkoff's other career-shaping coach, Joe Bernal, proved, if nothing else, that Shakira, the popular singer, wasn't the only Colombian expatriate with legal problems. Before he was Joseph Worthington Bernal, a handle befitting his eventual Ivy League pedigree, he was Hugo Bernard Calderon. Bernal coached on U.S. Olympic team staffs in 1984 and 1988, and was inducted into three Halls of Fame — all this before his lifetime achievement honors were rescinded after he was banned by USA Swimming on findings of sexual abuse.

At the time of his death in 2022 at 81, Bernal was the central figure in baroque litigation surrounding his former USA Swimming age-group team in Waltham, Massachusetts, once known as Bernal's Gator Swim Club and now just as Gator Swim Club. An ex-swimmer, Kimberly Stines, who'd been sexually abused by Bernal, sued in New York federal court to recover damages from various post-Bernal corporate entities. That case turned on the technical legal issue of whether, when Bernal sold his club's brand and assets in the wake of his scandal, he unloaded *only* the assets — or whether his successors also assumed financial liability for Bernal's malfeasance.

Five years earlier, his alter ego as Colombian native Calderon had surfaced in his own lawsuit in Florida circuit court claiming elder abuse by his son, Craig J. Bernal. Joe's complaint said Craig — described as a drug abuser who was in and out of rehab, had fathered at least one child out of wedlock, and sponged off his mother and "the girlfriend of the moment" — was trying to control his father's finances and convert his property to his own use after the "elderly, sick, and vulnerable" Joe was diagnosed with prostate cancer in 2014.

Joe Bernal had coached at Fordham University from 1966 to 1978, then at Harvard from 1977 to 1991 (where he was a seven-time Ivy League coach of the year). He founded the Waltham club in 1979.

His lawyer told the court that radiation treatments and chemotherapy drugs had left him "physically fatigued, emotionally unbalanced, depressed and mentally confused at times, and experiencing hot flashes and memory problems." Son Craig thereupon exploited him, taking over his home in Waltham. That's when things got weirder. Already a member of New York's Metropolitan City Hall of Fame and of Fordham's Athletic Hall of Fame, Joe Bernal was named to the American Swimming Coaches Hall of Fame in September 2015. Days later, however, he was informed by USA Swimming that he was under investigation for sexual misconduct; he got added to the banned list the next year.

By then, as the *Boston Globe* reported in a lengthy feature headlined "Without a Trace," he'd already disappeared from the neighborhood where he lived for more than two decades. "Multiple sources who knew Bernal before the ban said they have heard that he moved out of the country," the *Globe* story said.

In the 2017 lawsuit against his son, Bernal said he "felt as if his identity and livelihood he had ever known for his entire adult life [*sic*] had been stripped from him because of one allegation in a 44 year career."

According to Joe's lawyers, Craig pushed on him the idea that the press and police in Waltham would be "hounding him" every day at the front door of his house, and "that he was at risk of losing all his money because of the investigation, and further that there was going to be a global revolution and an ensuing economic collapse, that the U.S. economy was unstable and in danger of collapsing, that the real estate market was going to collapse, that banks were not safe, and Plaintiff needed to put his money into gold/precious metals or risk losing everything."

Craig packed Joe's belongings and drove him to New York, from where he flew to Mexico. Craig allegedly concocted a scheme for Joe to move to Ecuador with a new Ecuadorian passport. However, the "passport could not be obtained as quickly as defendant CRAIG wanted," the lawsuit complaint said, so the plan changed to obtaining a Colombian passport as Hugo Bernard Calderon, "the name that appears on Plaintiff's Colombian birth certificate." The passport was issued on October 22, 2015, according to this account, and Bernal/Calderon traveled to Colombia five days later, and he remained there for 15 months, "only returning to the U.S. or the Cayman Islands at the behest of defendant CRAIG."

CHAPTER 8

MICHAEL PHELPS'S HOME TEAM

By October 1, 2012, whispers about the misdeeds of Murray Stephens, founder of the North Baltimore Aquatic Club (NBAC), had amplified into full-blown disturbing stories. That day my colleague Tim Joyce decided to seek comment from Debbie Phelps, the mother of Michael Phelps. Joyce reached her at the Education Foundation for Baltimore County Schools, which she headed. Debbie had been a public middle school principal, but her duties as First Mom of swimming started interfering with that job, as viewers of NBC's coverage could see for themselves in the cameras' compulsive cuts to her cheers and wild gesticulations from the stands.

At the time, Joyce was doing special reports on swimming scandals for WBAL, a Baltimore radio station. Soon WBAL would ditch Joyce without explanation. Perhaps to ensure that this profile in caution would never get mistaken for anything else, the station additionally scrubbed the archive of all his reports. WBAL's self-censorship was part and parcel of the entire Baltimore news media's on all things NBAC.

But despite authorities' best efforts to keep swimming community dissidence under control, many of the team's families registered their concerns to management, until the head coach, Bob Bowman, felt obliged to issue a statement to them. While he "cannot comment" on the allegations broadcast on a Joyce WBAL report, Bowman told parents in a statement, "I can assure you that the safety, health, and well being of our athletes, your sons and daughters, are paramount to all of the staff at NBAC. NBAC is committed to creating, and protecting, a safe and healthy environment for all of our participants."

Bowman's superstar Michael Phelps, of course, was arguably the greatest Olympic swimmer of all time. As in the case of many famous jocks, there was little else noteworthy about Phelps: just because he was a historically accomplished athlete didn't mean he had aptitude for anything else, nor penetrating observations about anything else — at least, not ones he was interested in sharing. Later, in retirement, Phelps did do commercial endorsements for a company offering online therapy, in which he reflected on his own struggle with depression and anxiety, which had the admirable effect of helping destigmatize the subject of mental health. With respect to sexual abuse and other unpleasantness in swimming, he never said a public word. The only possible exception was a minor motif, in one of his painful, cliched, anodyne interviews, of the psychological revenge he savored against those kids who he remembered taunting him for having big ears, and how he figured most of them, unlike himself, must now be working in menial jobs.

"If [sexual harassment or assault] goes on in the swimming world," Phelps told The Daily Beast in 2017, "I don't know about it." That interview was arranged to hype his role as the face of a public service campaign on water conservation sponsored by Colgate-Palmolive Company.

One time, to his embarrassment, Phelps got caught inhaling marijuana from a bong at a party, in a photo captured on someone's phone. The image went viral, and USA Swimming disciplined him for this blot on the sport's presumably otherwise pristine reputation. The only real significance of the episode, as Chapter 10 develops, is that it got incorporated into Chuck Wielgus's false contention that swimming, prior to that picture of Michael Phelps with a bong, had never had to deal with any kind of problem stemming from behind-the-scenes video content. That statement proved actually much worse than false or bogus or any similar adjective one might conjure. It was said under oath, which made it textbook perjury.

In any event, when Tim Joyce was seeking third-party perspective on the accusation of Murray Stephens's predation of a girl swimmer, Joyce didn't bother trying to talk to the six-time gold medalist at the 2004 Athens Games. Joyce, though, thought Debbie Phelps might be different. After all, she was an educator. And her two daughters, Michael's sisters, also swam at NBAC. Maybe she'd have something thoughtful to say about Stephens, maybe even in his defense.

Debbie Phelps answered Joyce's call. He introduced himself.

Before he could complete the first sentence of his first question, she hung up.

≈

One of the most successful coaches in the sport's history, Murray Stephens was inducted into the ASCA Hall of Fame in 2006 and the International Swimming Hall of Fame in 2010. Like Rick Curl, and with a different model than that of prep school–affiliated Dick Shoulberg, Stephens established that a program in the country's colder northern region could achieve levels of success more likely to be found in the Schubert-esque clubs of sunny California and Florida. Phelps was only one of the Olympic legends who came out of NBAC, which Stephens started in 1968. Others included Anita Nall, Beth Botsford, and Katie Hoff. In 1987 Stephens purchased the Meadowbrook Aquatic Center, making NBAC a rare age-group team to own its own pool.

Stephens's wife and assistant, Patty, was the one who began coaching the precocious Phelps when he was six. Bob Bowman would go on to get most of the credit for guiding him to greatness (though his rivals thought it might have been just the luck of the draw, a case of the "golden fish" landing in his lap).

Bowman's coaching mentor had been Paul Bergen, whose career in swimming turned radioactive — not so much because of his sexual abuse of Deena Deardurff, which would be revealed to a wide audience only many years later, but because of what he went on to do to one of her Cincinnati teammates, who spoke up about the abuse in a more timely fashion.[1] Bergen returned for a time to his other passion, training horses. If there was one life lesson Bergen taught Bowman, it was that training swimmers was a lot like training horses.

"I thought, This is a guy who knows what he's doing," Bowman told *Sports Illustrated* in 2008. Bowman followed Bergen to Napa Valley, California. There the acolyte bought a pair of knee-high boots and helped out in Bergen's horse stables. In between cleaning stalls, Bowman picked Bergen's brain about the art and science of swimming.

Bowman wound up hooked on horses, too, and owned and trained nine thoroughbreds. In what could be considered something of a negative photo image of the brain map of his entire profession, he said: "The horses have taught me to be a better observer, because they can't tell you what they're feeling."

Together, Bowman and Phelps, stage manager and generational talent, built a business empire whose flagship was the Michael Phelps Swim School out of Meadowbrook. After Athens '04, as Phelps reached adulthood, the coach athlete base of operations shifted, first with the swimmer's and coach's move to the University of Michigan, and then with Bowman's to Arizona State University. In 2017 their company, Aquatic Ventures LLC, which had bought control of NBAC and Meadowbrook operations from the Stephenses nine years

---

1 The full story of Bergen and Deena Deardurff's friend and teammate Melissa Halmi is in Chapter 11.

earlier, turned it back over to them. The NBAC team then moved out of Meadowbrook in 2021. By that point, Murray had long been persona non grata at his own pool. However, this never prevented him from collecting a reported $57,000 a month as NBAC's landlord.

≈

In 2010 USA Swimming received a complaint by a former NBAC female swimmer. She said she'd been molested by her coach in 1975. The name of the coach wasn't known, but when word of the complaint spread, his identity was intuited. On-deck sightings of Stephens, now NBAC's éminence grise, promptly vanished. In October 2012, after WBAL successively published and disappeared Joyce's reporting on this and other matters, the *Baltimore Sun* ran a slanted story asserting that the alleged victim "did not follow up with" a USA Swimming investigator. Left unanswered by the article was whether the investigator likewise "did not follow up" with the victim. *Sun* reporters acknowledged to me that they already knew the name I offered as the accused coach — Stephens — but claimed the police had told them no document existed pertaining to the purported abuse. While devoting newspaper space to casting aspersions on the legitimacy of the complaint — or maybe it was the complainant's responsibility for follow-through — the newspaper didn't get around to mentioning that there was a conflict between the accounts of USA Swimming and police.

USA Swimming issued a statement confirming that "we reported the complaint and information received to the Baltimore County Police Department, Precinct 1." Swimming insiders, noticing that Stephens had receded from public view, speculated that he might have been added to USA Swimming's secret flagged list. The same sources said Stephens had left as CEO of the North Baltimore Aquatic Club, without fanfare or even a resignation announcement. Moreover, the complainant told Joyce and me that a Baltimore County police detective had contacted her in October 2011 — a conveniently leisurely full year after USA Swimming submitted "information."

At first, a police spokesperson said any such letter from USA Swimming could very well have been discarded, owing to the massive passage of time (that is, from 2010 to 2012). Eventually the cops acknowledged receipt of a letter from the organization. But they still insisted no police report was ever generated, "due to insufficient victim information." For its part, USA Swimming wouldn't release a police control number from its 2010 submission, or otherwise elaborate.

Cut loose in dangling dishonor, and in the usual vague way, Stephens was next spotted supervising his own son Henry in one-on-one swim practices at the natatorium of the exclusive McDonogh School in suburban Owings Mills. Henry was a student there; a plaque on a wall at the school thanked his parents for being major benefactors. Their financial support included fundraising for the construction of that very natatorium.

If Murray Stephens no longer was welcome on Meadowbrook's pool deck, then why was he being allowed on McDonogh's? Did he perhaps serve in some official capacity with the school or with the Eagle Swim Team, the USA Swimming club domiciled there? Scott Ward, head coach of the team and aquatics director at McDonogh, wouldn't answer that question. Raymond Brown, the general chair of Maryland Swimming, advised journalists to "direct any inquiries to the general counsel of USA Swimming." At the Bryan Cave law firm office in Denver, partner Richard Young said he would "be happy to respond directly to any USA Swimming LSC or club official who has a question." No such Maryland-to-Colorado query was forthcoming, or at least publicized.

During this period, Paul Yetter began following me on Twitter. Yetter had been a confidante of many of the top female swimmers

111

at NBAC, from his time on the coaching staff there. But Yetter was now an assistant at Auburn University, and NCAA rules forbade him from communicating with them as regularly and deeply as he once did — for that could be interpreted as an illegal overture for recruitment to Auburn after they graduated high school. Yetter's Twitter follow was curious, but in our single direct conversation he said nothing of moment or for the record. Today Yetter is head coach of the post-Stephens, post-Bowman, post-Phelps NBAC.

≈

Even as the Murray Stephens scandal roiled, NBAC was dealing with life and death. At 10 a.m. on October 28, 2012, a 14-year-old swimmer was found at the bottom of an auxiliary pool at the Meadowbrook complex. Louis Lowenthal hadn't been participating in a group practice session. Rather, he seemed to have been practicing breathing drills on his own. There was no lifeguard present, and study of the facility's layout made it obvious no official Meadowbrook person could have had eyes on him from the main pool. Young Lowenthal was given CPR on the deck before being taken by ambulance to Sinai Hospital in a coma. He died three days later.

Like Fran Crippen at the open water championships in Fujairah two years earlier, Louis Lowenthal found himself, fatally, at the tragic nexus of organized swimming's interlocking unsafeties.

There were no public statements from NBAC co-owner Michael Phelps. He carried on with a public relations tour of Brazil, site of the next Olympics. The priorities were evident in the days before and after Louis's emotional funeral, when Phelps, tastelessly, was the subject of online jocularity about his appearance that month on the cover of *Golf* magazine. Even if Phelps or his handlers didn't orchestrate the jokes, they had the capacity — but obviously lacked the motivation or will — to shut them down during the mourning period. Even if he didn't have it in him to say something serious and meaningful in young Lowenthal's honor.

The Maryland medical examiner ruled that the death was from "complications of near-drowning." Bowman announced to the NBAC community that the cause was Shallow Water Blackout Syndrome. The National Institutes of Health describes this condition as "loss of consciousness caused by cerebral hypoxia towards the end of a breath-hold dive in shallow water. It is typically caused by hyperventilating just before a dive, which lowers the carbon dioxide level and delays the diver's urge to breathe." NBAC arranged for an educational conference on the syndrome, which Bowman said "almost exclusively affects accomplished swimmers." The Lowenthal family didn't litigate. It's not known if they settled with the team and Meadowbrook for anything other than an ongoing memorial to Louis — who, as they say, had died doing what he loved.

≈

NBAC's director of operations was a long-time assistant coach, John Cadigan. Many years earlier, his girlfriend was Jill Johnson, a local swimmer who went on to compete in the 1992 Barcelona Olympics.

Jill Johnson became Jill J. Chasson. She matriculated and swam at Stanford, after which she practiced law and married Mike Chasson, one of her Stanford coaches. Mike Chasson moved on to Arizona State, then left that post to become owner and operator of the age-group club out of the university campus in Tempe. Meanwhile, Jill Chasson was named chair of USA Swimming's National Board of Review, the body that heard coach misconduct cases whenever chief Wielgus exercised his discretion to forward them.

In February 2013, reports broke of an investigation by Maricopa County police in Arizona of the molestation several years earlier of an underage girl swimmer. The perpetrator was a former ASU and Sun Devils Aquatics assistant coach, Greg Winslow, now the head coach at the University of Utah. The youth swimmer had followed him there before returning to Arizona, descending into substance abuse and a suicide attempt, and reporting Winslow's abuse. Appropriately, Jill Chasson said she would recuse herself from consideration of the Winslow case, should it reach her review board, because she was conflicted by marriage to the former boss of the accused.[2]

But Chasson's Baltimore history limned an entanglement too complex for the fix of a one-off recusal. Back when she had been NBAC assistant coach Cadigan's openly known girlfriend, she was as young as 15. On a technical point, if they had sex during that period, then Cadigan would have been prosecutable for statutory rape under Maryland law.

That technicality aside, the larger issue was how this background exposed the limits of solving youth coach sexual abuse via campaigns by elite female swimmers to make the sport more fair and equitable. Sexual and gender discrimination policy was less than a bullseye platform here. This complication is also evident in the work of the #MeToo movement generally; while related, the #MeToo agenda is by no means identical to the challenge of cleaning up youth sports. Women in leadership roles like Chasson's, set against their own particular life and career data points, can find themselves in nearly impossible positions when it comes to balancing privacy with peak transparency. Obviously, such difficulty doesn't apply to every woman in swimming who rose to power. But the difficult truth is that some — many — women in swimming have similar career arcs. Such were the times then. And they continue to overlay the culture now.

---

2 Chapter 15 has more on the implications of the Greg Winslow episode.

In stage 2 of conflict resolution, following her quick no-brainer recusal in the Greg Winslow case, Jill Chasson resigned altogether as chair of the National Board of Review.

The previous year, an aquatic sports convention proposal to ban *all* coach-athlete romantic or sexual liaisons, regardless of age, had gotten voted down. In 2013, that legislation would pass. Casual observers believed coaches comprised the single key opposition bloc, but that's an oversimplification. Another constituency for a pause button on this measure might well have been women who were or had been part of coach-swimmer couples. As with the issue of rape in the newly gender-integrated military, the issue of sexual assault by sports coaches will be largely, and properly, driven and resolved by women. Still, these are figures in the sport who might recognize the potential value of the ban on coach-swimmer relationships to reduce abuse, yet might also feel in a bind: viewing youth coach sexual abuse through that lens might also seem to invalidate their own life choices, in real time.

As at Dick Shoulberg's Germantown Academy and other places, the abusive culture of Murray Stephens and Bob Bowman's North Baltimore Aquatic Club was filled with the grist of discrete disturbing events. In Maryland in 2013, there was news of progress in enacting an anti-cyberbullying statute, to be known as "Grace's Law," after Grace McComas, a 15-year-old girl who'd committed suicide the previous year after being publicly humiliated by peers on social media. NBAC wasn't implicated in Grace's scenario, but, coincidentally, some of her cousins had swum there. And late summer and fall, as Grace's Law marched toward passage by the state legislature, a group of male NBAC swimmers were passing around a girl teammate for casual sex, and gleefully documenting it all on Instagram.

One of the boys — needless to add, the least competitively promising — got expelled from the team. The three others got off with slaps on the wrist.

Perhaps the most horrific episode — because of its serial nature and the documented indifference of Bowman — was the tormenting by a group of teenage boys of a male teammate who was on the autism spectrum. The prelude to more heinous acts was their engineering a 2011 Facebook post that called the kid "the biggest fagut [*sic*] ever!" From there, they moved to ridiculing him mercilessly on the pool deck at practices, calling him a "faggot" and an "asshole." They executed pranks and worse, such as stealing and hiding his gear.

These boys were in NBAC's Challenge group, a tier below the best of the best swimmers. One day an athlete in the top group, called High Performance, was outside the pool, doing dryland exercises, when he observed the taunting. Peyton Bailey didn't like it one bit. He told the High Performance coach, Jeffrey Lindner, who advised Bailey to take his observation directly to the Challenge coach, Erik Posegay.

(Later, Lindner would get fired by NBAC in retaliation for his whistleblowing. Posegay, readers will recall from the previous chapter, was the Allentown coach for whom Marie Labosky worked after she left her job at Germantown. Posegay himself was out in Allentown in 2011, and found a job on Bowman's staff in Baltimore.)

Bailey approached Posegay on the deck, outlined what he'd seen, and forcefully said, "This has to stop. If you don't do anything about it, I will." According to Bailey, Posegay screamed back at him, "Don't you talk to me like that! I'll have you thrown off the team!" Lindner confirmed Bailey's account. Bailey said Posegay misrepresented the exchange in reports to head coach Bowman and administrator Cadigan. The gist of Posegay's account was not the scene in the pool that underlay Bailey's confrontation of him, with attendant outrage; instead, it was the temerity of a swimmer to address a coach with less than maxed-out respect.

Three years earlier, Bailey had been so eager to swim for NBAC that his mother moved with him and his younger brother to the Baltimore area, while his father stayed behind in Virginia. Now, Peyton was so disgusted that he stayed away from practice for more than a month. Bowman told his mother, Sue Bailey, "Perhaps this break from swimming . . . is a good time for all parties involved to assess whether NBAC remains a viable choice for either [Peyton] or the other current members of the program."

Ultimately, Peyton Bailey, a high school senior, did quit NBAC. He went on to enroll and swim at Virginia Military Institute.

The harassment that he observed culminated in an incident at a February 2012 practice. According to the target's mother, one of the bullies repeatedly touched her son inappropriately under the surface of the water.

The mother pursued complaints to both NBAC and USA Swimming. To call the ensuing churn of justice turtle-slow would be to defame the speed of chelonian reptiles. The clique members were forced to write apology letters, before being immediately reinstated. When the victim returned to the pool after a hiatus, the verbal abuse picked up without missing a beat.

One member of the circle of offenders was part of a prominent NBAC family: his brother trained with Michael Phelps and went on to become an Olympic gold medalist; their mother was on the board of Maryland Swimming. Even while the case of the younger brat's alleged participation in the lengthy and multi-pronged harassment was under review, he was the subject of a fawning profile at the NBAC website. The victim's mother complained to Susan Woessner at USA Swimming, and Woessner prevailed on NBAC to take down the article.

In Baltimore swimming, the buck stopped, or didn't, with Bob Bowman. His callous email response to the mother right after the touching incident in the pool all but channeled the defiant line of John Leonard, the coaches association boss, about not having direct responsibility for the safety of youth athletes "in any way, shape, or form." Bowman wrote to the mom, in part: "We will not be held to your standard of moral superiority nor those of any other single member. NBAC is not a public school or institution. It is a private club whose members choose to join and participate and are also free to choose to join another organization if the program does not meet their personal needs."

Years later, the mother of the traumatized swimmer said that one thing she'd never forget was how two USA Swimming officials, Safe Sport director Woessner and a lawyer (a woman whose name the mom didn't remember), treated her in a telephone call. "They said if they put my son on the witness stand, he would be crucified and humiliated. I started to weep, I simply could not believe their callousness toward our son. They were going to try to break him mentally and emotionally. It was one of the worst days of my life, and I lost all faith in institutions and in the law. I remember I asked if either of them had children and they said no. I told them that I hoped that they never had to experience what we and our family had experienced with a child of their own."

≈

In the middle of my reporting on these events, I was sued in Maryland federal court by the family of one of the alleged tormentors. The Reporters Committee for Freedom of the Press helped me find pro bono representation by BakerHostetler, a Washington law firm. My attorneys counseled that a point of vulnerability for me was my publication of the names of the clique members, who were minors. In the end, we negotiated a consent order by which the plaintiff parents agreed to drop the case and I agreed to remove publication of the clique members' names. I did so by deleting content at my blog; this eliminated or altered content was flagged with my explanation and supplemented by the full text of the consent order from U.S. District Court Judge William D. Quarles, Jr. The consent order is also reproduced here:

CONSENT ORDER

Minor Plaintiff, John Doe, through his parents, James and Jane Doe (collectively referred to as "Plaintiff"), and his counsel, Anne T. McKenna and Andrew C. White, filed the above-captioned lawsuit against Defendants, Irvin Muchnick and Concussion, Inc. ("Defendants"). Plaintiff brought this action against Defendants as a result of blog and internet posts made by Defendants concerning an alleged incident during a North Baltimore Aquatic Club practice that was held at Meadowbrook Swim Club in Baltimore City, Maryland, in February 2012 (hereinafter referred to as "the alleged February 2012 NBAC incident").

Plaintiff's Complaint asserts the following claims against Defendants: defamation, invasion of privacy, intentional infliction of emotional distress, constructive fraud, and violation of 47 U.S.C.A. § 231; simultaneously with the filing of the Complaint, Plaintiff also moved for a temporary restraining order and preliminary injunction. On May 13, 2013, Judge Richard Bennett of the U.S. District Court for Maryland heard oral argument on Plaintiff's Motion for Temporary Restraining Order, and on May 14, 2013, Judge Bennett entered an Order which, by agreement of the parties, has remained in effect until today's date. Subsequent to May 13, 2013, hearing, Defendants retained counsel, Mark I. Bailen and Laurie A. Babinski, and the law firm of BakerHostetler.

By agreement of the parties and the Court, a hearing date was set on Plaintiff's Motion for a Preliminary Injunction of June 25, 2013. Prior to that hearing, however, the parties agreed to resolve this matter pursuant to entry of this consent Order and the terms contained herein.

Accordingly, the following IS HEREBY ORDERED, this 15th day of July 2013:

1. This Order and all its terms shall apply to Irvin Muchnick, Tim Joyce and any other individual associated with Concussioninc.net or any individual working on behalf of or at the direction of Irvin Muchnick; and for purposes of this Order, the terms "Defendants" shall encompass all such persons;

2. Defendants shall not publish in any format, whether written, spoken, or posted online, the following:

   a) Any and all references to the real name of the minor Plaintiff, John Doe, in any correlation whatsoever with the alleged February 2012 NBAC incident that underlies the allegations in the above-captioned case;

   b) Any and all references that discuss the details of any investigation by any Maryland government agencies or Maryland police departments of the alleged February 2012 NBAC incident, though references to the fact that the alleged February 2012 NBAC incident was reported to any Maryland government agencies or Maryland police departments and the disposition thereof are permissible;

c) any and all references to which information or records relating to the Minor Plaintiff John Doe may be in the possession of any Maryland government agencies or Maryland police departments involved in investigating the alleged February 2012 NBAC incident;

d) Any and all references that would identify by real name the minor, John Doe, as Plaintiff in the above-captioned matter;

e) Any discussions of the alleged February 2012 NBAC incident that refer to the matter as a "sexual assault" or otherwise state that:

- **Any criminal activity** occurred;
- **Plaintiff's conduct or any other minor's conduct was in any way criminal**
- **Plaintiff's conduct was in any way** tortious;

3. In no way does this Order restrict or preclude Defendants from publishing any other matters in connection with NBAC, USA Swimming, or other such matters that do not pertain to the alleged February 2012 NBAC incident, or that do pertain to the alleged February 2012 NBAC incident but otherwise comply with the terms of this Consent Order;

4. Within ten (10) days of entry of this Consent Order, Plaintiff shall file a Voluntary Stipulation

of Dismissal without Prejudice. This filing shall in no way preclude Plaintiff's rights to refile this matter or bring an additional cause of action in the event Plaintiff believes that the terms of this Order are being or have been violated;

5. The parties agree that Defendants are permitted to publish the following statements regarding the above-captioned matter:

Plaintiff brought this action against Defendants as a result of blog and internet posts made by Defendants concerning an alleged incident during North Baltimore Aquatic Club practice that was held at Meadowbrook Swim Club in Baltimore City, Maryland, in February 2012.

Plaintiff sought the issuance of a temporary restraining order, preliminary injunction, and filed a complaint asserting the following claims against Defendants: defamation, invasion of privacy, intentional infliction of emotional distress, constructive fraud, and violation of 47 U.S.C.A. § 231.

On May 13, 2013, Judge Richard Bennett of the U.S. District Court for Maryland heard oral argument on Plaintiff's Motion for Temporary Restraining Order; with the Court's permission Defendant Muchnick appeared pro se via teleconference. During the Course of that hearing, Defendant Muchnick argued that the blog posts were speech protected by the First Amendment, but agreed to remove any and all references to the names of minors involved in the alleged February 2012 incident and all references suggesting that he had access to information or records in the possession of Maryland government agencies that were involved in investigating the alleged incident pending hearing on Plaintiff's Motion for Preliminary Injunction.

On May 14, 2013, Judge Bennett entered an Order wherein he denied in part Plaintiff's Request for a Temporary Restraining Order but specifically reserved all matters raised in Plaintiff's Motion for Temporary Restraining Order for the full hearing on the Plaintiff's Motion for Preliminary Injunction. The Order further ordered the removal of the references described above as Defendant Muchnick had agreed pending the hearing on Plaintiff's Motion for Preliminary Injunction. Subsequent to May 13, 2013, hearing, Defendants retained counsel, Mark I. Bailen and Laurie A. Babinski, and the law firm of BakerHostetler.

By agreement of the parties and the Court, a June 25, 2013 hearing date was set on Plaintiff's Motion for a Preliminary Injunction. By agreement of the parties and with the Court's consent, the preliminary injunction hearing was continued while the parties attempted to reach settlement of plaintiff's claims. Prior to a preliminary injunction hearing being held, the parties mutually agreed to resolve this matter by entry of a Consent Order.

6. Defendants are permitted to post unsealed public records of the above-captioned proceedings and Orders of this Court, provided they do so in a manner consistent with the terms of this Consent

Order. However, Defendants may not post misrepresentative excerpts of the pleadings in this case. If Defendants publish excerpts, such publication should be accompanied by a link to the entire document.

7. Defendants will remove all publications, including internet posts and social media platforms, and all content that are inconsistent with the terms of this Order.

So ordered this 15th day of July, 2013.

William D. Quarles, Jr.
United States District Judge

CHAPTER 9

SEX, LIES, AND ALEX PUSSIELDI

Chuck Wielgus's perjurious invocation of the video of Michael Phelps taking a hit from a bong came in a 2010 deposition in Brooke Taflinger's case. She was the Indiana swimmer whose since-imprisoned coach, Brian Hindson, had a Peeping Tom video system in a locker room. Asked about USA Swimming's culpability in the matter, Wielgus did his best emulation of Captain Louis Renault, the character in *Casablanca* who was "shocked, *shocked!*" to learn that gambling had been taking place at his bar. Under oath, Wielgus said no video evidence of any kind was ever even "on the radar screen" for his organization prior to 2008, the year Phelps got caught participating in the dark arts of Cheech and Chong.

In the truthfulness department, at least two buckets of facts failed Wielgus. They weren't on the periphery of anyone's tracking, either, whether the technology was radar, sonar, or eyes not willfully shut against the obvious. The first was the extensive public record surrounding a coach named John Trites.

Wielgus began at USA Swimming in 1997. Trites, then 36, was directing the men's and women's swimming teams at Franklin & Marshall College in Lancaster, Pennsylvania. He also ran the Trident Aquatic Club's USA Swimming–sanctioned age-group program out of the college pool. Starting in December 1997, police gathered evidence implicating Trites in the production and maintenance of secret video and audio recordings of female swimmers as they changed in and out of their swimsuits in the locker room. The video cameras were obscured by towels. The targets of this invasive ogling were as young as 14. After being confronted with the allegation in January 1998, police said, Trites tampered with the videos. Franklin & Marshall fired him. On March 10, 1999, a local warrant sought his arrest on six counts of violating a state electronic surveillance statute. Trites went on the lam. In April, a federal arrest warrant was issued for unlawful flight from prosecution.

According to the FBI, Trites likely proceeded to commute among six U.S. states, Canada, and the Bahamas. (Early on, there was a sighting of him landing at Kennedy Airport in New York on a flight from Trinidad.) The FBI put him on a not-exactly-obscure bit of iconography known as the Most Wanted List. At the time, the bureau was supplying content for a television program, *America's Most Wanted*. Trites was featured on it.

In 2005 the feds acquired information that Trites might be trying to get back into swim coaching. They alerted USA Swimming, which issued an advisory to 7,000 coaches across the country to be on the lookout for Trites. (At 6'7" and up to 290 pounds, he would have been hard to miss.) With the organization's usual speed and dexterity, USA Swimming wouldn't get around to adding him to the banned list until 2013. It's an easy stretch to speculate that Trites had been "flagged" long before that; and, further, that the delay in publishing his name on the USA Swimming site had the dual benefit of containing embarrassment over the one-time presence of a heinous villain, while also giving Wielgus cover during the ordeal of the 2010 Taflinger case deposition.

(In 2015 the FBI publicized an award for information leading to the arrest and capture of Trites. The bureau said he was considered armed and dangerous.)

The other smoking-gun precursor of Wielgus's never-indicted perjury was a coach with seemingly superior resources and a more ambitious aquatic reach. No mere Peeping Tom, Brazil's Alexandre Pussieldi added to his portfolio the methods of a downright human trafficker. Much better connected than John Trites, both locally and internationally, Pussieldi moved to the U.S. in his mid-30s in 1999, and spent five years assisting the legendary coach Jack Nelson, whose program operated out of the International Swimming Hall of Fame complex in Fort Lauderdale, Florida.

Exposure of the conspiracy to paper over Pussieldi's crimes — collusions involving not only USA Swimming, but also the city Parks and Recreation department, police, and a journalist for a major local newspaper — came at the worst possible time for Chuck Wielgus, who in 2014 was on the cusp of induction into the Hall of Fame for long and meritorious service to the sport. Jack Nelson, retired and about to die in November of that year, was already in the Hall's coaches' wing. But a group of well-organized petitioners, coordinated by the Women's Sports Foundation and with abuse survivors at the top of the list of signatories, rose up and said "no" to honoring the executive who presided over a generation of cover-ups.

≈

Alex Pussieldi wasn't the only sketchy figure on Jack Nelson's staff. Another was Cecil Russell, a Canadian coach who twice over the years found ways to work around supposed lifetime bans in his native country. His first infraction was for playing a leading role in an international steroid-trafficking ring. He got a reduced prison sentence of a little more than six months in exchange for testimony at his drug-dealing partner's first-degree murder trial. There, Russell testified to the equivalent of the 400-meter individual medley of turning state's evidence: helping burn and bury the body of the murder victim, and disposing of incriminating bones and jewelry. After his jail term, Russell moved to Spain and coached there, before getting caught as the mastermind of the smuggling of massive quantities of ecstasy from the Netherlands to the American black market; he spent four more years *en celda*.

Jack Nelson himself — most famous for coaching the medal-garnering U.S. women at the 1976 Montreal Olympics — was, both before and after his death, under a cloud for his abuse of Diana Nyad, later a broadcaster, author, and celebrated marathon open-water swimmer, back when he coached her at the exclusive Pine Crest School in Fort Lauderdale in the late 1960s. The ways Nyad has processed her unquestionably irregular interactions with Nelson have ranged from an uncomfortable rambling monologue at a Hall of Fame gathering (in which she discussed, among other things, her traumatic flashback when her airplane, just prior to landing at Fort Lauderdale-Hollywood International Airport, hovered over the Pine Crest campus); to articles in places like *The New Yorker* and the *New York Times* (the latter, a first-person essay, which didn't name Nelson, later would get quietly and partially retracted by the *Times* for an errant detail); to an off-Broadway play dramatizing her crowning triumph over abuse with a successful 110-mile swim from Havana, Cuba, to Key West, Florida, at age 64; to a Netflix biopic starring Annette Bening.[1]

≈

---

[1]   In a 2007 article in the *Miami New Times*, the retired headmaster of Pine Crest equivocally supported Nyad in her accusations against Nelson. I'm convinced that something terrible indeed happened. At the same time, I've reached the difficult opinion that Nyad is a fabulist, an attention-hogger, and an oxygen monopolist, with respect to both youth coach sexual abuse and her impressive open-water swimming stunts. (In those, Nyad has done more than her share to ensure that objectively superior achievements of numerous other women marathon swimmers remain unfairly ignored.) The lesson here is that the tyranny of celebrity abuse testimonials – the true, the mostly true, and otherwise – can become both a moral and a strategic dead end for advocates of youth sports system reform. I wrote about this at length in a 2019 article, "My Diana Nyad Problem – And Ours," concussioninc.net/?p=13962.

Alex Pussieldi's deviations from the straight and narrow climaxed with his assault and battery, on the Hall of Fame complex pool deck and in the locker room, of a swimmer whom he'd brought from Mexico to Florida. The violence represented the coach's retribution after the swimmer discovered that Pussieldi had peeped on him, and acted on the discovery, refusing to follow Pussieldi's instructions at an early morning practice of the Fort Lauderdale Swim Club.

The background was that, after arriving from Brazil and getting settled in Florida, Pussieldi had conceived a side hustle that was both lucrative and fantastically exploitive: he recruited promising swimmers from all over Latin America, and he put up some of them at his own house. One was this fateful Mexican kid, Roberto Cabrera Paredes. Prior to his junior year in high school, more than three years before the 2004 incident, Pussieldi had had Cabrera Paredes designated as his legal ward. Like others', the swimmer's room and board were paid by his parents back home.[2]

Late one night near the end of 2001, Cabrera Paredes got up to go to the bathroom used by the tenant-swimmers. (Pussieldi had his own private bathroom in another part of the house.) He confronted Pussieldi holding a drill in the bathroom. Returning to the bathroom later, Cabrera Paredes found a hidden camera tucked inside a vent for the heating and air conditioning. Shortly after that, Cabrera Paredes, along with someone else, snuck into Pussieldi's bedroom when he wasn't there, and they found and played a VCR cassette. The video was of the tenant-swimmers using the bathroom. Later, a report by the Fort Lauderdale police Special Victims Unit would document that the two bedroom interlopers also came across a

---

2   The following details were constructed, in part, from a combination of Fort Lauderdale police reports and a heavily redacted copy of a report by a USA Swimming private investigator, Dirk Taitt, who also did work for the NCAA and the NFL. He was deposed in 2011 in an abuse lawsuit against the organization. Taitt's report also was part of the voluminous internal swimming files, submitted in discovery after the 2012 California Supreme Court order and subpoenaed by an FBI field office.

videotape of "Pussieldi having sex with teenage boys." The witnesses surmised that the three boys were teenagers "because they did not have facial hair" and that the video was not made in the U.S., since the surroundings weren't recognized and the people on the tape were speaking Portuguese (the main language of Brazil). One of the witnesses interviewed by police claimed that the parents of a girlfriend of a swimmer had also confronted Pussieldi about surreptitiously produced video of sex between the swimmer and the girlfriend, and Pussieldi had "admitted everything" to the parents. (In a telling sidelight, a swim team official assured the reporting parents that Pussieldi was undergoing psychiatric treatment for his problem. The official evidently defined the problem as not criminal voyeurism and abuse of underage victims, but rather homosexual proclivities.)

Cabrera Paredes reported his findings of, at minimum, the hidden bathroom video to a team coach (likely Nelson, but the name is redacted in the USA Swimming investigator's report). "[REDACTED] told [REDACTED] not to tell anyone because it could ruin the [REDACTED] Swim Club's reputation." There was further dialogue about Pussieldi's "personal problems and an unusual infatuation and personal attraction to [REDACTED]."

This aligned with an aspect of the 2007 *Miami New Times* article about Jack Nelson and Diana Nyad. *New Times* referred to what it called a "packet" of information, given to Fort Lauderdale city commissioners, which "paints an alarming picture of Nelson and some of the coaches he supervised. In 2004, a swimmer in Nelson's program told Fort Lauderdale police that one of the coaches had child pornography on his computer and that the coach secretly videotaped male swimmers who lived with him as the swimmers undressed in a bathroom."

A source for the *New Times* account was another Nelson assistant coach, Duffy Dillon; along the way of a business dispute between them, Nelson sued Dillon for defamation. "According to the packet,

Dillon told Nelson about the boys' accusations, but Nelson did not go to police. Instead, Dillon's wife did," the *New Times* article said. (It bears noting that Duffy Dillon and his wife Barbara would become sources of mine, as well, on a range of Alex Pussieldi scandals — that is, until Duffy Dillon wound up taking a job with John Leonard's American Swimming Coaches Association.)

Pussieldi's criminal assault was at a 5 a.m. practice on February 13, 2004. Now 20 years old and long since moved out of Pussieldi's house, and about to go to the University of Maryland on a swimming scholarship, Roberto Cabrera Paredes gathered with half a dozen others for drills supervised by Pussieldi. On Pussieldi's instructions, the teammates went into the pool, but Roberto kept his seat in the bleachers alongside. He said he'd take direction from other coaches but not from Pussieldi.

Pussieldi said, "You had better get into the fucking pool, I don't care what you think, you fucking no one." According to the USA Swimming investigator, Cabrera Paredes said Pussieldi "effectively choked" him with the towel around his neck, and "manhandled" and punched him.

> [REDACTED] reported that the incident ceased after [REDACTED] effectively pushed [REDACTED] to the floor and stated to the young man "get the hell out of my pool, you don't belong here." [REDACTED] reported that he was shaken, rose to his feet and ran to the locker room for the purpose of retrieving his cellular phone to contact the police for help. [REDACTED] reported that [REDACTED] followed him into the locker room and while [REDACTED] was attempting to open his combination lock on his locker, [REDACTED] banged on the locker with his fists and verbally abused the young man. . . . [A]nother swim

coach appeared in the locker room and intervened. [REDACTED] removed himself from the locker room and shortly thereafter two officers from the [REDACTED] Police Department arrived.

Cabrera Paredes was treated at Holy Cross Hospital but no charges were filed. In Fort Lauderdale's *Sun Sentinel*, swimming beat writer Sharon Robb reported the altercation but not the background. Nelson told her, "We have excused Alex from coaching and told Roberto not to return to the team until we find out the facts . . . until we know the total truth from both sides." Pussieldi, Nelson added, "is a fantastic coach, and I stand by him. It was a mistake on Alex's part and terribly unfortunate."

Documents acquired from the City of Fort Lauderdale through a public records request in 2014 included an extraordinary email, from Sharon Robb to Pussieldi, abetting the cover-up.[3] On February 17, 2004, the same date as that of the first of her two articles on the incident, the journalist messaged:

Hi Alex,

I think since you have a week off, it would be a good idea to go down to the police station, the records department and buy a copy of the police incident report . . .

The Case No. is 04-018791, unless you have a fax number, I can fax to you . . .

---

3 I disputed a portion of request responses for containing improper redactions of information. I sued in Florida circuit court, where I was represented by the Miami law firm Astigarraga Davis Mullins & Grossman. A settlement of that lawsuit followed the judge's *in camera* review of the unredacted versions of the documents, after which he ordered reversal of two of the redactions. The city agreed to reimburse my attorneys $5,000 in legal fees.

It's good to have a copy just for your files in case
this gets out of hand. . . . keep in touch and call me
when you are reinstated so I can write another story
saying you are back coaching . . .

sharon

Other documents from the public records requests made it clear
that complaints about Pussieldi preceded the 2004 incident. Local
sources filled in some of the spaces and went further than the documents. One swimming community figure, who was at the pool when
Pussieldi allegedly struck and choked the Mexican swimmer, told me,
"An atmosphere of 'sex, lies, and videotape' had been in the air for
several months at the Fort Lauderdale Swim Team." Many people were
talking about this swimmer's complaints that Pussieldi had secretly
videotaped him in the bathroom. Additionally, following a trip to a
meet in Orlando the previous fall, which Pussieldi supervised, videos
circulated (either on computers or via the mobile devices and social
media of that time) of a teenage girl swimmer performing fellatio on
two teen boy swimmers, one of whom was a national champion.

In an October 15, 2003, letter to Ernest Burkeen of Parks and
Recreation, Jack Nelson wrote in part: "We plan to ask the three
athletes who were most directly involved to write an essay on what
they feel their responsibility is on a trip to represent themselves,
their team and City of Fort Lauderdale in a dignified and morally
upstanding manner. Each of these three athletes has surely had a lot
of mental pain over this incident and we didn't feel that further negative punishment was required. I hope you agree."

As to the wrap-up of the Pussieldi–Cabrera Paredes altercation,
a memo by Parks and Recreation official Stu Marvin outlined, with
almost comic thoroughness, a paradigm of an information silo bar-
ricaded with bureaucracy, groupthink, and victim-blaming:

I promised Coach I would email these points, per our conversations yesterday and today, to keep him on track.

1. Accept the resignation ASAP.
2. Consult an attorney about wording an official statement to be released to the press (Sharon Robb)
3. Contact George Smith before contacting Sharon Robb concerning the resignation.
4. Call a staff meeting
5. Announce to staff that Alex is resigning "in the best interests of FLST", etc.
6. Make it very plain about the importance of all coaches projecting the same position on all matters concerning FLST
7. Sharing independent points of view can be very detrimental to the organization
8. If any coach has a problem concerning FLST, for any reason, they MUST share it with the Director.
9. The Director will then share the information with City staff. The relationship with the City is of the utmost importance.
10. Contacting Commissioners outside the chain of communication embarrasses the Department & City, damaging FLST
11. Communication breakdowns are detrimental to any organization, creating distrust among staff members.
12. At this time there is obvious distrust among all staff members on many levels, including the Director.
13. Entire staff is put on notice that any internal problems within FLST must be communicated properly.

14. Failure to communicate properly will result in discipline or dismissal
15. FLST is a Team. There is no "i" in "team". Staff needs to act like a team and work together towards a common goal.
16. "A house divided cannot stand".
17. Formal written notice should be given to CoachG, Roberto that their actions are not "in the best interests of FLST".
18. Delay further action on these two individuals at this time.

In accord with the wise counsel of the *Sun Sentinel's* Robb, Pussieldi lay low for a while and was soon back coaching. In fact, his career took off to greater heights. Picking up all the footprints is complicated by chaotic records, but it's clear that one of his many roles was as head coach of the national swimming team of Kuwait. Locally, a prominent lawyer, Norman Tripp, who got wealthy by helping launch Alamo Rent a Car, and whose children swam in Jack Nelson's program, was a long-time patron who fundraised for the building of the Hall of Fame aquatic complex, and sources said he helped fix Pussieldi's employability. Pussieldi landed the Kuwaiti post, it was said, through the good offices of swimming federation (as well as Hall of Fame) board member Dale Neuburger — he of TSE Consulting in Indianapolis and eventual infamy in the Fran Crippen death in Dubai. Through this period, Neuburger was networking with deep-pocketed sheiks newly enamored of the Olympic movement.

Fort Lauderdale's public record disclosures included a police report calling Cabrera Paredes a "victim" — the scare quotes are those of the report's author, a police sergeant — and saying the whole matter was now moot because the sergeant was told by another officer that "the suspect coach is no longer at the pool and is a coach overseas now. The case is going to be closed as Unfounded."

Pussieldi coached at Fort Lauderdale's St. Thomas Aquinas High School from 2000 until 2004, the year of the assault incident — and possibly beyond. A spokesperson for the Archdiocese of Miami said Pussieldi left in '04 because "he didn't wish to continue coaching at the High School level. There were no complaints on Mr. Pussieldi while he worked at St. Thomas Aquinas High School." But one version of an online biography he published for a while (which, it must be said, was rife with hype and exaggeration) claimed a second stint at the school, 2005–07, as "co-head coach."

Pussieldi coached at the Lauderdale Isles Yacht Club's summer program from 2003 to 2009. One of the most intriguing aspects of his work was his association with another coach, Roberto Caragol, including with the age-group team out of Pine Crest School, the setting of Nyad's historical allegations against Nelson. Pussieldi resigned from Pine Crest in 2008, in the middle of an investigation by a regional, multi-agency law enforcement task force, which achieved Caragol's federal conviction and incarceration on charges of child pornography and solicitation of minors.

A member of the task force from Broward County Sheriff's Office was honored for her protection of the region's kids from sexual predators. But it appears that the extent of Detective Jennifer Montgomery's enterprise was confiscation of Caragol's computer and the coach's arrest — she did no investigation of the perpetrator's full employment history and associates. Caragol, who also coached at state boys' champion Cypress Bay High School, joined Pine Crest in 2006, where he was primarily responsible for swimmers from ages eight to 14, and he and Pussieldi were listed as co-contacts. According to a federal government source of mine, the FBI's North Miami field office, one of the task force agencies, had been tipped about Pussieldi's own activities in the years prior to the investigation of Caragol (which began with a tip from a user of the online service AOL). The source, however, didn't know if any of the Pussieldi information — which the FBI ultimately didn't act on due to the failure of victim witnesses to emerge — was ever shared with the group of officers who targeted Caragol. And Detective Montgomery admitted to me, "The investigation did not expand into additional suspects."

Upon leaving Pine Crest, Pussieldi started his most celebrated program, the Davie Nadadores, in a town just south of Fort Lauderdale. He brought to Florida many swimmers from Brazil and other Latin American and Caribbean outposts, and from the Middle East. Haphazardly, many of them lived in dormitories at Nova Southeastern University in Fort Lauderdale.

Among the hoodwinked local observers was *Miami Herald* sports columnist Linda Robertson. In a lengthy feature article, Robertson told readers that Pussieldi was running a local athletics jewel, a model of swim world comity. "Swimmers from 53 countries have found a second home at this global hotspot in west Broward as members of the Davie Nadadores club. Coach Alex Pussieldi not only trains them but he also accommodates their multicultural needs," Robertson gushed.

Less than a year later, in 2013, the Davie Nadadores were kaput. After a series of chaotic incidents tied to the poor supervision of swimmer-boarders, Nova Southwestern ended the housing arrangements. "The great Alex Pussieldi," winner of two straight ASCA Coach of Excellence designations, was retiring, SwimSwam said. The Nadadores "sort of came apart," SwimSwam later elaborated. For years, coaching rival Duffy Dillon had been registering complaints with USA Swimming's regional affiliate, Florida Gold Coast Swimming, over Pussieldi's fraudulent manipulation of team rosters with ringers who buzzed in and out of the state and the Nadadores roster. In December 2013, Florida Gold Coast suspended the "retired"

Pussieldi and his partner, Tomas Victoria, and fined them $17,750 for 355 violations in meet entries.

After the full facts and context of the 2004 Cabrera Parades assault were published at my website in early 2014, South Florida swimming parent J.P. Cote, a former Canadian national team member, told of having observed Pussieldi's inappropriate touching of a young male swimmer at a 2012 meet in Plantation. He'd filed complaints with both the Plantation police and USA Swimming. Now Safe Sport director Woessner told Cote that a USA Swimming investigator, Nancy Fisher, was undertaking a fresh probe. "I understand your frustration and I can only offer frustration myself when I review the file and wonder why more was not done then," Woessner emailed. "I can tell you that we are committed to trying to right that wrong now."

Pussieldi had moved on to become a freelance swimming journalist and commentator. He was on the masthead of *Swimming World* magazine as its Brazil correspondent. In 2015 the publication's CEO Brent Rutemiller said, "We are reassessing the status of all of our contributors as we have new people coming on board from around the globe." The next year, Rutemiller said Pussieldi was no longer a contributor, but not why.

Pussieldi worked extensively on air, including at both summer and winter Olympics, for Brazil's ESPN-type network, SporTV. In 2020 CNN Brasil broadcast a report on Pussieldi that fell far short of the original parameters contemplated by the correspondent — who, while arranging to interview me for the same report, confided that he'd already cornered Pussieldi into a compromising interview. The Pussieldi interview wound up not being shown, as CNN largely focused instead on Leo Martins, a former swimmer under Pussieldi and a fellow native Brazilian. Martins had gone on to become an abusive coach himself, getting added to USA Swimming's banned list in 2016.

The 20-minute CNN Brasil report — padded with rehashes of broad subjects such as U.S. Congressman George Miller's fizzled investigation of years earlier — failed to share with viewers that Martins had been well known in the Florida swimming community as "Pussieldi's boy." The older man often referred to the younger one as his "son," an instructive point in light of the evidence that Pussieldi had installed himself as legal guardian of some of the swimmers he imported from around the world. Martins was one of the swimmers living in the house when Mexico's Cabrera Paredes discovered the Peeping Tom practices. And Martins was believed to be the person who, in the subsequent covered-up Fort Lauderdale police investigation, said Pussieldi had inappropriately touched him. Local sources said that Martins then started receiving a stream of expensive gifts from Pussieldi, including a car. Another swimmer and a girlfriend of another of Pussieldi's house tenants (the ones victimized by Pussieldi's Peeping Tom video of them having sex) were notably disgusted at a poolside celebration of Martins's impending departure to Arizona State University on a swimming scholarship. Martins got a business degree in travel management at ASU and advertised himself as a consultant for international travel packages. Florida state business records listed him as a partner of Pussieldi in a venture called Best Swimming.

CHAPTER 10

HALL OF FAME? OR HALL OF JUSTICE?

The cover story of the June 5, 2014, editions of the weekly alternative newspapers *Miami New Times* and *Fort Lauderdale New Times* carried the headline "An Underage Sex Scandal Leads to South Florida's Swimming Hall of Fame." The article, by Deirdra Funcheon, jumped off from the reporting at my site about Alex Pussieldi by Tim Joyce and myself. The impact of the article was evident in a note added to the version posted at the *New Times* website:

> **Update:** Minutes after this story went to press, Chuck Wielgus, the longtime head of organized swimming, withdrew from his planned induction into the Swimming Hall of Fame.

The induction had been scheduled for June 13. The walkback of Wielgus's honor by the International Swimming Hall of Fame (ISHOF) rewarded a burst of anti-abuse activism, which highlighted in major media the cover-ups of the cases of largely forgotten survivors. The central tactic of this triumph was a public petition skillfully orchestrated by Nancy Hogshead-Makar, then senior director of advocacy for the Women's Sports Foundation. (A few months after the Wielgus / ISHOF campaign, Hogshead-Makar, who embarked on a legal career after winning three gold medals at the 1984 Los Angeles Olympics, left the foundation to start her own group, Champion Women.)

In the view of some activists, however, the output of the campaign was hollow, with some going so far as to label it a sellout. This was because Wielgus, though publicly embarrassed at levels exceeding those of even the ABC *20/20* broadcast, remained otherwise unscathed. He stayed in his post at the top of USA Swimming.

The stakes of the compromise that saved Wielgus's job were told in the numbers in IRS nonprofit filings. Even as he scratched himself from the Hall of Fame final after winning his nomination heat, his USA Swimming paychecks that year totaled $853,923. This broke down as $772,263 in base compensation, $15,900 in "other reportable compensation," $47,587 in retirement and other deferred compensation, and $18,173 in "nontaxable benefits." In 2015 he'd go on to make $882,008. In 2016, $960,047. In 2017, the year of his death, $1,142,405.

≈

The petition, entitled "Rescind Chuck Wielgus' Hall of Fame Nomination," was uploaded on May 31, 2014. By the end of its first weekend online, more than 500 people had signed it. The skeletal form of the petition is viewable to this day at Change.org, along with the names of nearly 2,000 ultimate signatories. Savvy in social media, Hogshead-Makar and her team drove an associated Twitter hashtag, "#funnestsport." The petition was in the form of an open letter addressed to Hall of Fame executive director Bruce Wigo and the 12-person board of directors, who included Olympic legends Mark Spitz and Donna de Varona. Front and center for the petition launch were 19 survivors of swim coach abuse, with Diana Nyad's name topping the list. Another 30 initial individual and institutional supporters included Lisa Burt, mother of Sarah Burt, the Illinois girl who took her own life in 2010.

"Wielgus isn't inspiring a protest merely because he was at the helm," the petition text read. "Instead, the protest is about Wielgus' failure to protect swimmers from coaches with well-known, long histories of sexual abuse. Not until Wielgus was pressured by the United States Congress, by heart-breaking media stories on the unrelenting parade of victims, by lawsuits, and by new United States Olympic Committee (USOC) rules, did USA Swimming start to protect victims. It does not take leadership to move an organization under that type of scrutiny; it requires leadership to avoid it."

The full-length version of the petition, with backup attachments, laid out that Chuck Wielgus, in his then 17 years at the helm, had consistently failed to rid the sport of known serial molesters. The keystone of the argument was Andy King. In 2010 Chuck Wielgus lied to ESPN's *Outside the Lines* by claiming that USA Swimming had never heard of King until his arrest. With much the same effect of *20/20*'s unveiling of swimming leadership's cynical priorities behind the scenes, *Outside the Lines* detailed a 2003 email exchange demonstrating that Wielgus knew full well about King and, indeed, ordered the cover-up of a complaint about him. The petition also name-checked Everett Uchiyama, Mitch Ivey, and Rick Curl.

Allowing "a culture of sexual harassment and abuse to foster by condoning sexual relationships between coaches and the swimmers they coach," the petition said, was "inconsistent with the USOC's Coaching Ethics Policies," as Wielgus failed to protect swimmers "the way students and employees are protected." Even after the Andy King trial and a significant rule change by the aquatics convention in 2013, "many coaches still see nothing untoward about having sex with the athletes they coach."

Moreover, the petition charged, USA Swimming's national legislative strategy, led by Wielgus, was "hostile to victims." Attempting to reform a burdensome regime of short statutes of limitations for bringing civil cases in many individual states — a condition benefiting molesters because victims, commonly, were slow to come forward — anti-abuse forces lobbied for, at the very least, one-off special new windows for litigation by the last generation's victims. Yet in 2013, the petition pointed out, USA Swimming hired one of California's most influential lobbying firms to join the Catholic Church in killing legislation that would have extended statute of limitations deadlines.[1]

Swimming policies were likewise hostile. The petition zeroed in on two in particular, for which Wielgus, under existing law, exercised wide executive discretion, but which he interpreted to the narrowest extent possible. One of them "grandfathered" a provision not to sanction abusers who were no longer USA Swimming members and whose abuse findings dated back in time. This policy made it "impossible for victims to remove their abusers from the Swimming Hall of Fame, and also leaves these molesters in good standing within the swimming community. More importantly, USA Swimming's failure to oust these molesters provides them with ample opportunities to be around swimmers." The second pernicious discretionary policy was USA Swimming's weak protection of whistleblowers and advocates for victims. The latter could be retaliated against with impunity, all the way up to the very filing of an official complaint. For example, an assistant coach discussing

---

1   The California legislation that year passed in the state legislature but was vetoed by Governor Jerry Brown, who was once a seminarian. The lobbyist paid by both swimming and the Catholic Church was the Sacramento law firm Nielsen Merksamer Parinello Gross & Leoni. A database of federal lobbying, maintained by the Center for Responsive Politics, also listed more than $100,000 in payments by USA Swimming in 2009–10 to FaegreBD Consulting, an Indianapolis firm that was an offshoot of the Baker & Daniels law firm. Baker & Daniels was where Jack Swarbrick practiced law and advised USA Swimming before becoming athletic director of Notre Dame.

possible abuse he or she witnessed, with the goal of remedying the problem, was wide open to dismissal or demotion.

Personally and callously, Wielgus's hostility extended to individual victims who reported abuse, the petition said; Deena Deardurff Schmidt, Paul Bergen's accuser, was a prime example. Following her revelations on ABC's *20/20*, Wielgus told journalists he would "call her up and talk to her." What actually happened was that he engineered having her served with a subpoena, which led to grueling cross-examination at a deposition — even though Deardurff Schmidt, who'd spoken out in an effort to improve the sport, "never hinted at litigation." Wielgus didn't apologize to her or to any other victim.

Steeped in devastating detail, the petition estimated that USA Swimming paid defense lawyers $3.5 million to defend a single case, Jancy Thompson's.

≈

Wielgus's statement to ESPN's T.J. Quinn, "We didn't hear of Andy King until April of 2009," was a major Pinocchio, of course. But as with Donald Trump's blatherings on the stump and in media interviews, this Wielgus lie itself didn't rise to the level of what should have been legal culpability. The word "perjury" comes from Latin *perjurium*, "deliberate giving of false or misleading testimony under oath." For that, you had to turn to things like Wielgus's one-word answer, "No," to a question in a 2009 interrogatory, "Were you ever made aware of prior claims of abuse by King?" The interrogatory was in the Jane Doe case concerning the coach who'd spend the rest of his life at Mule Creek State Prison.

What the record clearly laid out was an alert to Wielgus of allegations against King no later than January 20, 2003. On that date, Wells O'Brien, then USA Swimming's general counsel, advised a coach named Clint Benton to forward to Wielgus a lengthy email from former swimmer Katie Kelly detailing her experiences with King.

Wielgus emailed back to Benton a week later. This document was another one of those snapshots by bullet point — like that hapless Fort Lauderdale Parks and Recreation official's regarding Alex Pussieldi — filling in the gaps between USA Swimming's version of the truth, the whole truth, and nothing but the truth, and everyone else's lying eyes:

1. No formal complaint is being filed, so there is no formal action for you or us to take.
2. You should monitor the situation and alert us if any new information comes forward.
3. USA Swimming will open a file on this matter, and while we will take no action at this time, we will remain alert for any new information.
4. This matter should be kept confidential by both you and us.
5. If/when any new information comes forward, we will assess the situation at that time and determine if any action is required.

Even earlier than that, in 2002, Wielgus had deflected an email complaint about King from a Washington State parent. And in 2006, USA Swimming would enact those coach background checks, which would prove somewhat less than waterproof. Returning to a team in California two years later, King passed his with flying colors.

When he was asked about Rick Curl, Wielgus took incuriosity to the depths of the Mariana Trench. The head of organized swimming in the U.S. not only didn't know why this prominent coach got fired at the University of Maryland — "I never even knew he worked at the University of Maryland." Wielgus likewise "never received any information about" Curl's having had illicit sexual contact with one of his swimmers. And there was no file on him — "Not — not that I'm aware of. . . . I have — I have heard, just within the past three to four weeks, that there was some sort of a settlement between Rick Curl and a victim or a victim's family. And that's the first I heard of that." Wielgus later amended that to, "I shouldn't say I learned. I heard a rumor." From whom did he hear the "rumor"? "That's a good question. I don't recall. . . . I just — I — I think I heard it in the context of somebody saying that they had seen his name on a blog or something to that effect."

≈

The news media fallout of the Hall of Fame affair was even worse than the dual-national TV interview pratfalls of four years earlier — bad press around the same theme, by accumulation and reinforcement, both adds and multiplies. In his first recorded reaction, Hall director Wigo said, "The petition raises disturbing, grave questions that we take most seriously. The International Swimming Hall of Fame has great compassion and empathy for all survivors of sexual abuse [and is] reviewing the petition."

Wielgus's own response was by proxy: a letter signed by five current and former USA Swimming board presidents who'd worked with him across two decades. Their statement assured one and all, "Without hesitation, we attest that Chuck is a man of impeccable character who consistently exhibits a value system steeped in ethics and personal accountability. His integrity and leadership have been inspirational to us, and we have seen first-hand his positive impact on USA Swimming's 400,000 members that include athletes, parents, volunteers, coaches and staff."

Petition organizer Hogshead-Makar emphasized to the media that any incremental improvements under Wielgus had been achieved "at the point of a gun," from a congressional investigation, an FBI investigation, and lawsuits. "That was not 'admirable leadership,'" she said.

This interlude also backed USA Swimming into damage control on multiple ancillary scandals. The spotlight fell on the discreet 1998 firing of director of club development Will Colebank — enabling his rebound to a job as a middle school teacher in Colorado Springs, before finally being arrested and convicted for molestation and child pornography. Now, the organization was quick to soothe public concerns with a promise that no such thing would happen again.

The petition's impact was swift, and the denouement was coordinated:

> After significant reflection and discussion, International Swimming Hall of Fame (ISHOF) chairwoman Donna de Varona and President/CEO Bruce Wigo, and USA Swimming Executive Director Chuck Wielgus jointly announce that Mr. Wielgus' name will be withdrawn from consideration of the Hall of Fame. The induction ceremony should be a time to celebrate our sport and the outstanding accomplishments of the individuals being honored. Both ISHOF and USA Swimming believe our mutual decision is in the best interest of the swimming community as a whole and we are committed to working constructively together with other organizations, including the Women's Sports Foundation, to end sexual abuse and ensure a safe culture for athletes.

In accepting this olive branch on behalf of the foundation, Hogshead-Makar called the decision "a difficult action taken by both parties, [but] without a doubt the appropriate outcome." She added that it sent a powerful message of zero tolerance for abuse and of the responsibility of leaders to "do all within their power to protect the victims, perform competent investigations and remove abusers from positions of access and power."

But did it? A number of activists were not celebratory but angered. They felt this modus vivendi blunted momentum for pushing Wielgus not just out of the Hall but out of office, and beyond that, for scrutinizing the voluminous ongoing and historical cover-ups. Tony Austin, a Southern California swimmer whose blog, including original and forceful content on the sexual abuse issue that gained a following inside the swimming community, accused ISHOF board member de Varona of concocting a dirty deal whose tacit upshot was getting the Women's Sports Foundation inside the door for potential consultancy revenues and sponsorship support.

Over time — as one jerry-built abuse solution after another got rolled out, knocked down, and reconstructed under new names with the same rotating cast of characters — events would prove that Tony Austin got that one right. Chuck Wielgus kept his million-dollar-a-year job. At the Women's Sports Foundation's next fundraising banquet, USA Swimming bought a premium table.

CHAPTER 11

ABOUT PAUL BERGEN

International Swimming Hall of Fame chief Bruce Wigo could hardly claim that the continued honoring of Paul Bergen was any kind of newly risen issue. ISHOF's passive criteria for coaches with abuse baggage was long controversial. With respect to Bergen specifically, the criteria controversy had come to the fore a year prior to the announced Chuck Wielgus induction and the Women's Sports Foundation campaign that aborted it. The Bergen story also blew up three years after Wielgus's admission to ESPN's T.J. Quinn of never having reached out to Deena Deardurff Schmidt following the press conference at which she laid bare the abuse. Back then, Wielgus said, "Sounds like I should call her up and talk to her" — punctuating the remark with a smarmy smirk for the camera.

Here's what David Berkoff wrote in his 2010 research memo to the USA Swimming board, which likely mirrored the background of Wielgus's "flagged list" of shadow-banned coaches:

> Bergen is a Hall of Fame coach who is credited with coaching dozens of world record holders and Olympians in the US and abroad. In 2010, Bergen was impliedly accused by former swimmer and 1972 Olympian, Deena Deardurff (Schmidt), of sexual abuse beginning when she was just 11 years old (she alleged abuse by her coach

during the period of time she was coached by Bergen and stated that her coach was a Hall of Fame coach, but did not directly use his name).

A 2008 interview of Bergen, posted on YouTube but since taken down, called him an "internationally-renowned coach, currently working as a coach in Canada." Bergen talked about the lessons he learned from fabled Indiana coach Doc Counsilman, the first to develop certain methods for communicating stroke technique to swimmers and using video. Bergen said he was also influenced by George Haines: "I can remember paying my own tickets to go on the deck and watch him with his kids." Text accompanying the video interview said the "spirit of mentoring young coaches has come full circle. Bergen has been a mentor to some of the United States' best coaches, including Bob Bowman and Sean Hutchison."

≈

For 14 years, the swim club out of the Tualatin Hills Aquatic Center in Beaverton, Oregon, hosted the annual Paul Bergen Junior International SCM Championship. The meet was described on the club's website as "the only one of its kind held in the United States, bringing together young swimmers (ages 18 and under) from around the world. Since its inception in 1999, this competition has included swimmers from the United States, Canada, France, Germany and Mexico, many of whom have achieved World and/or Olympic championships." For the last edition of the event under that title, in 2012, the team's magazine, *The Current*, emptied the hagiography tank in a photo caption: "A real celebrity was sighted on deck at this year's Junior International as the man himself, Coach Paul Bergen, made an appearance."

By then, the club known as the Thunderbolts was headed by son Linck Bergen. The lead sponsor was Nike, the corporate sports marketing titan, whose headquarters were in Beaverton.

In June 2013, Deardurff Schmidt renewed the allegations she'd been raising for years. Now, in an open letter to Wielgus in the wake of his Hall of Fame controversy, her lawyer Bob Allard was again demanding action on Paul Bergen. The response came not from Wielgus but from USA Swimming lawyer Richard Young:

> USA Swimming is a membership organization, not a law enforcement authority. USA Swimming's ultimate authority is to expel from membership individuals who have violated its rules. Mr. Bergen is not currently a USA Swimming member, and has not been since 2005. Ms. Schmidt has stated, and your letter confirms, that the alleged abuse took place from 1968 to 1972. This was well before USA Swimming came into existence. USA Swimming has no authority to initiate a National Board of Review proceeding against an individual who is not currently a member (and is therefore not a risk to USA Swimming member swimmers) and where the alleged bad acts occurred before USA Swimming came into existence. However, based on Ms. Schmidt's information, if Mr. Bergen were to seek USA Swimming membership at some future date, Ms. Schmidt's allegations would be investigated and addressed in a hearing before that membership would ever be allowed, assuming, of course, that she would be willing to participate.

"USA Swimming," Young added, "has no control over the International Swimming Hall of Fame or who it inducts into the Hall or who it may choose to expel."

There wasn't any question, though, that local swimming and parks and rec authorities had control over the honorific of their junior invitational meet. As the 2013 Tualatin Hills event approached, Deardurff Schmidt shared with me graphic details of what Bergen had done to her decades earlier. The pool where he coached her in Cincinnati had an under-surface filter room; thanks to a side window, it doubled as a pool viewing room. From there, Bergen would critique the strokes of the swimmers in the water. At times, simultaneously, he'd hide behind the filters with Deena and physically violate her. It was a scene of subterranean evil, evoking what traumatized Irish swimmers from the same era used to call "the boardroom": a storage area where a coach, Derry O'Rourke, worked his depravity on child athletes, as described by writer Justine McCarthy in her 2010 book *Deep Deception: Ireland's Swimming Scandals*.

In Cincinnati, Bergen "controlled everything with fear and intimidation," Deardurff Schmidt remembered in an email. "I wanted to keep a journal but he made us all turn the journals in to him so he could read them and I knew I had to just write what he wanted."

The Bergen meet contretemps got the attention of the U.S. House of Representatives' Suzanne Bonamici of Oregon's First Congressional District, which included Beaverton. Almost imperceptibly as the year wore on, the Tualatin Hills promos pivoted to referring only to the "Thunderbolt Junior Internationals." But other swimming sites continued to use the Bergen name. Neither the team nor Nike responded to media queries.

On December 10, SwimSwam addressed public curiosity over this stealth switch. The upcoming edition of "the Tualatin Hills–hosted Short Course Meters meet that is internationally attended," the swimming news site reported, was no longer being referred to as the Paul Bergen International, "a brand that had become well-known in the Northwestern United States and more globally."

It took two more days for Portland's *Oregonian* to weigh in with the addendum that the name change followed "USA Swimming's suggestion that the club disassociate itself from a former coach who has been accused of sexual abuse." Yet the Thunderbirds' website persisted with other Paul Bergen references, including encomiums. Rome wasn't built in a day, and neither was the deconstruction of the Bergen classic executed overnight.

Congresswoman Bonamici, who served on the House Education and Workforce Committee with California's George Miller —who was purported to be investigating USA Swimming — said, "I am deeply concerned about reports of child sexual abuse by athletic coaches, particularly in public and private swim clubs."

Tualatin Hills Parks & Rec general manager Doug Menke said letters of agreement in place since 1997 described the relationships of the district with five affiliated aquatic clubs, one of which was the Thunderbirds — "a separate independent entity." Taking the irrefutable to the breaking point of plausibility, Menke told me Parks & Rec was unaware of the Bergen allegations "until we received your November 30, 2013 communication." Whereupon, on advice of counsel, he dutifully informed the Tualatin Hills club and its head coach, Bergen's son.

Having established sufficient, if risible, legal distance from the controversy of an acclaimed coach long associated with his facility, Menke didn't seem to feel the need to bother appending the ritual verbiage that child abuse was reprehensible. And that, if Paul Bergen was indeed guilty of it, then that too would be oh-so-regrettable.

A prominent swimming couple in the Beaver State, if so inclined, might have been able to contribute more to the public's understanding. Larry Liebowitz, head swim coach at Oregon State University, was a long-time associate of the omnipresent Mark Schubert, including at Schubert's summer camp in Southern California as recently as 2011.

Liebowitz was part of Schubert's founding staff at the Mission Bay Aquatic Training Center in Boca Raton, Florida, nearly 30 years earlier (about which more shortly). Schubert steered a number of swimmers to Liebowitz's program at Oregon State.

In 2013, Liebowitz's university athletic department bio said one of his assistant coaches was his wife Mary Anne Gerzanick-Liebowitz. Maybe the bio author didn't get the memo that OSU had moved on from Mary Anne the year before. This inconvenience caused Schubert to work his recruiting magic in the opposite direction, by helping some of Gerzanick-Liebowitz's swimmers transfer to other schools. In the meantime, whatever had caused Gerzanick-Liebowitz to be removed from the campus in Corvallis, Oregon, didn't stop her from serving on the board of directors of the American Swimming Coaches Association.

≈

Days after the umpteenth iteration of Deena Deardurff Schmidt's account of Bergen's molestation of her finally succeeded in getting his name scrubbed from the international junior invitational in Oregon, her lifelong friend Melissa Halmi shared another ghastly Bergen episode. Halmi (who later took a different surname — I'll proceed to refer to her as Melissa) actually had put herself out there much earlier than Deardurff Schmidt, even if the swimming world had succeeded in hushing it up. Melissa became another Bergen abuse victim when she swam for him at the University of Wisconsin-Milwaukee in 1973–74. She'd be interviewed about Bergen by the Hamilton County, Ohio, district attorney. Later still, her testimony would cost Bergen a lucrative coaching contract and send him into horse-training exile.

Deena and Melissa swam together under Bergen with the Cincinnati Marlins club in the early '70s. There, according to Melissa,

Bergen was widely thought to have engaged in sexual misconduct not only with Deena, but also with another swimmer who was the first national champion out of that city. Rumors escalated to the point where the team's major benefactor, Charles Keating (the financier who would become infamous for his role in the national savings and loan collapse and government bailout of the 1980s), forced Bergen out. Bergen became the university swim coach in Milwaukee.

In her late high school years, Melissa had focused more on water polo than on swimming; she and Deena played together on an Amateur Athletic Union national championship team. But when Melissa graduated from Cincinnati's Ursuline Academy in 1973, Bergen recruited her for his collegiate swimming program. Melissa recalls driving to Wisconsin with Bergen, his wife, and their three kids. One of them was the now-notorious Linck.

"That's when the brainwashing began," Melissa told me. "It's such a hard thing to understand if you haven't lived through it. Bergen put me on a pedestal, gave me constant attention, and demanded total control of my life. He wanted to see me every day, and not just at practice. He would have me go to his office between classes and sit on his lap. He touched me, nuzzled my neck, dropped objects into my shirt that he then had to 'retrieve.'" She called Bergen's behavior and its effects "cult-like. He was a Jim Jones figure."

In February 1974, Melissa's father died in a plane crash. Returning to Cincinnati for the funeral, she had long conversations with Deena, who helped her understand how Bergen was manipulating and abusing her. "Something clicked," Melissa said. "I realized I was done with him."

Melissa told Bergen as much when he picked her up at the airport upon her return to Milwaukee. He didn't take her back to her dorm — instead, he put her up overnight at his house, in a downstairs den with a foldout couch. In the middle of the night, and with the rest of the family asleep upstairs, Bergen, wearing only a Speedo bikini, showed up in front of Melissa, crawled into bed with her, and fondled her. (They never had intercourse or oral sex.)

The next day they drove together to the university pool, late for practice. On the drive, Melissa said, Bergen held her hand. "If things were different, I would have married you," he told her.

As soon as the car was parked, Melissa fled directly to her dorm room, from which she was afraid to emerge for days. Two months later, she withdrew from school and returned home.

Some years later, at her mother's urging, Melissa was interviewed by Ohio prosecutor Simon Leis. He concluded that Bergen couldn't be prosecuted in Ohio because of jurisdiction and statute-of-limitation issues.

In 1988 Melissa was living in Florida when she came across the news that Bergen had just signed a four-year, $125,000-a-year contract to succeed Mark Schubert as head coach of the prestigious Mission Bay Aquatic Training Center in Boca Raton. The deal was voided after Melissa called Mission Bay developer James Brady with information about Bergen's sordid past. Bergen backed out with a cover story that he couldn't take the job, after all, because he had to care for his sick mother.

At the conclusion of the Mission Bay drama, Bergen called Melissa. In her memory, he said to her, "You just never could accept the fact that I was in love with you."

Overcoming her anger and revulsion, Melissa said simply, "You've got a problem."

"I know," Bergen replied. He said he was getting out of swimming and turning to the horse business.

CHAPTER 12

WHERE THE BAD GUYS GO

While USA Swimming and the American Swimming Coaches Association are separate organizations, the boundaries between them aren't exactly as impermeable as the human body's blood-brain barrier. In 2013, not long before the lawsuits started piling up at the Germantown Academy, forcing the hand of the school administration to put the elderly Dick Shoulberg out to pasture (and a decade after he first postured that, heaven forfend, swimming must never become like the Catholic Church when it came to protecting child molesters), Shoulberg was president of ASCA's board of directors. This was a year when the annual ASCA World Clinic was being held at the Riviera Hotel in Las Vegas, a week prior to USA Swimming's national aquatics convention in Greensboro, North Carolina. For ASCA, coaches flew in to lead or participate in seminars about both the coaching techniques and the commerce of various models for teams and instructional programs. Rick Curl's ex-employers at Australia's Carlile Swim School came all the way from New South Wales.

The schedule of events listed a meeting of the ASCA board, immediately followed by another of the USA Swimming Steering Committee. ASCA president Dick Shoulberg adjourned the first. Following a break, USA Swimming Steering Committee chair Dick Shoulberg called to order the second. It's a small world, after all.

ASCA was a full-service provider. Coaches trying to make their way into the U.S. could avail themselves of ASCA's visa trouble-shooting support and experience. So, too, could coaches moving in the other direction: those seeking out of the U.S., either for innocent globetrotting or to evade the radar and heat from scandals at their jobs back home. In 2014 the organization began a new partnership for visa services with the Bratter Krieger law firm. According to the announcement, Bratter Krieger "specializes in legal work to secure USA Visa's, Greencards and Citizenship, and has already had significant success working for both athletes and coaches who wish to come to the USA for school, to train and to work. We are very pleased that a law firm specializing in this area is now at work on behalf of our sport. The hiring of an attorney for such needs is an important decision and we are happy to work with a highly professional and experienced firm to bring this service to American clubs and coaches."

For coaches under the siege of abuse allegations — sometimes landing on the USA Swimming banned list, sometimes on the secret flagged list — ASCA's John Leonard offered more direct benefits: workarounds to stay in gainful employment. Mitch Ivey was the most famous and controversial beneficiary of Leonard's generous definitions of his trade group's boundaries, geopolitical and ethical.

In the annals of serial abusers, Ivey distinguished himself by being the only one known to have two victims who were unrelated but had the same surname. As a teenager in the late '70s, Noel Moran was America's fastest female backstroker. In 2009, at age 48, she committed suicide — handing USA Swimming the excuse, three years later, that a case against Ivey lacked sufficient evidence on the basis of "no witnesses," and because the Women's Sports Foundation's Nancy Hogshead-Makar, a third party, was "the only person" claiming a coach conduct violation by Ivey. At least, that's what Hogshead-Makar said Safe Sport director Susan Woessner told her in the spring of 2012.

A "new" investigation of Ivey must have gotten opened four months later. It was driven by the other Moran — Suzette Moran — who persisted in her own pursuit of accountability and finally achieved Ivey's official banishment. Suzette Moran was represented by swimming's civil litigation antagonist Bob Allard. Bryan Cave attorney Lucinda McRoberts told Allard that Woessner spoke to Suzette "on June 12, 2013, at which time Ms. Moran confirmed that she had engaged in a sexual relationship with Mitch Ivey while he was a USA Swimming coach and she was his athlete." On the other hand, McRoberts asked Allard, how could he reconcile his demand for Ivey's ban "with your client's wishes that Mr. Ivey not be banned? [Your client told others that she didn't want to see Mr. Ivey banned. In fact, we received sworn testimony to that effect during the hearing.]" (The brackets in the previous sentences were those of McRoberts.)

Suzette Moran did confirm a single contact by USA Swimming. But she said the organization twisted its upshot: "I never said I did not want him banned. I said I was going to think this through and get back to her. After a few minutes I knew I needed [to retain Allard]." Moreover, Hogshead-Makar said she'd provided USA Swimming with the names of people who could be helpful in the investigation of Ivey, as far back as 2011. Suzette Moran was one of them.

Late in 2013, Ivey was banned. The move was conveniently timed: just before his 65th birthday and in the middle of USA Swimming's PR campaign, its "independent" review of its Safe Sport program, and its Olympic Committee–buttressed lobbying — all designed to blunt Congressman George Miller's investigation.[1] Before then, Ivey was seen on pool decks in Canada but not the U.S. The presumption was that he was "flagged," while ASCA was keeping his hand in the sport with contracts to write instruction manuals.

---

1   Chapter 15 fully covers the Miller investigation.

As Leonard liked to say, ASCA had no "direct" role with children "in any way, shape, or form." Its indirect role manifested, in part, in a publication called *News for Swim Parents*. The May 11, 2009, edition of this periodical was devoted to the topic "Adjusting to Different Stroke Techniques." The content included an advice column, in which a parent asked: "My daughter's coach has been changing her strokes and now all of her times are slower. Does the coach know what he is talking about?" Guest columnist Mitch Ivey, identified as "a member of the 1984 Olympic Coaching Staff," soothed this parent's concerns.

≈

John Leonard's Rembrandt — the masterpiece of ASCA's enabling of alternative career tracks for coach abusers — may have taken the corpulent shape of Dustin Perry. Well north of 300 pounds, Perry had a flaccid physique that didn't intuitively connote acuity at teaching how to streamline through the water. What Perry did have, in abundance, was aptitude in peripatetics; he traversed state and national borders like a Houdini. In the process, he became something of a poor man's Alex Pussieldi, minus the known clandestine videotapes.

In 2003–04, Perry served an 18-month USA Swimming suspension for sexual abuse and other improprieties. After doing the time, he went on to coach in five additional states far and wide. Especially instructive was his employment during the suspension itself. Thanks to an ASCA job board, Perry found work as a coach in Mexico under Jack Simon, an ASCA Hall of Fame coach who himself worked in five foreign countries in the course of his career, according to his bio at FINA, the international swimming body.

The original 2002–03 investigation of Perry pertained to misconduct at the Extreme Aquatics Club in Edmond, Oklahoma.

Among the findings were a hazing incident in which naked boys were locked outside a dormitory room, and another in which three boys, wearing only socks on their genitals, ran in front of parent-chaperones. Images of the latter event, on Perry's cell phone, were shown to others. It was further alleged that Perry supplied underage boys with alcohol on a trip to a swim meet, and allowed gambling by kids on another such trip, to Las Vegas.

After complaints lodged by Oklahoma parents, Perry relocated to Harrisonburg, Virginia, with the Valley Area Swim Team. USA Swimming's investigation also discovered that Perry had been abruptly terminated from his previous job at a YMCA in Oklahoma City, where he worked from 1994 to 1998.

Perry got off with a mere suspension following a written apology to executive director Wielgus. In that email, Perry informed Wielgus of accepting a position with Simon in Mexico during his U.S. suspension. Wielgus was not known to have blinked an eye. To my colleague Tim Joyce in 2014, Perry said, "Just FYI, [the original allegation] was 2000 and still bitter about this accusation!"

Upon USA Swimming reinstatement, Perry became a coach in Washington State with the Walla Walla Swim Club. This was the setting of perhaps his most sordid Svengali act, with a boy we'll call "Benton." Born to a mother addicted to phenobarbital, Benton was raised by foster parents. When he was four, he had a severe seizure, part of a sequence of drug withdrawal symptoms. When he was six, he went into swimming and excelled, eventually earning a partial athletic scholarship at a major university. When he was 14, Perry started abusing him. Benton remained under Perry's spell for many years of adulthood, following the coach around to several states in an ambiguous arrangement that Perry sometimes falsely represented as a father-son relationship. Somewhere in there, Benton changed his surname, as well. He had a rap sheet that included a plea deal on charges of providing obscene material to minors.

From 2009 to 2013, Perry coached the Tiger Aquatic Club in Pocatello, Idaho. One of his predecessors there was Bobby Goldhan, himself an abuser who later committed suicide.

In the spring of 2013, Snake River Aquatics, the local swim committee of Idaho, received complaints against Perry — ranging from sexual harassment to threatening and retaliatory behavior. After much delay, in late summer USA Swimming's investigative consultant, double-dipping retired FBI agent Paulette Brundage, started interviewing concerned parties in Pocatello. According to one witness interviewed by Brundage, she expressed surprise when informed that Perry had already moved from Pocatello to Carson City, Nevada. Perhaps the investigator assumed Perry would stick around in the state of Idaho, since he worked on the board of Snake River Aquatics, along with Patty Stratton, treasurer of a club out of the Y in Boise — and wife of USA Swimming board president Bruce Stratton. (One more thing: Carson City's Tiger Sharks was also one of the many coaching stops of ASCA world traveler and luminary Jack Simon, Perry's Mexican employer during his USA Swimming exile.)

In Pocatello, parents told Brundage — and Joyce and me — that Perry had talked the team board into allowing him to use a separate site, more than a mile from the pool, for dryland exercises. He called this space the "Tiger Den." The auxiliary rental was necessitated when Perry got kicked out of former office space used for non-pool workouts, in the aftermath of frequent verbal altercations with other tenants. Groups of boy and girl swimmers, almost all underage teenagers, alternated days using the Tiger Den before and after pool practices. According to a local source, the space had no weights or much other workout infrastructure. Its primary purpose was Perry's hosting of "movie nights" for older swimmers. The windows of the Tiger Den were always shuttered, and the coach had a strict policy of allowing no parents around.

Benton wasn't the only boy who lived with Perry in creative arrangements. Not all these co-habitants were confirmed to be swimmers. Some were foreign exchange students. From the investigation that led to the 2003 suspension, USA Swimming was aware that Perry boarded at least two foreign youngsters in Oklahoma. In a public document, a Mexican national, who went on to swim and matriculate at the Missouri University of Science and Technology in Rolla, said that he met Perry while he was coaching in Mexico and that the swimmer moved to Idaho to swim with Perry's team there.

After Perry's movements and machinations got publicized and he disappeared from the pool deck in Carson City, too, he applied to be a lifeguard and aquatics director — a position that would also include USA Swimming club coaching duties — for the Waverunners in Craig, Alaska. Team board members contacted Safe Sport director Woessner after reading the coverage of Joyce and myself. One of them told us Woessner stressed that "we don't make recommendations about coaches." She also said that Perry's most recent alleged infractions were merely "administrative." Ultimately, the gatekeepers of this town on Prince of Wales Island decided to take a pass on Perry's application. A club board member and city councilman emailed us, "We had Bob Goldhan as a coach back in the late 90s and we are a little gun shy." Goldhan was that Perry predecessor in Pocatello who took his own life in a hail of abuse charges.

There's much, much more redundant material on the multi-state and multinational meanderings of Dustin Perry. Back in Oklahoma, one of his earliest victims, "John," told Joyce that the coach was a "master manipulator," adroit at insinuating himself into kids' lives and creating an atmosphere of trust and freedom. John said a typically confused teenager could easily be coerced into thinking that sexual activity with an adult male was normal. He met Perry when he was 15, at the YMCA in downtown Oklahoma City, where John became an unofficial lifeguard intern.

At 16, John started cyclically running away from home and staying with Perry. The parents would call the police, and John would be picked up and returned. At times John would hide in Perry's place while undercover cops searched for him. Perry helped orchestrate these runaway episodes, sometimes picking him up at a pay phone booth. Perry guided John in seeking emancipation from his family, and the boy lied to social workers that it was his parents, at home, who were the abusive ones. After a few years, Perry moved on to another victim, and John returned home and was able to rehabilitate a positive relationship with his parents, and a hinged adult life.

What remains unknown is whether the Oklahoma City police did much of anything in terms of sharing their information with either YMCA or swimming authorities.

≈

When Jesse Stovall got the boot at Bear Swimming in California, he knew just where to head next: the U.S. Masters Swimming (USMS) program on the campus of his alma mater, the University of California in Berkeley. Alex Pussieldi wannabe Dustin Perry and Dick Shoulberg assistant Joe Weber landed at YMCA's. Many others slid over to Masters, which is likewise unencumbered by USA Swimming. Despite their designation as "national sport governing bodies" under the Amateur Sports Act, NGBs are really just a motley assortment of nonprofits recognized by the Olympic Committee for running programs with the mission of tracking and developing talent for international competition. They are only national sport governing bodies when the puffery suits them.

Bill Volckening, who edited the USMS magazines *Swim* and *Swimmer*, said the skulduggery of that group might even be termed the worst of all, in the sense that "what people are doing isn't illegal, but it is reprehensible." Rapists and molesters, he said, "retire" into what he called "the 'Shady Pines' for sexually deviant, alcoholic, morally corrupt people who like to swim."

Volckening's own high school coach at the Peddie School in Hightstown, New Jersey, Jeff Lowe, got dismissed for inappropriate conduct with a 15-year-old girl. Another coach in the region, John Trembley of Mercersburg Academy, later would be fired by the University of Tennessee for misdeeds that included soliciting underage boys on the internet. In 1998, Volckening moved to Oregon and started coaching masters at the Tualatin Hills of the infamous Bergens, father and son. "I arrived at the same time as Paul Bergen and Sean Hutchison. During this period, Don King came to Tualatin Hills and was coaching for a brief period. He disappeared as mysteriously as he appeared — midseason."[2]

One-time USMS members on the USA Swimming banned list have also included Darek Hahn, Scott Gaskins, Aaron Bartleson, and Brian Williams. A local favorite in Oregon was David Burleson, described by Volckening as "an anesthesiologist who went to jail for fondling patients while they were sedated. Dave was a member of the Multnomah Athletic Club Masters, and at one time was suspended for getting caught on club premises in a sexual situation with a woman who was also a member of the masters team." Volckening noted that nothing would have prevented Burleson from re-upping with USMS when he got out of jail.

General sexual misconduct, of course, is a different category than child sexual abuse. But the path and pattern were clear, as was the studious non-vigilance for juveniles and adults alike. Sarah Kwon, a Masters swimmer who set national records, launched a Change. org petition to reform vague USMS rules that she said provided "no guidance, repercussions, definitions, or imperative to actually care

---

2   In symmetry with Mitch Ivey, who victimized multiple females with the surname of Moran, the USA Swimming banned list features multiple coaches with the surname of King. Don King was, perhaps, marginally less despicable than the aforementioned Andy King.

for swimmers who have experienced wrongdoing." She said that in 2020, "a man undid my swimsuit and exposed my breasts from another lane at practice. I immediately reported this to my coach. My team president at the time took it upon himself to berate me for being 'irrational.'" Kwon continued:

> When I went to the regional-state governing body, they kicked me to the National office (based in Sarasota, Florida) where Jessica Reilly, Senior Business Director, said there was nothing they could do and offered me a refund to leave. I went to the police after the Chair of the Florida regional governing body said she couldn't believe me until I had a police report. Due to the specificity of the law, this is not considered sexual assault and the police couldn't help me. After nearly two months of being harassed, asked to leave, receiving threatening texts from team mates, I was finally called into the pool and reprimanded that I reported wrong, but told that "something was done" about this man. To this day I still don't know what that is. The only thing I do know is that my team elected a new team president who re-published the rules on sexual misconduct and told me the way this was handled was not acceptable.

Another Masters figure, Don Jacklin, mostly buried his grim legacy in a journey from Oregon to California and back again. At David Douglas High School and its associated USA Swimming age-group club in Portland, Jacklin mentored his star, Kim Peyton, to the Olympic team; she won a freestyle relay gold medal in Montreal in 1976. But in October of the same year, allegations arose that Jacklin had molested another David Douglas swimmer. Jacklin

abruptly resigned and moved to the De Anza club in the part of
California soon to be known as Silicon Valley. Later, several of the
female Douglas swimmers who'd defended Jacklin admitted that
the accusations were true, and indeed that they were themselves
survivors of his abuse. (Kim Peyton went on to swim at Stanford.
She died of cancer in 1986. It's unclear whether she ever claimed to
have been abused by Jacklin.)

At De Anza, according to swimming sources, Jacklin attracted
a number of athletes whose parents checked them out of the Santa
Clara Swim Club after getting smart to the predatory ways of Mitch
Ivey. Jacklin himself coached only a few years at De Anza. He
returned to Portland, opened a travel business, and went the Masters
route. Early in 2024, I received a tip that Jacklin was married to the
mayor of a small town, Maupin, 100 miles east of Portland. Mayor
Carol Beatty's office didn't respond to email queries.

≈

The ultimate in Masters swimming chicanery — sleight-of-hand
with names — may have been pulled off by a character named
Phillipp Djang. Or was it Lincoln Djang? And did anyone care?

Lincoln's USA Swimming membership ended in 1999, after
he was found to have repeatedly grabbed the butt of a 16-year-old
female underwater during a water polo scrimmage at Carlsbad High
School in New Mexico, where Djang was an assistant coach. As a
casual employee under the high school's head swimming coach, his
then-wife Shea Djang, he'd already been at the center of an investigation of sexual relations with another swimmer, age 18. There was
evidence that Lincoln had groomed this girl from an even younger
age, and these indiscretions were administratively actionable even if
there wasn't enough evidence to prove that it crossed the line into
statutory rape. Still, the school had let him off the hook.

The 1999 incident had a different arc through criminal justice. The family of the water polo player swore out a police complaint, and Lincoln Djang was charged with four counts of felony sexual contact with a minor. In a plea bargain, he copped to three counts of misdemeanor aggravated battery and was given a three-year suspended sentence, conditioned on agreement to attend Alcoholics Anonymous and to explain the facts of the incident to a meeting of the entire swim team. The next summer the family settled a civil lawsuit against Djang, the school district, and USA Swimming.

No USA Swimming membership — no problem. Late in 1999, *Swimming World* magazine reported: "New Mexico Masters Phillipp (Lincoln) Djang set a world mark in the men's 45-49 100m back, his 1:03.39 besting the 1:04.14 set by Britain's Eddie Riach last year."

Alas, no such person as "Phillipp (Lincoln) Djang" existed. There *was* a Phillipp Djang, who in 1976 had been a National Association of Intercollegiate Athletics All-American swimmer at Southern Oregon State College. Lincoln Djang, seemingly Phillipp's younger brother, had been a top swimmer at Columbia University who made the 1980 Olympic Trials in the 800-meter freestyle. At best, "Phillipp (Lincoln)" was a confused amalgam; at worst, yet another one of swimming's impenetrable absurdities.

Phillipp Djang — if that's who he was — didn't respond to inquiries sent to what appeared to be a good Gmail address under his listing as "Sanction Manager" of New Mexico Masters Swimming. The same email address showed up online on the curriculum vitae of a researcher who used Djang as a reference from their time together at the U.S. Army Research Laboratory. The content of my query: What was Phillipp's relationship to or association with Lincoln Djang? Or were they one and the same person?

The plot thickened in 2021, when *Men's Health* magazine highlighted the uncommon geriatric athletic prowess of Phillipp Djang under the headline "An Elite Swimmer Shared the Secret to Smashing

World Records at Age 66." Nicknamed "The Phish," he was one of the marquee stars of the 2022 National Senior Games held in Florida.

Lincoln Djang, or should we say the real Lincoln Djang, was also an elite Masters swimmer, boasting four world-record times at that level, according to a 2010 article in a newsletter covering programs in western Washington State. At that point, Lincoln and his new wife Amanda co-owned Tri City Atomic Sturgeon Master Swim Club in Richland. (Need it be added that they were certified ASCA Level 2 coaches?)

Extraordinarily, both Lincoln and Phillipp Djang in 2010 held Masters record times for their respective age groups in the 200-yard backstroke: Lincoln at 2:01.39 for men 50–54 and Phillipp at 2:05.90 for men 55–59. This would support the theory that they were two separate people, and that *Swimming World*'s report of "Phillipp (Lincoln)" reflected either a reporter's error or a switcheroo of the type deployed by a dastardly old pro wrestling tag team competing behind masks.

In the meantime, Lincoln's son Doug Djang grew up to swim under and serve on the coaching staff of Sean Hutchison, the Ariana Kukors abuser, in Seattle.

Lincoln's LinkedIn profile, before going dormant, called him a software engineer at Nuclear Waste Partnership LLC in Carlsbad, New Mexico, presumably in a period before a move to Washington State. The U.S. Masters Swimming public database showed no times for a number of years for "Lincoln P. Djang." (The P stood for Peter, not Phillipp.)

Phillipp had a LinkedIn profile that, for whatever reason, spelled his name with a single L, and called him a semi-retired contractor in Las Cruces, New Mexico. In 2015, Phillipp swam Masters in Adelaide, Australia, and later moved to Florida.

The main takeaway from all this is that somehow, somewhere along the way, Lincoln probably either faded away from competing in the water or morphed into Phillipp for the purpose of Masters listings. The only absolute certainty was that organized swimming, again, proved it could effortlessly transpose to the whole population its inattentiveness to children's safety.

≈

Some situations allow no time for a visa, a coherent exit strategy, or a translucent name; you just have to head for the hills. Such was the case for Simon Daniel "Danny" Chocrón. His resulting hopscotch from North America to Europe to South America was told in USA Swimming's 68-page dossier on him.

In 2001, Chocrón, a 25-kilometer open-water swimming champion out of Florida State University, was a 27-year-old member of the swim coaching staff of the Bolles Sharks, the age-group program of the Bolles prep school in Jacksonville, Florida. Bolles was the cradle of many American Olympic champions (including women's sports advocate Nancy Hogshead-Makar). Gregg Troy developed numerous stars at Bolles before becoming one of Mitch Ivey's successors at the University of Florida. A long-time stalwart of John Leonard's ASCA board, Troy married a swimmer he'd coached at Bolles.[3] Another Bolles head coach, Sergio López, trained under Rick Curl in Washington, D.C., and won a bronze medal for Spain at the 1988 Seoul Games.

According to a March 2, 2001, Jacksonville Sheriff's Office arrest report, a 16-year-old male swimmer said Chocrón had "masturbated in front of him and . . . also encouraged him to masturbate in front of the suspect." On another occasion, "the suspect showed him pornographic video tapes prior to them masturbating. [The victim]

---

3   Kathleen Troy went on to co-own the Gator Swim Club in Gainesville. A coach there,
    Bryan Woodward, was arrested for soliciting sex with a minor over the internet, and later
    banned by USA Swimming.

continued to explain that he has performed penile/oral intercourse on the suspect and that the suspect has reciprocated him by performing penile/oral intercourse on him." Upon being interrogated by police, Chocrón signed a written confession. A second police report five days later said Chocrón acknowledged "consensual penile/vaginal intercourse with an additional minor, female." This 17-year-old subsequently reported having had sex with Chocrón on multiple occasions at his apartment. Eventually, a third victim came forward. The total of felony counts reached 14. Chocrón was held at Duval County jail on $250,000 bail. After he posted bond, police seized videos and computer equipment as part of his conditional release.

The general chair of Florida Swimming, Jim Kelly, reported by email to USA Swimming's Wielgus that he'd been contacted for comment by the Associated Press. Apparently proud of his verbal wizardry, Kelly said, "I told them I hadn't heard anything about it, which was true at the time."

Chocrón missed two March court dates; he'd fled to Spain. In June, an attorney representing families at the Bolles School sent a packet of news articles about Chocrón's arrest to Dale Neuburger, the USA Swimming vice president who also served on the board of FINA, the international body. Neuburger forwarded the information to Richard Young, USA Swimming's chief counsel, and to FINA's executive director. In October, USA Swimming's National Board of Review issued a slam-dunk ritual order banning Chocrón.

Three years later, Chocrón was spotted at a swim meet in Barcelona and arrested. He was on the brink of extradition back to the U.S., where civil lawsuits by victims were also in the offing, but slipped away again, this time to his native Venezuela, with which the U.S. had no extradition treaty. For more than another decade, he carried on as a coach in Venezuela, smiling out from dannychocron.com and associated social media sites. The failure of USA Swimming to publish its banned list until 2010 contributed richly to his ability to hide in plain sight.

In 2017, fellow countrymen following the coverage at my website Concussion Inc. reported Chocrón to the Venezolana de Deportes Acuáticos, which suspended him for a year from "any activity related to the sport." A federation source explained that the second-hand nature of the case presented against Chocrón didn't permit a lifetime ban under the evidentiary rules. (Chocrón's lawyer challenged the prosecution material, printouts of my articles, as "simple copies," and also pointed out that the U.S. had defaulted on a six-month window in 2011 that a Venezuelan court had approved for ad hoc cooperation in extraditing him.)

≈

Chocrón's American review board formality was USA Swimming's administrative "prosecution." The prosecutor was a young lawyer at Holme Roberts & Owen (later Bryan Cave) by the name of Travis Tygart. And what a coincidence: Tygart was a Bolles School alumnus. After graduating and before law school, he'd even served as an assistant coach in the Bolles athletic department. Tygart never answered the question of whether he considered asking to be recused from handling the Chocrón hearing because of this obvious conflict of interest. For all the public knew, USA Swimming's legal brain trust considered Tygart's background to be far from disqualifying — indeed, some specially knowledgeable qualification. Tygart simply directed the notice of the hearing to the several speculative postal addresses of the accused, before, at the hearing itself, reading into the record the evidence of Chocrón's criminal prosecution and his rubber-stamped addition to the banned list.

A year later, Tygart, having established his competence as an Olympic bureaucrat, joined the staff of the U.S. Anti-Doping Agency as director of legal affairs. In 2007 he was promoted to CEO. In 2012, Tygart famously directed USADA's takedown of Tour de France bicycling champion Lance Armstrong for doping violations. Tygart earned heroic media profiles, including on CBS's *60 Minutes*.

Whether the long arm of anti-doping law is applied with equal and persistent fervor across the board is debatable. What's undeniable is that the "independent" U.S. Anti-Doping Agency became a model for its cousin, the "independent" U.S. Center for Safe Sport.

CHAPTER 13

GEORGE GIBNEY —
MOST NOTORIOUS AT-LARGE
SEX CRIMINAL IN SPORTS HISTORY

In 2010, the 16th year of former Irish Olympic swimming coach George Gibney's second act as a quasi-fugitive from justice residing in the United States, USA Swimming executive director Chuck Wielgus was asked about him at a deposition in a coach abuse lawsuit. Wielgus projected his customary muddled forthrightness. The Gibney name, he first responded, "does not ring a bell." But Wielgus quickly gathered himself. "Actually — sounds like a — sounds like an Irish — is he an Irish coach?... Yeah, I think I've heard the name."

The exchange with deposing counsel resumed:

Q   Was he ever a USA Swimming coach?

A   Not — I don't know the answer to that.

Q   You don't know if he's a member now?

A   I do not know he's a member now, but he was a coach in Ireland.

Later in the year, David Berkoff's research memo to fellow USA Swimming board members — a document believed to correspond to much of the content of the organization's secret "flagged" list — characterized Gibney as "arrested, released & on the run." Gibney, Berkoff wrote (incorrectly referring to him as British), "is alleged to be one of the worst pedophile coaches in British swim history. He is alleged to have had seven [*sic*] child rape charges dismissed in Great Britain on legal technicalities and is alleged to have raped an Irish female swimmer he held captive in a Florida hotel room in the early 1990's while on a training trip. Gibney apparently lives in Florida but Irish officials are seeking his extradition. The list of his victims is alleged to be substantial. Gibney is asserted to have coached in the US for North Jeffco Aquatics."

(The passage was riddled with mistakes: Gibney, of course, is Irish, not British, and his charges were dropped in Ireland. The original prosecution encompassed 27 criminal counts. And at the time of Berkoff's memo — and as of the writing of this book — Irish officials had not sought his extradition.)

In 2021, from the safety of retrospective transparency around a figure no longer so easily passed off as obscure, USA Swimming spokesperson Isabelle McLemore conceded to the hometown *Colorado Springs Gazette* that Gibney had been a member in 1995. "Prior to 2013, USA Swimming's rule prohibited sexual misconduct by a member," McLemore said. "The rule was then changed in 2013 to sexual misconduct at any time — past or present. Unfortunately, given Mr. Gibney has not been a member since 1996, he has never been subject to the updated rule." Gibney might have been a beneficiary of Wielgus's discretionary "grandfathering" of past allegations in order to provide the benefit of the doubt to a contemporary accused abuser.

In the 11 years between USA Swimming's first accountings — Wielgus's evasive deposition response plus Berkoff's mistake-strewn, but broadly accurate, item about Gibney — and the ultimate acknowledgment of his existence in their own ranks, the American government added significant data points regarding his immigration timeline and status. These were the output of my Freedom of Information Act lawsuit against the Department of Homeland Security, which settled at the Ninth Circuit Court of Appeals in 2017. Three years hence, a popular podcast series, co-produced by the British Broadcasting Corporation and the Irish media company Second Captains, cemented Gibney's villainous profile for a new generation of infotainment consumers.

From his San Francisco bench, Charles R. Breyer, the U.S. District Court judge who reviewed Gibney's immigration records *in camera* prior to ruling in the FOIA matter, discussed a preview of a decision he called "mostly" in my favor. Breyer, brother of U.S. Supreme Court justice Stephen Breyer, had been an assistant prosecutor on the Watergate Special Prosecution Task Force in the 1970s. The money passage of his remarks: "I have to assume that if somebody has been charged with the types of offenses that Mr. Gibney has been charged with, the United States, absent other circumstances, would not grant a visa. We're not a refuge for pedophiles."

In his order releasing certain documents, some in redacted form, while withholding others, Breyer said the goal of the plaintiff was "to uncover how American authorities allowed an alleged sexual predator to enter and reside in the United States despite the scandal swirling around him in his native Ireland." Breyer observed that the litigating journalist suspected part of the answer was "that the American Swimming Coaches Association greased the wheels for Gibney's relocation."

The judge seemed unlikely to have memorialized this last point had his own private review of all the documents not turned up corroborating information on which he didn't feel at liberty to elaborate publicly. Indeed, the collective "other circumstances" behind Gibney's odyssey, covering three regions of the U.S. and approaching the three-decade mark as this book was being written, emphatically suggested it was rooted in an ASCA operation. Peter Banks, Gibney's old assistant coach with the Trojans club out of the

Newpark Comprehensive School in Blackrock, County Dublin, had been an ASCA official under John Leonard and got inducted into the ASCA Hall of Fame; and Banks has never availed himself of multiple opportunities to refute that it was he who assisted the visa application and was behind Gibney's short and disastrous coaching stint in Colorado.

The George Gibney scandals thus spanned the wide pool of the Atlantic Ocean; they were where global swimming's systematic transborder sex crimes and official cover-ups went not to drown but to float with world-record sophistication. Ways and means involved not just clueless local swim clubs, not just their money-eyeballing regional and national governing bodies. Here, there was also the element of the serviceably selective enforcement practices of both local police agencies and the national governments above them.

Late in 2023, Irish news media reported that the country's director of public prosecutions was considering, for the umpteenth time, a new prosecution of Gibney. The possibility seemed more real than ever this time, since some of the same reports said that American officials had been alerted to prepare for a possible extradition request. No matter how that proceeded to play out, history needn't be kind to his relay team of enablers on two continents.

They started with the Irish Amateur Swimming Association, the country's counterpart to USA Swimming. In the 1990s, IASA was disgraced by the exposure of rampant sexual abuse by some of its top coaches. Several, unlike Gibney, went to prison. One, Frank McCann, was convicted of murdering his wife and their baby niece (whom they were seeking to adopt) by burning down their Dublin house with the woman and little girl inside — thus ensuring they'd never learn he raped and impregnated a teen girl swimmer with special needs.

Rendered no longer functionally viable under its old banner, IASA pivoted from a carefully couched government report on the scandals to a "rebrand." Henceforth, it would be known as Swim Ireland — still run by essentially the same gang who sat by and did nothing while Gibney and his peers preyed on untold dozens of child swimmers. For a time, Peter Banks returned from Florida — back from ASCA, American citizenship, and a stint on the U.S. Olympic coaching staff — to serve as Swim Ireland's High Performance director and the head coach at the 2012 London Games.

It was all good, with the rule of thumb being: no one need fear for their own careers among their countrymen's lords of the rings — a cadre known in Ireland as the "Blazers," in reference to their Olympic-signaling garb and pretensions. All good, that is, so long as the public could be guided simply to demonize the presumably singular sick shadow of John George Gibney.

≈

Gibney was head coach of the Irish Olympic swimming team at the Summer Games in both Los Angeles, 1984, and Seoul, 1988. No Irish swimmers won medals at either Olympiad, but two members of the '88 team would go on to have an impact on the sport's history, especially out of the water.

The first was Michelle Smith. She didn't advance to the finals in any of her four events in Seoul nor, post-Gibney, her three at the 1992 Barcelona Games. But at Atlanta 1996 she won four medals, including three golds, for the largest hardware haul in Irish Olympic history in any sport. Smith's feat became somewhat tainted in 1998, when FINA, the international swimming body, banned her for four years for tampering with her urine sample for a drug test. She retired from swimming and practiced law.

Smith's husband and coach, Erik de Bruin, was a Dutch shot putter and discus thrower who'd been banned for performance-enhancing drugs himself. ASCA's Leonard and the American swimming establishment in general have always been far more passionate about catching doping cheaters from other countries — especially and preferably Russians — than about perpetrators of sexual assault, wherever they came from or landed.

The other impactful swimmer, Gary O'Toole, was Ireland's top Olympic hopeful of 1988, though he placed no higher than 18th in any of his three events. Today he's one of the country's most in-demand orthopedic surgeons. Though not himself a Gibney abuse victim, O'Toole became a key organizer of and spokesperson for those pressuring IASA and the criminal justice system.

Gibney began coaching in the 1960s at the Guinness employee swimming pool (today part of the St. James's Gate Health & Fitness Club); he worked as a machinist at the brewery. His earliest known abuse victim was an 11-year-old boy, Francis "Chalkie" White, who won his age group in the annual Liffey Swim, a race held in Dublin's main river, and was a top national swimmer and coach. It was White who, by wisely choosing O'Toole as a confidante, loosened Gibney's stranglehold on Irish swimming.

Toting up the number of juveniles on whom Gibney preyed during his quarter-century reign of terror is simply impossible. Among them was Chalkie White's sister Loraine, when she was nine years old. In 2019, over lunch on Kevin Street in Dublin, Loraine Kennedy explained to me how she had long earlier determined the best course for talking about her family's toxic Gibney entanglements and navigating the anguish they caused — most particularly to Chalkie, who eventually went into self-imposed exile in South Africa. "I decided to take it to my grave," Loraine said. Just three months later, she died of lung cancer at 62.

Another early victim was at the Glenalbyn club in the Stillorgan neighborhood, where Gibney coached in the early 1970s. The abuse of this swimmer, who was 13, got kick-started when she stayed with Gibney for a month while her parents were away. As a priest had counseled her, the girl confronted Gibney and told him to stop. In her account, Gibney responded by slapping her, calling her a whore, and continuing to molest her for two more years.

Many other survivors, frustrated by the swimming and legal systems, gave up; made renewed and belated runs at being heard; gave up again. The same arc of despair applied to those under the thumbs of Gibney's IASA cohorts, one of whom was Derry O'Rourke, the Olympic head coach before Gibney, at Moscow 1980, and after him, at Barcelona 1992. One woman, suppressing memories, got re-triggered when she accidently encountered O'Rourke at her local supermarket, but she remained too traumatized to take legal action. On the basis of other victims' testimony, O'Rourke would be convicted of 27 charges of sexual abuse and imprisoned for 12 years.

≈

As his own criminal chapter unfolded, in 1976 Gibney moved up to running the Trojans team at Newpark — a Church of Ireland (Episcopal), not Catholic, parochial school. The manager of Newpark's Sport Centre just before the Trojans' launch was John Furlong, who went on to an even more formidable career in the Olympic movement, as CEO of the 2010 Winter Games in Vancouver. It's not known whether Gibney and Furlong directly overlapped on the Newpark faculty or had other interactions. Furlong parlayed his high Canadian Olympic position into celebrity authorship of a best-selling memoir, *Patriot Hearts*. Canadian journalist Laura Robinson showed errors in the airbrushed biography therein; she revealed Furlong's several-years-long interlude when he returned to his native Ireland, as well as the backstory.

In a 2012 investigation for the *Georgia Straight*, a weekly newspaper in Vancouver, Robinson wrote of Furlong's secret past in rural British Columbia. While Furlong's book sketched an emotional arrival in his adopted homeland in 1974, Robinson documented that Furlong was actually in Burns Lake, B.C., in 1969, straight out of graduating secondary school in Ireland. Absent formal training, he was a physical education teacher at the missionary Immaculata Elementary School, operated by the Catholic Oblates of Mary Immaculate. A bishop in the diocese of Prince George, B.C., had founded a proselytizing movement called the Frontier Apostles, whose mission was to save the souls of the region's First Nations "pagans." (In the U.S., Indigenous peoples are more often called Indians or Native Americans.) Robinson wrote of former students' multiple allegations that Furlong brutally berated, demeaned, and physically abused them. Between Burns Lake and his permanent move to Canada in the mid-'70s, Furlong worked in sports administration in Ireland, including that position at Newpark.

Furlong sued Robinson for defamation but never followed through on the legal steps that would have brought the case to definitive resolution. The lawsuit did, however, succeed in burying the writer under punishing legal bills.

Later, the recollections of Furlong's former students led to a complaint to the country's Human Rights Commission. Investigations also showed multiple grave sites at other Catholic residential schools. A measure of these probes' critical mass was a 2022 apology tour by no less than Pope Francis. Speaking in Maskwacis, Alberta, the Holy See said: "Sorry for the ways in which, regrettably, many Christians supported the colonizing mentality of the powers that oppressed the Indigenous peoples. I ask forgiveness, in particular, for the ways in which many members of the church and of religious communities cooperated, not least through their indifference, in projects of cultural destruction and forced assimilation promoted by the governments of that time, which culminated in the system of residential schools."

Reparations negotiations and other next steps have proceeded. In major Canadian media, these have only rarely referenced the contributions to this sordid history of George Gibney's one-time possible colleague, John Furlong, whose stature as a national lord of the rings has continued, controversially, without missing a beat — most recently as a top lobbyist for the respective bids by Calgary and Vancouver to host the Winter Olympics of 2026 and 2030.

≈

Thirty-five years after the fact, an Irish woman offered chilling and explicit details of an incident with Gibney in 1982 when she was 11, at the pool of what was then named the Burlington Hotel in Dublin's upscale Ballsbridge district. The long delay by "Julia" in coming forward had all the formula elements — shame turned inward, collateral damage to loved ones, fear she wouldn't be believed nor her information acted upon — plus some unique ones. She was out of the country during the period when the swimming scandals first broke in the news media there, and "I didn't see the point after the injustice the others were dealt out. I didn't want the upheaval in my life," Julia said. "I had a hard childhood and just wanted to forget about everything I went through and get on with my life. What Gibney did to me was minor in comparison to other things that were done to me so I didn't see the big deal about it when I was young. I sometimes thought about it but never saw myself coming forward — until two years ago when I saw a picture of Gibney and Ger Doyle in their younger days on the internet and recognized them."

Julia's recall was far too specific and vivid to be discounted. At first, a spokesperson for the Dalata Hotel Group, most recent owner of the property formerly called the Burlington Hotel, said he didn't believe there was ever a swimming pool there. This assertion incensed Julia, who proceeded to give me a diagram of the pool complex and its dressing rooms and relation to the main hotel area, and pinpointed the spot where the sex crime occurred. With legwork by Olga Cronin of the Irish site Broadsheet, I even acquired a picture of Gibney with 11-year-old Gary O'Toole at an event at the Burlington pool (see this book's photo section). The hotel group's deputy chief executive Stephen McNally then amended his earlier statement: "I can only remember the hotel since 1989. And there was no pool then. However, there could have been a pool in 1982."

In Julia's telling, Ger Doyle was another Irish coach who that evening served as the Burlington pool's "lifeguard," in which capacity he was something of a Gibney wingman. Julia's father had brought both her and her older brother to the pool. Gibney introduced himself to the brother and impressed him with the information that he was a national team swimming coach. The brother relayed this exciting nugget to Julia, who was already in the pool. She remembered:

> The man approached us and started splashing me with water so I splashed back. I asked him was he really an Olympic coach and he said yes. We thought it was amazing that we had met somebody like this. The man said he lived in a luxury apartment and would bring us there to show it to us if we came back the next night. He told us that he came here every night to swim.
>
> He said he wanted to see me swim, so I swam up and down the pool. He said I was a good swimmer but needed some lessons to be better. He made my sibling and me race against each other.
>
> The lifeguard blew the whistle after an hour was up. Gibney told me to stay — that he would give me a free swimming lesson. My brother left, leaving me alone with Gibney and Ger Doyle. Gibney called him "Jerry."
>
> Gibney became angry and bossy. He brought me to a corner of the pool where the lifeguard was sitting and put his hand inside my bathing suit. He probed me

everywhere and then put his finger inside me. While he was probing inside me, the lifeguard was watching before he finally said, "Enough." Gibney said, "Just give me a few more minutes, Jerry." The lifeguard was getting annoyed with Gibney and said to Gibney every few minutes, "Time is up, enough." Gibney would keep answering, "Just give me another minute, Jerry, I'm nearly finished."

There was something violent about him and I was afraid so didn't protest. He was ordering me around. I froze while he abused me.

When he was finished he told me to come back tomorrow night and he would bring my brother and me to his apartment. He told me to get out and get dressed. I was frightened and dressed as fast as I could. I just wanted to get out of there.

I met my sibling in the front hall of the hotel waiting. He asked me why I took so long to get ready. We waited for my father to pick us up. I watched Gibney from the hall, he seemed to know a few people at the hotel; the workers from the bar and the receptionist knew his name, he talked to them. He left the hotel with two other men. My brother tried to wave to him but Gibney ignored him and walked on.

My father came shortly after that to pick us up. My father said he would bring us back there the next night. The next day I pretended to be sick and have an earache. I knew he would do something worse to me the next time and dreaded it. After protesting, I got my way. My mother was there when I was pretending to be sick and said not to bring me swimming if I had an earache.

I didn't fully understand what had happened to me and just thought every man did this to girls and that it was normal. I didn't know any different because I had been sexually abused throughout my childhood; my first memory of abuse was when I was four.

Julia ran away from home in 1987, at age 16. She returned to Dublin in the 2010s and spent two years piecing together the puzzle in an attempt to make sense of everything from childhood. She didn't follow up on my suggestion to make an official report, and fell out of touch for several years.

Ger Doyle, not one of the core coaches named in the 1990s abuse scandals, directed the Irish Olympic team at Sydney 2000 and Athens 2004. In 2010 he was convicted on 34 counts of sexual assault (these victims were all male), and sentenced to six and a half years in prison. In 2020, Doyle committed suicide (though Irish newspapers, which customarily don't publish this cause of death, didn't explicitly say so).

At a grocery store, Julia saw a photo of Doyle on the front page of a tabloid reporting his death. She wrote to me remorsefully, saying she felt it had been wrong of her to sit on the sidelines of the swimming abuse cases; she now wanted to file a complaint about the 1982 Burlington Hotel incident, with the goal of helping others. I put her in contact with Jonathan Hayes, a detective sergeant of the Garda National Protective Services Bureau. I know that a live investigation was opened but nothing else. Julia again fell off my radar.

≈

In December 1990, Gary O'Toole was sitting next to Chalkie White on a long airplane flight to the world championships in Sydney, Australia. Elliptically, White began chatting about sexual abuse.

He asked O'Toole if anything like that had ever happened to him. As their conversation deepened, O'Toole came to appreciate that White was telling his own story, in his own way, and seeking help. Heretofore focused on athletic excellence alone, O'Toole started connecting fragments of observations of Gibney and his teammates over the years, some of whom were also good friends. Having satisfied himself that he was identifying an unimaginable pit of darkness previously taking up residence only in the recesses of his consciousness, O'Toole realized he was well positioned to do something about it. And he did. Upon their return from Australia, O'Toole quit Gibney's Trojans club, ending their 13-year athlete-coach relationship. During the same period, February 1991, Gibney stepped down as national team coach, with the explanation that he wanted to focus on his team at Newpark.

Through a survey mailed out to fellow swimmers, cleverly structured to maintain the anonymity and trust of hesitant witnesses, O'Toole compiled anecdotes of the astounding breadth of Gibney's predatory conduct. O'Toole's advocacy and measured outspokenness would be indispensable to the campaign to crack the code of the Irish criminal justice system and its unfortunate history of suppressing knowledge of abuse in high places.

The other foundational figure in breaking the Gibney story was Johnny Watterson, a sportswriter for the now-defunct *Irish Tribune* (today a sports columnist for the *Irish Times*). Watterson had been a student at Newpark School before matriculating at Trinity College, Ireland's great Protestant institution of higher learning. He'd heard the Gibney stories from friends at Newpark and was haunted by them. Overcoming media taboos on reporting sexual abuse scandals in real time, and bucking the draconian regime of Irish defamation law, was a task underappreciated by Americans, who enjoy the protections of the First Amendment.

Before Gibney could be brought down, the coach managed a final spasm of on-the-job depravity. On a trip to the Netherlands in 1990, Gibney sexually assaulted one of his swimmers, a 16-year-old girl. The next year, during a school break, he took a group of his top athletes to train at an Olympic-length 50-meter pool in Florida (the Newpark pool was 25 meters and Ireland had no swim facilities congruent with Olympic competition). On that trip, in a Tampa hotel room, he raped the girl again. Three months after their return, she discovered that she was pregnant. She told a doctor who was an Irish swimming official, and was plied with tranquilizers, whisked to England for an abortion, and warned not to talk about it.

The Tampa rape would serve as the Gibney saga's signature nexus. This was not only because of the victim's on-and-off determination and capability, across a long period, to seriously prosecute the crime against her. It was also because the entire scenario brought into high relief the passive lack of coordination between the law enforcement assets of two countries: there's no evidence that Ireland's Garda ever shared information or sought assistance from police or prosecutors where the crime occurred. When I began reporting all things Gibney in 2015, the state attorney's office of Hillsborough County, Florida, verified that the statute of limitations in that state didn't automatically foreclose pursuing Gibney in the 1991 matter. There were, chief of policy and communications Rena J. Frazier said, "exceptions and circumstances that can extend the statute of limitations. The circumstances of a specific case would need to be analyzed to determine whether its prosecution would be time-barred."

In this case, special circumstances included the crime's transnational nature, the agony of Gibney's centrality in Ireland's national swimming sexual abuse narrative, and the confused tale of Gibney's visa and long-term U.S. green card residency. Yet various starts and stops of investigations by Ireland's director of public prosecutions never clarified any of these crucial details; never demonstrated to a curious public a purposeful effort to document, corroborate, and act on the Tampa incident *in the relevant jurisdiction*. When Maureen O'Sullivan, an Irish legislator, took up the cause of Gibney's survivors, one focus was implementing the provisions of the legal treaty between the U.S. and the constituent countries of the European Union, which codified procedures for the sharing of information between different nations' police agencies. Without a doubt, this could and should have been occasioned, if not at the time of the very crime, at least at the time of renewed scrutiny, in the 21st century, of the legitimacy of Gibney's American residency.

In adulthood and as part of Watterson's reports for the *Irish Tribune*, the Tampa victim swore out an affidavit. Unfortunately, she never demonstrated consistent competence to pass as an unimpeachable trial witness. Overwhelmed by trauma, she was in and out of mental hospitals in the wake of multiple suicide attempts — one of them during a phone conversation with the swimming scandals' other prominent Gibney scandal journalist, Justine McCarthy, then of the *Irish Independent*.[1] At one point the woman lodged a civil lawsuit against Swim Ireland and the Irish Olympic Council, which the court deemed untimely and threw out. The defendants were even awarded costs against the accuser. During appeal, the woman's financial liability got decreased by the country's minister of sport, Leo Varadkar, later the taoiseach (prime minister).

≈

---

[1] McCarthy, who went on to become a columnist for the Irish edition of London's *Sunday Times*, and is now a columnist for the *Irish Times*, wrote the powerful book about Ireland's swimming scandals referenced in Chapter 11. In his U.S. court opinion in the Gibney FOIA case, Judge Breyer footnoted McCarthy's *Deep Deception*.

In 1988, four years before the prosecutorial walls began closing in, George Gibney had begun the process of acquiring one of the prize possessions of Irish–American relations: a U.S. residency visa; it would become something of a get-out-of-jail-free card. Through the 1980s and 1990s, prior to Ireland's so-called Celtic Tiger tech boom era, large numbers of undocumented Irish immigrants roamed America. A succession of special visa programs, engineered by Irish-American politicians in the U.S. Congress and blessed by the Immigration Act of 1990, legitimized their presence and opened doors to more by setting aside disproportionate visa slots for applicants from Ireland. (Such measures, calculated to facilitate the ingress of European groups, are worth bearing in mind during controversies surrounding the current purported overrun of the U.S. by black, brown, and yellow people.)

Gibney's visa came via a diversity lottery — which meant that this well-connected Blazer might have been keeping a shamrock in his pocket, or a four-leaf clover, or more. Peter Banks, Gibney's Newpark assistant, had moved to Fort Lauderdale in 1989. In Florida, Banks's prize pupil was Brooke Bennett, who won three distance freestyle gold medals in 2000 and 2004. Banks attained American citizenship, in part so he could be part of U.S. Olympic coaching staffs. And in 1992 — as he would confirm many years later — Banks met with Gibney in Florida and discussed his old boss's own visa application.

Another thing Gibney had in his pocket was a letter offering an American coaching job. This would become known when it got released in redacted form in 2016, on order of Judge Breyer in the FOIA case. The date, the sender, and everything following the key verbiage were deleted. "Dear George," the letter stated, "[REDACTED] would be very interested in your services as coach to there [*sic*] team."

As part of his visa application, Gibney further swore that he'd never been convicted of a crime nor, importantly, *ever been arrested or prosecuted.* That was a cinch. Foreshadowing the Florida swimming official's later report to the USA Swimming chief about what he'd disclosed to an inquiring journalist regarding Venezuelan bail jumper Danny Chocrón, Gibney could, with a clear conscience, assure his prospective hosts of his clean bill of criminal health — for it "was true at the time." The Dublin Phoenix Park precinct of the Garda even chipped in with a "certificate of character," dated January 20, 1992. This was just days after IASA denied Gary O'Toole's request for a meeting to discuss the growing body of allegations against Gibney, stating that it couldn't "act on mere rumour and innuendo and the person concerned has a basic right to his good name and reputation."

By the time Gibney had to renew U.S. visa and green card paper-work years later, the only things that needed to be re-certified were possible changes of address or marital status. Changes in criminal status were a loophole.[2]

Late in 1992, six swimmers swore out statements to gardai in Blackrock. The next April, Gibney *did* get arrested and indicted. The director of public prosecutions, Eamonn Barnes, brought 27 counts of indecent assault and unlawful carnal knowledge of females under the age of 15. Within months, however, an Irish Supreme Court panel made it all go away, ruling that Gibney's right to a fair trial would be compromised by the long passage of time since the earliest allegations. It was a statute-of-limitations principle, but a highly controversial application, and one called into question by more recent legal scholarship.

Technically, the Irish Supreme Court issue was whether to accept Gibney's petition for a judicial review on remand to the lower court (called the High Court). If granted, the High Court, in

---

2   As to his domestic life, in Ireland Gibney was married and adopted a daughter born in Africa. She swam at high levels and was later set up in a public relations post at Swim Ireland. The Irish news media made the call that it would be inhumane to hound her concerning the sins of her father. I concur.

all likelihood, would dismiss the case. That's what Declan Costello, the High Court judge, ruled. Prosecutor Barnes didn't appeal.

The Supreme Court members who deliberated Gibney's fate were Thomas Finlay, the chief justice, and justices Susan Denham and John Blayney. A barrister representing Gibney at the hearing was Patrick Gageby, the brother of Denham (who later became chief justice). Their father, Douglas Gageby, was the former long-time editor of the *Irish Times*. Until the alternative news site Broadsheet blew the whistle in 2016, no Irish news media entity ever reported this blatant conflict of interest on the 1993 Supreme Court panel (arguably, a lapse on the level of U.S. Supreme Court Justice Clarence Thomas's lavish gifts from right-wing benefactors). In 2019, Ireland's Judicial Council Act finally added a judicial ethics code provision, modeled after the United Nations' Bangalore Principles and stating: "A judge shall not participate in the determination of a case in which any member of the judge's family represents a litigant or is associated in any manner with the case."

Now a free man, but a Flying Dutchman due to his infamy, Gibney moved away in August 1994, landing the job of head coach at the Warrender Baths Club in Edinburgh, Scotland. Within five months, he was sacked there, after swimmers' parents got wind of his background.

It was time to pull that American diversity lottery visa out of his pocket.

What happened next could have been that Gibney consulted an atlas of the U.S. and decided that the next place where he had to live was the Denver suburb of Arvada, Colorado. Whereupon he flew 4,000 miles, walked cold into the office of the Apex Park and Recreation District, home of the North Jeffco Hurricanes, submitted an application, and underwent a background check and a rigorous interview, after which it was determined that a new swimming coach, whose English speech was distinguished by soft vowels and hard consonants, was exactly what the crisp Colorado air needed. Or, maybe it was the case that North Jeffco was long ago lined up to hire him should he ever need to repair to America.

In any event, by October 1995 Gibney was out in Arvada, too. "A citizen" called in notice to police that Gibney "had previously been accused of child abuse in Ireland," the department later disclosed. While the cops were investigating, they learned that the swim club was in the middle of adjudicating an incident in which Gibney was suspected of either pinching a girl swimmer or snapping the bra strap of her suit. The police investigation was unable to establish that a crime had occurred. Nonetheless, Gibney either resigned from the team or was fired. And the police said they "had no other involvement in this matter."

The City of Arvada rejected a public records request for a copy of the contemporaneous report by Sergeant Jo Ann Rzeppa, on the grounds that state public information law exempted reports of child abuse. No one could square this rationale with the released narrative summary, which claimed, on the contrary, that "the APD investigation was not triggered by a complaint."

Irish journalist Watterson told me, "After Gibney left Scotland, he went to Colorado. I contacted the police there and they claim to have carried out a background check with regard to his green card. The police officer I spoke to told me they checked everything but that it was all in order. I was led to believe the club was frequented by police officers and their families."

One way to summarize George Gibney's short time with the North Jeffco Hurricanes was that he got informally busted for abuse for the last time. In the alternative explanation, he simply agreed, with a friendly handshake, that he wasn't such a great fit after all. Either way, what ranks as the most dangerous and damaging career in coaching kids' swim teams, anywhere at any time, was over.

CHAPTER 14

GIBNEY SLIPS AWAY AGAIN

With top national swimming coaches either headed to prison or in hiding once the stories of a generation of abuse went above ground thanks to the determination of some Irish journalists, the government hopped right to it. In 1998 the sports ministry set up a comprehensive investigation by an independent commission, whose findings were submitted under the title *First Interim Report of the Joint Committee on Tourism, Sport and Recreation: Protection of Children in Sport.*

A prominent judge, Roderick Murphy, was the peculiar choice to chair the commission. Like Bolles School alum Travis Tygart for USA Swimming's National Board of Review hearing on Bolles School coach Danny Chocrón, Justice Murphy had counterintuitive credentials that the powers-that-be, who were more interested in perpetuating the cover-up, might have been considered, au contraire, to be spot-on rather than inapt. To the *Independent*'s Justine McCarthy, a government spokesman confirmed that everyone was well aware of Murphy's membership at Glenalbyn Swimming Club, setting of some of George Gibney's earliest crimes. Additionally, Glenalbyn was in the Leinster Branch of the Irish Amateur Swimming Association, where a lot of the worst revelations were clustered. Frank McCann, the coach who murdered his wife and baby niece in the course of covering up his impregnation of a girl swimmer, had held forth at the Terenure College pool, also within Leinster, and served as president of the branch when the Gibney allegations started bubbling up in early 1991. Carol Walsh, a coach in whom Chalkie White confided, said that when she pressed McCann to take action on Gibney, McCann replied that "I hope to fuck" the scandal wouldn't break publicly on his watch.

Murphy's "extensive involvement in swimming," McCarthy summed up, "is a conundrum which is puzzling many lawyers" in anticipation of the report. For good measure, Murphy also was once a member of Opus Dei, the controversial Roman Catholic group that would be featured in Dan Brown's novel *The Da Vinci Code* and the movie thriller adaptation. And Murphy's sister-in-law, McCarthy reported, had worked on the committee that earlier drew up "The Code of Ethics and Good Practices for Children's Sport in Ireland."

For better or worse, the Murphy Report it was. Clocking in at 161 pages, the report spent four chapters clearing its throat. Starting with Chapter 5, 29 pages were devoted to Gibney, who was called "the first named coach," someone "who seemed to dominate Irish swimming." On overseas trips, the report said, his swimmers were "locked into their rooms" and "conditioned not to protest." The Tampa trip rape victim was the fifth of six witnesses who gave testimony to Murphy.

"Why did victims not complain?" the report asked rhetorically in the headline of Chapter 8. In a nutshell: some victims *did* complain, or at least expressed dissatisfaction in some form, which invariably fell on deaf ears. Regarding cases where the victims didn't speak up, this was explained by issues of age, experience, power imbalance, trust, and fear — pillars of our understanding of abuse dynamics and dysfunction.

The conclusive finding: "In light of the charges arising out of the Garda investigation, the complainants were vindicated."

In a conversation some years later, McCarthy gave poor grades to the effectiveness of this rhetorical dance. A major concern, she said, was that "swim officials who played secondary roles in the cover-up have remained in positions of influence. I think this was made possible by the restrictive terms of reference for the Murphy inquiry [by which no one at all was named]. The effect was to add to the secrecy and to allow individuals — such as Dr Moira O'Brien, the swimming association's honorary doctor and a former president who was personally told about abuse and did nothing — to elude any accountability."

≈

Gibney remained in Greater Denver following the North Jeffco Hurricanes debacle. He found work as a temp hired out to corporations to support their human resources departments. Some of the assignments were at the Coors Brewing Company in Golden, hearkening back to his days with Guinness. The region had a substantial population of Vietnamese immigrants, and the ranks of young clerks at Coors included Vietnamese women. Gibney hit on several of them. He bragged about, among other things, connections he claimed to have to priests high up the Catholic Church hierarchy.

In 2000, Gibney signed on to work full-time for an agency in Wheat Ridge, another Denver suburb, that contracted HR and accounting temps for area businesses. But the day he started, the owner came upon references on the internet to Gibney's criminal charges in Ireland. The most authoritative versions of these postings were generated by a native Irishman, Evin Daly, who'd retired from a 22-year career in global advertising and marketing to start One Child International, a nonprofit child protection agency headquartered in Fort Lauderdale, Florida, with auxiliary offices in Dublin and Sydney.

Daly was the exception to the rule of this book's general criticism of the phenomenon I call "Child Abuse Inc." In lieu of churning out general anti-abuse manuals for institutions writing consultancy checks, One Child actively pursued and exposed people like Gibney. Daly got in Gibney's face more than once in more than one part of the U.S., handed him copies of press reports tracking his movements and the progress of his possible legal liability, and demanded (though never received) answers to the questions swirling about him. Daly also took most, perhaps all, of the candid-camera photos of Gibney that accompanied Irish newspaper reports through this period (one of them is in this book's photo section). Eventually, Daly's work would bring about Gibney's climactic crisis with American immigration authorities.

When the Wheat Ridge businesswoman read One Child's and others' information about Gibney online, she fired him and went to the local police. As it turned out, the Wheat Ridge police had received another tip about Gibney two years earlier. (In 2015, police said the report emerging from that first tip got destroyed in a routine purge of inactive records, before the start of computer storage in the 21st century.)

This time, Detective Lila Cohen was assigned to run down the information provided by Gibney's former boss. It included a résumé with two intriguing representations. The first was that he was "Director of the Advisory Board for the Youth Detention Center in Golden, Colorado," formerly known as the Lookout Mountain Youth Services Center, under the auspices of the state Office of Children, Youth & Families. The second Gibney résumé claim was that he was "Chairman of the International Peru Eye Clinic Foundation." The Wheat Ridge police informant said Gibney told her he'd traveled to Peru on a humanitarian medical mission, along with other members of his Denver-area parish.

Detective Cohen's report was a blizzard of butt-covering and muted curiosity. She said her interviews with officials associated with the Lookout Mountain youth center confirmed Gibney's role there. But Cohen was silent on Gibney's claim regarding the church mission in Peru. Her supervisor, Wheat Ridge police division chief Dave Pickett, said in 2015, "Because there were no allegations regarding any crime in this jurisdiction, no investigation outside of notification was done." Notification *to whom*?

In 2019, Cohen — who left the police force to become a child therapist, and whose name was now Lila Adams — emailed me, "I will tell you that I was worried about Mr. Gibney's contact with children and spent a lot of time and effort to make sure children who lived in my city and any children I could protect were safe. I have spent my career trying to protect children from offenders like Mr. Gibney. I will also say that it appears that you have everything I recall and I did try to make my report detailed and complete in case it was needed in the future. I currently work with crime victims, primarily children, to assist in the healing process so they can process their trauma and obtain safety skills to prevent future victimization."

I wanted to ask Lila Adams more about the Peru angle, on which her report had zero clarity or "notification" evidence, unlike with the Lookout Mountain element. We scheduled a telephone interview. The morning of the interview, Adams reneged on her agreement to talk further.[1]

≈

That church mission to Peru remained swathed in mystery. Catholic Relief Services, the umbrella charity, said it had no information: ad hoc humanitarian initiatives by individual parishes weren't in CRS's purview. Similarly, the Archdiocese of Denver said it didn't centrally record such localized undertakings under the broad flag of Catholicism. I

---

1   The end of this chapter reproduces a facsimile of the 2000 Wheat Ridge police report. It includes the name of the local informant, which I didn't publish during my reporting from 2015 to 2019. Since the woman was named and interviewed on the 2020 BBC podcast, there's no point in blacking out her name here.

reached out to all of the approximately 140 parishes in the archdiocese, which serve more than a half-million members of the faith. I wasn't able to find the name of Gibney's parish. But I did receive a useful email from a monsignor, who advised me to look into the area's associations with a Peruvian-based Catholic sect, Sodalitium Christianae Vitae ("Fellowship of Christian Life"), whose local base, Holy Name Church near Fort Logan, he said, "did medical mission trips to Peru."

Separately, I learned that the Marian Sisters, a female affiliate of the Sodalitium, had started a Denver chapter in 1998, at the invitation of Archbishop Charles J. Chaput. A former Marian fraterna told me that she personally traveled to Peru in the couple of years prior to George Gibney's 2000 résumé invoking his leadership of the eye clinic, and volunteered in a medical mission there. This source said that while she didn't know Gibney, "I think you're on the right track."[2]

In Catholic governance, Opus Dei is a one-of-a-kind "personal prelature." Sodalitium Christianae Vitae, which started in Peru in 1971 in reaction against the emerging "liberation theology" movement, won recognition by Pope John Paul II in 1997 in the different and more numerous category of "societies of apostolic life." This meant the Sodalitium gained formal recognition by the pope as a consecrated organization in which seriously dedicated lay observers lived fraternally around common spiritual and social goals. These included humanitarian service to the less fortunate. (A related lay group, sharing similar principles, is known as the Christian Life Movement.)

At the now-disowned beginning of their history, sodalits gathered in celibacy and obedience to their lay founder, Luis Fernando Figari, an admirer of Hitler and Mussolini who sympathized with

---

2   Archbishop Chaput would move on to the same position at the Archdiocese of Philadelphia, which became the second U.S. stronghold of the Sodalitium. Many heads of the most populous archdioceses get elevated to Cardinal, but Chaput never was. He retired in 2020, reportedly as part of a widespread effort by Pope Francis to replace conservative leaders with more reform-minded voices.

Falangism, the ideology of Spanish fascists. Their proselytizing met with the most success among youth upset by progressive societal trends. Some came from prosperous or well-connected families.

Father Daniel Cardó, pastor of the Denver archdiocese's Sodalitium affiliate Holy Name, was the son of a member of the Peru government's cabinet. In 2019 he told me that any possible Gibney-led mission "was not sponsored by Holy Name." Of course, it wouldn't have been, since, as Father Cardó himself went on to note, "the Sodalitium was not present in the United States in the 90's." On further follow-up, the priest said, "I am sure there have been many missions to Peru and other places throughout the years, organized by different people or groups, but I have no documentation, nor know of anyone who might have that information."

For purposes of tracking Gibney's international travels in relation to the broad subject of child abuse, the Sodalitium's history bears deeper review. In the 2010s, stories emerged of emotional, physical, and sexual violence by Figari and other sect leaders. These found voice in an explosive 2015 book by two Peruvian journalists, Pedro Salinas and Paola Ugaz, *Mitad Monjes, Mitad Soldados* ("Half Monks, Half Soldiers"). By 2017 the Sodalitium was commissioning an independent investigation, authored by a former FBI agent, which concluded, "Figari sexually assaulted at least one child, manipulated, sexually abused, or harmed several other young people; and physically or psychologically abused dozens of others." Charges of kidnapping, abuse, and criminal conspiracy trailed at least seven of Figari's underlings. The Vatican prohibited Figari from further contact with the Sodalitium. A biographical page at its website went blank except for this acknowledgment: "Due to the recent news of the accusations against our founder, we have removed the information in this section." Figari, who was born in 1947, "retired" around 2007. But in Rome, where he moved upon fleeing Peru, he's been a consultor to the Pontifical Council for the Laity, and according to the Catholic News Agency, may still to this day have consultant positions at the Vatican.

Figari's appointment to the Pontifical Council was engineered by Cardinal James Stafford, whose promotion of the Sodalitium's inclusion in the Denver archdiocese was continued by Chaput, his successor as archbishop. The affiliated Marian Sisters chapter was established in Denver in 1998 and, five years later, a retreat center started at Camp St. Malo in the Rocky Mountains, followed by the Holy Name parish.

In 2016, as part of a campaign by a group called SNAP (Survivors Network of those Abused by Priests), which said it had 28,000 members worldwide, demonstrators leafletted archdiocese headquarters, the Denver Catholic Cathedral Basilica of the Immaculate Conception. SNAP publicized the many ties between international and local Sodalitium leaders. A scrubbed Facebook page showed one of the accused abusers under Figari, former "superior general" Eduardo Regal, at an event at Holy Name with Father Cardó. Regal also attended the 2012 installation ceremony of the current archbishop of Denver, Samuel J. Aquila. Father Cardó told me: "I am not aware of unpleasant allegations at a local level. At a global level, I know generally what has been said."

≈

My FOIA case against the Department of Homeland Security for material from Gibney's alien file got boosts when Judge Breyer rejected the federal government's attempt to dismiss it and then pushed for more document disclosures and an improved index of withheld documents. Among the documents produced in these releases were Gibney's visa, the Garda "certificate of character," and the American job offer letter.

Gibney's 2010 citizenship application was a major puzzlement. That year there was one of the periodic surges of Irish media coverage of his abuse survivors' campaign to get the director of public prose-cutions to reconsider going after the coach — on the basis of either challenging the law of a decade and a half earlier that concluded Gibney couldn't get a fair trial; or processing new evidence in the old cases; or investigating and acting on fresh evidence from entirely new cases. At the same time, Gibney's neighbors where he now lived, central Florida, were catching up to the informational postings of Evin Daly's One Child International. Daly also was fueling the Irish news coverage and publishing ads appealing for Gibney survivors to come forward purposefully. The upshot was that, after a period of residence enabled by green card renewals, Gibney now decided to apply for naturalized citizenship — perhaps on the theory that this would inoculate him, once and for all, from calls for his extradition back to Ireland.

At the time of his visa application, Gibney had answered — with technical truthfulness — that he'd never been convicted of a crime, nor ever arrested and indicted. But his 1993 indictment could no lon-ger be hidden from a 2010 citizenship application, which asked the same question about a criminal past. In a notice dated September 27, an Officer Benabe of the U.S. Citizenship and Immigration Services field office in Orlando warned Gibney that required information might be missing from his application, and invited him to try again. (USCIS already had the sordid details of the dismissed Irish case, thanks to Daly.) The notice reminded the applicant that he needed to list "ALL arrests, charges or incident report(s) made by the arrest-ing or other officer(s) for violation of any law in the United States and in any foreign country, at any time in your life," as well as:

- The information or indictment and the judicial court judgment and sentence, including ALL probation orders and evidence of completion of all probation, and evidence of completion of any Court ordered fines, community service, counseling or any other sentence. All court records must reflect the charge. Include ALL judicial judgments that were:

- o Dropped
- o Record Sealed or Expunged by the Court
- o Deferred Judgment
- o Completed a Pre-Trial Diversion Program
- o Dismissed
- o Adjudication Withheld
- o Pardoned[1]
- o A "Nolle Prosecui" letter was issued
- o Plead Guilty
- o Not Guilty
- o Deferred Adjudication
- o A "No Information" letter was issued
- o Plead Nolo Contendre (No Contest)

- Your own personal statement, typed or printed, describing, in detail, each incident, exactly what happened and your involvement in each offense; date and have your signature notarized.
- If you claim there is no record, you must submit verification by obtaining a statement, on official government letterhead stationery, certified by the clerk of court, from both the felony & misdemeanor divisions, and also from BOTH the police department and sheriff's office in the county of the arrest certifying that no records exist.
- If unobtainable, sealed records must be re-opened. Also, you must submit an original, certified letter on official government letterhead from both the police

and sheriff verifying that there are no existing records
of any violation of law.

In the summer of 2016, to his credit, the assistant U.S. attorney
litigating our FOIA dispute revealed that the government had just
come across a previously unknown letter by a government agency
concerning Gibney's immigration. Judge Breyer's private review
of that document, and the entire stash of withheld records, drove
his fall decision "mostly" in my favor, as he put it. The government
appealed, but as these things go it was a fairly soft and friendly
demurral. With the help of the Ninth Circuit Court of Appeals
mediation service, a settlement was arranged a year later. (The
settlement also reimbursed $70,000 in fees to the attorneys who
represented me: Roy S. Gordet, who filed and litigated the FOIA,
and Thomas R. Burke, chair of the media department at the San
Francisco firm Davis Wright Tremaine, who managed the appeal.)
The guts of the settlement were two heavily redacted documents,
which had the bottom-line findings and decisions of two agencies
with immigration portfolios, while blacking out all the background
and supporting commentary.

The first was a July 20, 2010, letter from someone at Immigration
and Customs Enforcement. The ICE official wrote: "This case
involves GIBNEY, who applied for naturalization; [REDACTED]
no criminal convictions which would render him removable
from the U.S. [REDACTED] this referral does not meet the current case acceptance criteria [REDACTED] is being returned
[REDACTED] for action deemed appropriate."

The second document was a December 2, 2010, letter to
Gibney from Margaret Iglesias, director of the USCIS Orlando
field office. Headed "DECISION ON APPLICATION FOR
NATURALIZATION," it said: "[REDACTED] Pursuant to an
investigation and examination of your application . . . [REDACTED]

On [REDACTED] an officer of the U.S. Citizenship and Immigration Services (CIS) interviewed you under oath in regards to your Application for Naturalization."

The reasonable inference from the combined documents, especially in light of Judge Breyer's comments in open court, was: USCIS spotted that Gibney lied on his application by failing to disclose his aborted sex crime case in Ireland. USCIS forwarded the file to ICE for possible revocation of his green card and deportation from the U.S., on the basis of the lie on the application. ICE told USCIS that Gibney was not removable for lying, as he hadn't been convicted of any crimes. USCIS then told Gibney, merely, that his citizenship application was rejected.

In a supreme irony of Catch-22 proportions, Gibney almost certainly would have been in more danger of removal had he *succeeded* in gaining citizenship based on his untruthful application. Under President Donald Trump, ICE established an office targeting *citizens* who attained their status under false pretenses (though the focus there was surely on Central Americans who'd snuck through, not white Europeans). The agency's 2010 Gibney opinion letter indicated a different posture for *green card holders* in similar straits. Or at least it did in this instance. Judge Breyer had suggested a stricter standard for guests of the U.S. who fibbed to the government about material facts. In full truth, the resolutions of knotty problems in the immigration arena are far squishier and less consistent than is assumed.

What might have put the Gibney extradition campaign over the top was major American media coverage, but that never happened. Federal agents following the FOIA case and all the reporting at my blog decided to investigate Gibney's purported Peruvian travel and whether anything untoward happened there. FBI agents flew to Peru and asked around. Jane Khodarkovsky, an experienced prosecutor who was the human trafficking finance specialist at the Justice Department's Money Laundering and Asset Recovery Section, opened an investigation. However, no media outlet with any juice reported any of these developments. Then again, the *New York Times* and its fellow elite news churners also let things closer to home, such as the federal grand jury investigation of USA Swimming, just sit there, too, until they possibly reached parallel bland denouements amidst the apathy.

The FOIA outcome did catalyze what was, before the 2020 British-Irish podcast, the last flurry of real activity in Ireland on Gibney — or, at least, it sparked the last insufficient gestures toward same. On the floor of the Dáil Éireann, the principal house of the Oireachtas, Maureen O'Sullivan, the supporter of Gibney survivors, challenged Simon Coveney, the tánaiste (deputy prime minister) and foreign minister. Coveney said: "This is a case we will continue to follow closely and [your] questions about the circumstances which facilitated George Gibney moving to the United States need to be clearly understood. This morning is the first time my Department or office has had any correspondence on this issue. We will follow it closely and provide . . . any information that may come to light."

The headline in the Irish edition of London's *Times*: "Government is ready to take action in Gibney case." And a few days later: "Ireland TD O'Sullivan demands action from US on Gibney."

It took nearly three more years for American news organizations to show up, weakly. Their hook wasn't the FOIA findings of 2017 but the new BBC podcast. The *New York Times* assigned its Dublin stringer to write the story "True-Crime Podcast Puts the Spotlight on Irish Coach Accused of Abuse." When the *Colorado Springs Gazette* gave me a crack at the only long-form Gibney article to run in an American publication, the headline was "Podcasts stir new sex abuse allegations against former Irish Olympic swim coach in U.S."

≈

Where Is George Gibney?, the podcast, fulfilled the expectations of its genre, providing listeners with useful oral history, on a platform of accessible but cheesy production values. There were significant additions to the record, the most notable of which was producer-narrator Mark Horgan's interview of Peter Banks, who was back coaching in Florida after his top post with Swim Ireland ended badly.

For all its strengths, the audio documentary series, which included the disclaimer that sexual abuse could be an uncomfortable subject for listeners, should have been accompanied by a second: "No sports institution, government agency, or current figure in power was discomfited in the making of this podcast." For even as Horgan admirably tracked down Gibney's old coaching assistant, and cornered him into not denying that he might have had a hand in his former boss's American relocation, the crucial ASCA context went missing. At the time of Banks's probable intervention on Gibney's behalf, he was an ASCA director under John Leonard. The podcast didn't say as much, nor mention ASCA at all.

Also willfully ignored by Horgan: USA Swimming . . . the nepotistic Irish Supreme Court panel . . . the tardy and bland Murphy Commission . . . the Colorado police failure to alert the community or explore the medical mission to Peru by Gibney's local church group . . . the Denver archdiocese's simultaneous new ties with Sodalitium Christianae Vitae. (After former detective Lila Adams ducked out of her promised interview with me, she sat down with Horgan — who left their entire interview on the cutting-room floor and didn't refer at all to it or her on the podcast.)

And that Justice Department investigation of Gibney in the wake of the 2017 FOIA revelations — including the dispatch of FBI agents to Peru and the probe by the human trafficking finance specialist at the DOJ? So far as the listeners of *Where Is George Gibney?* knew, these things never happened.

Nonetheless, the podcast pleased the crowd, racked up millions of listens, and won genre awards. It amounted to a victory lap for figures like journalist Johnny Watterson and whistleblower Gary O'Toole: the most recent reprise of what they'd been saying at intervals of major media interest for many years. (Somehow, podcaster Horgan disappeared writer Justine McCarthy, author of the definitive book on the Irish scandals.)

In addition, the allure of the BBC megaphone induced fresh on-the-record participation by several previously silent victims or their family members, and their voices and accounts were often moving. For years, one survivor, Trish Kearney, an Irish newspaper columnist, had written and tweeted advice to others from the Gibney generation to the effect that, should a journalist knock on your door to inquire about those days, then you should feel free to tell him to go take a hike, for it was nobody else's business and the journalist was probably only out to exploit you. Now, Kearney herself was deciding it was OK to talk with the BBC, after all, conveniently coinciding with publication of her memoir of her own ordeal.

The podcast's real twin stars were its original musical score, oscillating between maudlin and ominous, and Horgan's contrived dramatic superstructure of stalking Gibney, a reclusive geriatric doing mundane things. The title *Where Is George Gibney?* posed a question to which the answer was already long known, though Horgan's listeners had no idea (and, of course, titles and headlines are always just shorthand). He didn't share with them that 14 years earlier, in Napa, California, Clare Murphy of Ireland's RTÉ TV, on the program *Prime Time*, had already pulled off the ritual of chasing down the old monster coach and sticking a microphone in his face. This was a trope straight out of the *60 Minutes* playbook, and, it seemed, an expected element for the podcast.

So for their very own Gibney "gotcha" moment, Horgan and his sound technician parked at night near Gibney's house on

Breakwater Drive in Altamonte Springs. Evin Daly of One Child International, who had a lot of experience shadowing Gibney, had advised the crew that they should notify the police about their project, so as not to unsettle the neighbors. Horgan ignored this advice. Throughout the 10-episode package, the podcast interspersed reports of the spying from the car, devoid of substance but breathless with hype. From chopped-up audio of this much-ado-about-nothing, later serially spliced into each episode, it was impossible to tell whether Hogan and colleague, in real life, were camped out there for weeks or just a night or two. A curious neighbor, quite understandably, approached the car to ask them what the hell they were doing. Narcissistically, Horgan broadcast this non sequitur encounter, too.

The last episode delivered the pièce de résistance: Horgan trailing Gibney, out on a shopping trip, for the big confrontation. Just as he had with RTÉ in 2006, Gibney remained close-mouthed and stone-faced — but at least that time there was also video showing the target in all his icy stoicism. This time there was only radio silence, literally. In voiceover, Horgan filled in the spaces by assuring listeners that Gibney's face clearly showed deep anguish at being so called to account; while Horgan himself was sticky-wet with nervousness, and in awe of what his BBC budget had wrought.

In 2022 the producers staged an event, "The Making of *Where Is George Gibney?*," at Dublin's National Concert Hall. They said "all proceeds" were earmarked for One in Four, an Irish anti-abuse group. All in all, another triumph for the fang-free watchdogs of Child Abuse Inc. And the next year, as Irish authorities finally seemed poised to pounce on a Gibney prosecution 2.0, the podcasters were — as the Murphy Commission wordsmiths might have put it — "vindicated."

Offense Report		Felony ☐						
		Misdemeanor		Reporting Agency			Case Report No.	
Incident Report	X	Petty Offense ☐		Wheat Ridge Police Department			00-21023	

Connecting Case Report No.	Offense / Incident Classification		Reporting Officer
	Suspicious Incident		L. A. Cohen

Location of Occurrence: WHEAT RIDGE POLICE DEPARTMENT

Date/Time	On	Month	Day	Year	Time	Date/Time	Month	Day	Year	Time
Occurred	or	09	20	00	1500	Reported				
	Between						09	20	00	1500

Code: V - Victim RP - Reporting Party W - Witness SB - Subject (Incident Report Only)

Code	Name (Last, First, Middle)			Age	DOB	Sex	Race
RP	Turner, Marilyn					F	
	Address		Zip Code			Phone (xxxx)	
	Res.						☐
	Bus. 2000 S. Colorado Blvd. Suite 200 Denver, CO		80222			303-296-4333	☐

Code	Name (Last, First, Middle)			Age	DOB	Sex	Race
S	Gibney, George John			52	032648	M	W
	Address		Zip Code			Phone (today)	
	Res. 5503 W. 43rd Ave. Denver, CO		80212				
	Bus. 2000 S. Colorado Blvd. Suite 200 Denver, CO		80222			303-296-2000	

Vehicle:	Year	Make	Model/Style		Color Top/Bottom		Teletype No.
Stolen ☐							
Victim ☐	License No.	Type	State	License Colors Prime/Numeral	Identification No.		
Suspect ☐							

Describe Unusual Features (Exterior/Interior)

OFFENSE STATUS

							OFFENSE STATUS
Are Witnesses able to assist in solution of	Yes	No ☐	Can suspect vehicle(s) be identified?	Yes ☐	No ☐	X	Open
Can a suspect be described?	Yes	No ☐	Is stolen property traceable?	Yes ☐	No	☐	Cleared By Arrest
Can a suspect be named?	Yes	No ☐	Is physical evidence present?	Yes ☐	No	☐	Exceptional Clear
Can a suspect be located?	Yes	No ☐	Recommend Case Review	Yes	No ☐	☐	Unfounded

Item Number	Quantity	Brand Name	Description		Serial Number	Value Stolen	Value Recovered	Value Damaged

Weiner, Bill
MSCD Lab School
2901 Ford St.
Golden, Co 80401
303-273-2636

On September 20, 2000, Sergeant David Goracke received a phone call from Marilyn Turner, President of Temporary Accounting Personnel Inc. reference some strong information concerning an alleged pedophile living in Wheat Ridge. Sergeant Goracke forwarded the information to me.

ORIGINAL

Reporting Party Signature: I affirm this information is true and correct				Send Copies To	3 Total		
Officer Signature L.A. Cohen	Unit X-3	Number 91-12	Supervisor Approval and Date	Assigned To L. A. Cohen	Page 1 of 3		

Continuation	■	Reporting Agency	Reporting Officer	Case Report No.
Supplement	☐	Wheat Ridge Police Dept.	L. A. Cohen	00-21023
Connecting Case No.		Victim Name Original Report		Date This Report
				100500

I called Marilyn back and learned that she was an employer to a man named George Gibney. She advised that while she was on the internet she tripped onto some information about George Gibney that was very concerning to her and she thought I should know about. Marilyn advised that George Gibney used to be an Olympic Swim Coach in Ireland but was arrested or charged with sexually assaulting children there and then came to the United States. Marilyn said she used to be a swim coach as well and this is how she got to know George better.

Marilyn said she fired George Gibney the day prior to this call because he lied to her. She said he was working as a temporary employee for her company and then, after getting to know George, she hired him full time. She said one of the things they had in common is that they were both swim coaches for children.

Marilyn advised that she knew that Gibney went to Peru on behalf of an eye clinic for children. She said Gibney works with children in his parish and his is a volunteer in Golden at a Youth Detention Center. Marilyn further advised that the internet articles she read said he also coached the North Jeffco Swim Club in Colorado. Marilyn said the articles she found on the internet were on Google under Gibney. She said she found further information in Irish Times.com and Ireland.com. She said she thought Gibney was the director of an Advisory Board for the Youth Department of Corrections. She said he is also the Chairman for the International Peru Eye Clinic Foundation.

Marilyn advised that Gibney and his wife adopted an African girl who is now on the Irish Olympic Swim Team and is currently competing in the Olympics. Marilyn said the girl's name is Chantal Gibney. Marilyn said she knows that George has a brother who is a professor at Trinity College.

I told Marilyn that I had been sent articles last year concerning Gibney and concerns that he lived in our city at that time. I told her that he did not have to register as a sex offender and that he had not committed any crimes here that I knew of. I did tell her that I was very concerned that Gibney was working with children, especially children with issues such as being in detention or having eye problems. I further advised her that I was concerned that Gibney may travel with children in his parish to Peru. Marilyn did not know the church Gibney belonged to. She agreed to send me the information she located on the internet.

I attempted to find an advisory board through the Youth Department of Corrections but it is a State run agency and therefore does not have one. I called Lookout Mountain as was told the same. I know the members on the board for the Jefferson County Juvenile Assessment Center and Gibney is not on that. I called Arvada Police Department concerning the North Jeffco Swim Club and received a call back from Sergeant Joann Rzappa advising that she had investigated those allegations in 1995 and did not learn of any victims.

Marilyn advised that Gibney had access to a computer at work and when he was fired he was escorted to the door and did not have access to the computer. She asked if I wanted to come out and have someone look at it. I told her that I would have to send it to CBI and she would be without it for several months as it would take low priority because a crime did not exist at this time. Marilyn said she could be cooperative but she could not be without a computer for that long. She said she would have her computer expert check it and get back to me.

ORIGINAL

Reporting Party Signature: I affirm this information is true and correct				Send Copies To	$ Total	$ Total	$ Total
Officer Signature	Unit	Number	Supervisor Approval and Date	Assigned To	Page		
L. Cohen	X-3	91-12	Amtws 100500	L. A. Cohen	2	of	3

Continuation ■	Reporting Agency	Reporting Officer	Case Report No.
Supplement ☐	Wheat Ridge Police Dept.	L. A. Cohen	00-21023
Connecting Case No.	Victim Name Original Report		Date This Report
			100500

Marilyn told me that the place Gibney volunteers with young people is at the Lab School at Lookout Mountain. She said Bill Weiner is in charge of that and gave me his phone number, 303-273-2636. She said Gibney is the on the board for the Metropolitan State College Lab School at Lookout Mountain. On October 5, 2000, I called and spoke with Bill Weiner who advised that George Gibney is in fact on that board. I told him that Gibney had not committed a crime here that I knew of but had some information that he should be aware of if Gibney was having contact with kids. He provided me his address and I mailed him a copy of the information given to me by Marilyn Turner.

Nothing further to report at this time.

ORIGINAL

Reporting Party Signature I affirm this information is true and correct				Send Copies To	$ Total	$ Total	$ Total
Officer Signature	Unit	Number	Supervisor Approval and Date	Assigned To		Page	
L. A. Cohen	X-3	91-12	100900	L. A. Cohen		3 of 3	

8/97

CHAPTER 15

CONGRESSMAN MILLER
AND CONGRESSWOMAN SPEIER
BACKSTROKE FROM CONTROVERSY

First elected to the House of Representatives as part of the 1974 "Watergate class," George Miller, from California's district in Contra Costa County, northeast of San Francisco, was one of that body's liberal lions. For many years in Washington, in oft-told Capitol Hill lore, he sublet portions of his row house to roommates who included fellow legislators Marty Russo, Dick Durbin, Leon Panetta (later White House chief of staff, defense secretary, and director of central intelligence), and Chuck Schumer (later Senate majority leader).

In 2013–14, as ranking member of the Standing Committee on Education and the Workforce, Miller was in a good spot to bring the disinfectant of daylight to organized swimming's stench of long-normalized coach sexual abuse and cover-up. Since the Republicans held the House majority in the 113th Congress, Miller lacked the broad discretionary powers of the committee chair, including the ability to stage the kinds of hearings that get televised on C- SPAN. But even so, after the congressman heeded the opinion of the *Washington Post* editorial page that the public interest required an investigation of USA Swimming, his staff insisted he had plenty of arrows in his quiver. Nothing could stop Miller from publicly releasing information from his investigation, for example. He could have press conferences with abuse survivors. He could hold remote ad hoc "field hearings" at which others told their stories and moved the public to appreciate that major changes were in order. Even when Miller let it be known he'd be retiring from Congress, the impression was that he intended to go out with a bang. If anything, retirement meant freedom from facing voters again — leverage for the ambition of his swimming investigation.

Instead, Miller's investigation fizzled, seriously setting back the prospects for meaningful congressional action. Rather than sprinting to an exposé, he staggered to the wall, a toweled-off dud. Public understanding of and engagement with the abuse problem got advanced by a stroke and a half, if that.

In a 2017 *Post* article headlined "Government probe of sex abuse prevention in Olympic sports went nowhere," Miller reflected on what had gone wrong. By then, the U.S. Center for Safe Sport was off to its inauspicious start, and the USA Gymnastics scandals were unraveling. In Miller's telling, the fault lay with the collective anonymous bureaucrats of the Government Accountability Office, from which he'd requested what he thought would be a hard-hitting report to support his investigation. Released way too late, the document spat out 46 wonky and toothless pages under the title "Youth athletes: Sports programs' guidance, practices, and policies to help prevent and respond to sexual abuse." GAO researchers failed in their one job, which was to examine how the federal law governing Olympic organizations, the Amateur Sports Act, impeded measures to protect children in sports programs. The report neither included interviews with victims nor reviewed the voluminous internal USA Swimming records revealed in court cases. "Miller," the *Post*'s Will Hobson summed up, "expressed frustration . . . that his 2013 request didn't trigger a more aggressive review."

"I think the GAO had a congressman on his way out of office," Miller rationalized. "I don't know that they really poured the coal into this problem in the manner that they usually would."

Left unsaid by George Miller: he, too, did nearly nothing with the acquired thousands of pages of USA Swimming files. His passivity guaranteed that the work of his own office would also be a big hat with no cattle. In retrospect, this lawmaker, belying decades of experience in raising the profile of favored causes, seemed to have interpreted his relationship to the GAO as akin to the politesse of the old comic strip characters Alphonse and Gaston ("After you." "No, *you* go first"). While Miller and the GAO were busy faking each other out, the crimes of swimming got no spotlight and no human face to energize bland and abstract concepts — for which, in the first place, no one seemed to have much enthusiasm anyway. Or maybe the explanation was that Olympic-affiliated coach abuse wasn't really a favored cause of Miller's, but just a fleeting news cycle–inspired attention grab?

Most perplexing of all for a veteran of the ways of Washington, the House Democrats' self-appointed champion of youth sports safety found himself preempted, outmaneuvered, and outgunned by the USA Swimming and U.S. Olympic Committee lobby. And when Miller finally did pull together a letter asking the FBI to investigate further, it was so weak and thin — containing a tiny fraction of the robust tips and materials fielded by his office — that the FBI director, James Comey, didn't even feel compelled to weigh in. Deflating the hopes of activists in the most humiliating way, Comey delegated the bureau's reply to a low-profile assistant, who told Miller not to worry his pretty little head, since the bureau was already all over it. The special agents on top of these matters, of course, came from the same personnel pool ticketed for post-FBI retirement gigs as minimalist internal investigators for USA Swimming.

Miller's milquetoast intervention — before he headed off to collect his own congressional pension, supplemented by the obligatory lobbying sinecure (his was a position as "senior education adviser" for Cengage Learning) — added up to something worse than an innocent missed opportunity. To those hankering for action on USA Swimming's documented and widespread coach abuse, it was a profound betrayal. In their view, the *Washington Post* editorial writer could have done better summoning the Peter Sellers character Inspector Clouseau, or the myopic old cartoon figure Mr. Magoo.

≈

USA Swimming's Colorado Springs apparatchiks may have known from the get-go that they had Miller's number. Even before his investigation got organized (if that could be said to have ever truly happened), the national sport governing body already smelled what its scandals were cooking. Moreover, it knew the recipe for making them go away. Into the maw of national scrutiny, executive director Wielgus and board president Bruce Stratton poured an urgent initiative to beef up USA Swimming's operation in the crucial area of . . . public relations.

They outlined their "SafeSport Action Plan" in a memorandum to the board dated July 2, 2013. The sport's leaders said their strategy moving forward "will have the ultimate goal of improving the overall perceptions of USA Swimming's Safe Sport Program efforts."

Of all of swimming's measures to counter the season of the Miller investigation, "by far the most expensive piece" would be the commissioning of an "independent review" of the Safe Sport program. In addition, Wielgus and Safe Sport director Susan Woessner would undergo "intensive media training." This element and related crisis communications services were contracted to GroundFloor Media, a Denver marketing and PR firm. Other resources would be targeted to local teams and regional governing affiliates for whenever "an issue of sexual misconduct arises [and] there is a flare-up of local media attention."

Other key category observations:

We recognize that some of the issues we face today are an increasing **unfortunate fact of life** for all youth-serving organizations and that our evolving role and responsibilities related to inappropriate conduct by our members is permanently with us. [Emphasis added.] ...

While we believe that our Safe Sport program is a model for other sports and we are proud of the progress we have made, we acknowledge that there is always room for improvement. Therefore, we will engage a reputable and independent entity to undertake a thorough review of our entire Safe Sport Program and provide a report back to us that will evaluate our program against the best practices of other organizations, as well as make recommendations for how USA Swimming's program might be improved. This review will help USA Swimming gain greater public trust with our membership, the media, and the general public. This is a big project ...

There is a financial impact to this plan. ... [Y]et we are confident that it will be worth the cost in order to be able to improve our program and help victims of abuse. ... In total, we estimate the expenses could run between $100K and $200K. It's still early in the quad and we're hoping to be able to find the funds to cover the necessary expenses from the Executive and Business Development budgets.

≈

A month after board approval of the "SafeSport Action Plan," USA Swimming commissioned the "independent review." The prize went to Gundersen Health System in La Crosse, Wisconsin. The announcement described Victor Vieth, executive director of the Gundersen National Child Protection Training Center, who was in charge of the undertaking, as "one of the nation's foremost experts on the prevention of child neglect and abuse."

Vieth's designation ensured that the paradigm of the examination would be an academic study. In this way, it promised to evoke generalized motifs of media sensationalism around such phenomena as child kidnapping and parental abuse — while accounting little for the subtle dynamics of the institutions of youth sports, where kids are vulnerable to exploitation by authority figures for particular reasons and in particular ways. Wedding USA Swimming to usual-suspect expert voices was a smart move, and it would be an ongoing strategy. As with the organization's FBI agent–laden seminars on stranger danger, there was a rueful nod to a "society-wide problem," and an inclination to give the sport a pass for the wrinkles of its own mission-specific contributions to bad outcomes.[1]

Asked at the time of the USA Swimming review announcement about the federal government's timeline for support of Congressman Miller's parallel investigation, the GAO's managing director for public affairs, Chuck Young, showed that the plodding government bureaucracy was no match for the nimble and deep-pocketed national sport governing body and its soothing resources from Child Abuse Inc. "The [congressman's] request that we do the work has been accepted," Young said, "but it won't get underway until early in 2014."

Published in January, the Vieth report checked the boxes of "policies and procedures," "screening and selection," "education and

---

1   Vieth began building his portfolio as a prosecutor in rural Minnesota. Today he's chief program officer of education and research for the Zero Abuse Project, a 501(c)(3) nonprofit based in St. Paul. He authored a 2018 book, *On This Rock: A Call to Center the Christian Response to Child Abuse on the Life and Words of Jesus.*

training," "monitoring and supervision," "recognizing, reporting and responding," and "grassroots engagement and feedback." It compared USA Swimming's Safe Sport program with guidelines proposed by the Centers for Disease Control in 2007, as well as — in an apples-to-apples exercise of grading one low bar against another — with child protection policies in international swimming bodies. Vieth said his team "reviewed several thousand pages of documents pertaining to every banned or suspended coach in the history of USA Swimming as well as files of coaches or others investigated that were not sanctioned. We also interviewed 57 witnesses connected to the sport of swimming or who were subject matter experts that could assist us in our analysis. We also had our final report reviewed by a number of child protection experts."

Over the course of five months, the Gundersen gumshoes seem to have spoken with exactly five survivors of coach abuse. They simply extrapolated from the records in front of them "that there are 30 cases in which there is evidence a survivor or parent of a survivor expressed gratitude to USA Swimming for their efforts. There are also 13 cases we reviewed in which a survivor was critical of USA Swimming." In one of these, they were quick to point out — in a line that must have pleased their patrons — "the survivor was critical because USA Swimming was taking action *against* a coach."

The report pooh-poohed the "frustration" of advocates of standards for action against accused coaches where the known evidence fell short of that required for criminal conviction. Thereby, it reinforced the baked-in assumption that special administrative standards for disciplining abuse were off the table.

Prospectively, the report recommended:

- "equal layers of protection for all abused children"
- "a workable definition and response to cases of psychological abuse"

- "materials to assist clubs in this process"
- the addition for parents of "information on asking questions about pre-employment screening"
- a version of Safe Sport "accessible to children or parents with a disability"
- strengthening of "the physical abuse portion of Safe Sport training"

And last but not least: "incorporation of Adverse Childhood Experience (ACE) research." For no corporate report diddling with the fraught subject of abuse could be considered complete without the insertion of a new acronym.

Wielgus saluted the Vieth team's diligence. "This review," he said, "demonstrates USA Swimming's ongoing commitment to raise awareness and reduce the risk of abuse in sport. Our SafeSport program continues to evolve and an independent review of our program allows us to learn from the past, see what we're doing well and make improvements for the future."

On page 6, Vieth disclosed that Gundersen Health System was being paid "approximately $25,000." A footnote added this feint toward transparency: "The contract does allow for a higher fee as GNCPTC exceeded a set number of hours. Because these hours were exceeded, it's possible the final payment will be slightly higher. Expenses were also covered." Of course, the USA Swimming board memo the previous August had called the review by far the biggest financial bite out of a PR initiative estimated to total as much as $200,000. The exact fee, however, was less important than the patent mutual back-scratching. Since USA Swimming was paying Gundersen, the idea of independence wasn't just a conceit; it was a fiction. In all likelihood, the report was the opening volley of a future consultancy relationship. Like the Women's Sports Foundation and the other constituent nonprofits of Child Abuse Inc., Gundersen could be counted on to continue nibbling at the dangling carrot of Olympic movement funds in this never-ending quest for "improvement." Or, at least, improved "perceptions."

Two months before Gundersen issued "When the Athlete Is a Child: An Assessment of USA Swimming's Safe Sport Program" and deposited its check of "slightly" more than $25,000, Victor Vieth got contacted by the mother of a girl who'd been abused by her coach in Massachusetts, in a case that would become the cover story of a national magazine. He refused to engage her on the details. Presumably, this mother was one of Vieth's 13 asserted examples of those who were "critical of USA Swimming," and to boot, needed to be educated that the gold standard was criminal-beyond-a-reasonable-doubt. Five days after her conversation with Vieth, the mother received a FedEx package from the Safe Sport assistant director in Colorado Springs, informing her that the investigation of her daughter's coach was being closed as a mere unfounded accusation.

Never missing an opportunity to hype a new task force, USA Swimming appointed one to implement the recommendations of the Safe Sport review. The chair was Jay Thomas, a swimming official in Plantation, Florida. Plantation had been the setting for the incident in which parent J.P. Cote failed to get local authorities to follow up on his observation of the inappropriate touching of a young male swimmer by Alex Pussieldi, the Peeping Tom and human trafficking coach. Cote's follow-ups on the matter were during the exact period when the Thomas task force was beginning its work. Simultaneously, Safe Sport director Woessner was emailing Cote, "I can tell you that we are committed to trying to right the [Pussieldi] wrong now."

≈

Meanwhile, it was hard to tell just what Miller was up to. Major news media, including the *Washington Post*, and familiar special-interest groups didn't help by making no ongoing inquiries, which might have held the congressman's feet to the fire. The most timid and puzzling performance of all was by ESPN.

Early in 2013, Tim Joyce and I broke the story of a criminal investigation by the police in Maricopa County, Arizona, of Greg Winslow, for molesting a girl he'd coached in the age-group program on the Arizona State University campus. When we solicited comment from the University of Utah, where Winslow was now the head swimming coach, he was immediately pulled from the pool deck of the Pac-12 swimming championships being held in Washington State, and suspended; he was eventually fired and added to the USA Swimming banned list. Unusually for the news-gathering practice of top media players, which routinely "big-foot" lower ones on the information food chain, Winslow accounts by the Associated Press and the *New York Times* credited "Concussion Inc." But not ESPN's. When its *Outside the Lines* magazine show interviewed the victim and confronted Utah officials, the report vaguely explained that "it came out" that Winslow was a bad guy.[2]

The long *OTL* Winslow segment lacked any mention of the larger contemporaneous investigation of USA Swimming by Miller and what the impact could be from yet another instance of high-profile coach rape. I implored the ESPN producers to broach this angle, at minimum, in the post-report talkback panel segment conducted by anchor Bob Ley. The correspondent for the Winslow report, Steve Delsohn, was an old friend of mine. Delsohn said he'd recommend me to the producer for inclusion on the talkback panel. Delsohn either did or didn't follow through on this promise, but in any event, I wasn't chosen. Nancy Hogshead-Makar of the Women's Sports

2 The Winslow story was introduced in Chapter 8.

Foundation was selected, and she was obviously a worthy addition to the panel.

Leading up to the broadcast, I pushed to Hogshead-Makar the importance of supplementing general talking points with an explicit connection of the Winslow story to USA Swimming's larger problems with Miller and the federal government. She said she would, but when the time came, she didn't. (Hogshead-Makar would explain to me that she "ran out of time.") On the panel, anchor Ley pompously banged on in a self-promoting riff about how it had taken USA Swimming too long to ban Mitch Ivey after the *OTL* report that busted him 20 years earlier.

The next year, the worldwide leader in worldwide leading whiffed again following the petition that forced Wielgus to stand down from the Hall of Fame. The USA Swimming chief put out one of his vaporous apologies for possibly not having been as attentive to past abuse complaints as he should have. There was nothing the least bit mysterious about this latest canned PR, equivalent to a hostage video. Yet when ESPN threw on the air T.J. Quinn — the *Outside the Lines* correspondent who'd ably confronted Wielgus on the air four years earlier about Deena Deardurff — for analysis of the apology, Quinn had none. His take was that the Wielgus statement seemed to have come out of nowhere. ESPN's expert barely connected it to the Hall of Fame flap. And he said nothing at all about the looming Miller investigation.

ESPN was far from alone in declining to reinforce a good story, even one it partially owned, so long as such a message might land half an inch off the bullseye of its viewers' biases and the overall project of sports rah-rah. Inspired by the success of the Women's Sports Foundation campaign in the Wielgus Hall of Fame matter, a group calling itself Victims of USA Swimming Coaching Sexual Abuse open-sourced their own Change.org petition. They said that, as a follow-up, they were asking for two more things. First, they wanted to amend the Ted Stevens Olympic and Amateur Sports Act in a way that would "protect girls and women from sexual abuse in club and Olympic sports, the same way that Title IX protects females against abuse in schools and that Title VII protects employs." Second, in view of Wielgus having "arguably committed perjury," at the very least in the Andy King cover-up — thereby "violating 18 U.S.C. 1621–1622 and 18 U.S.C. Code 1001 and 1519 and other laws" — they wanted to ensure that such individuals were held fully responsible. The petitioners said that the best way to accomplish meaningful change in a sport that "has insulated itself to a small group of 'swimming insiders'" was "through Congressional action."

The Women's Sports Foundation didn't lift a finger to help *that* petition. It died on the vine.

≈

Especially in the absence of a push from behind — from parties who were all for stamping out abuse, but only when it was convenient — the ranking member of the Education and Workforce Committee was chum in the water. Miller didn't attend a meeting between USA Swimming officials and his staff. "The Chuck Wielgus Blog" (yet another new toy from the toolbox of his new PR handlers) crowed: "The fact is that USA Swimming pro-actively asked for the meeting. The meeting was cordial, informative and constructive. The staff members were well-informed, interested and asked a lot of smart questions related to our Safe Sport efforts, as well as those across the entire Olympic movement."

With the clock ticking on his departure from Congress, Miller chose July 9, 2014, as the date for sharing with the FBI the low-energy findings of his low-calorie investigation. This report took the form of an 11-page letter to FBI director James Comey. (Miller would wait three months before publicly releasing it, probably because the upshot from it was so unflattering.)

Much of Miller's letter was boilerplate, adorned with prissy footnotes. Miller said he was summarizing information his staff had recently conveyed to the bureau's Child Exploitation Unit. "Based on my prior work on child protection, I am confident that the alarming allegations and high-profile reports of sexual abuse in the ranks of USA Swimming necessitate closer scrutiny by the Federal Bureau of Investigation," Miller wrote. Closer than his own, for sure.

Despite the existence of the Safe Sport program, "problems persist," the congressman said. Wielgus had recently apologized "in a highly publicized manner" for possible lapses in this area. A measure of the letter's half-heartedness was the way it contextualized the apology in the rollback of Wielgus's Hall of Fame induction — lowballing the mass petition campaign against him as "19" victims who'd "recommended," rather than demanded, he stand down from the Hall honor.

Page 6 of the Miller letter sought to puff up the Gundersen Health System review of Safe Sport into a "warning" of the "dangers" of an "informal complaint resolution process." Page 7 had a vague reference — there were no names in any of the very few specific examples — to an Alaska woman's complaint to USA Swimming of "sexual abuse by her estranged husband"; this must have been Bob Goldhan, the Dustin Perry predecessor in Idaho who committed suicide. The Massachusetts woman who talked to Victor Vieth also got a mention, minus the detail that he blew her off just before Safe Sport informed her that the file on her daughter's accused abuser was being closed.

Pages 8 and 9 bowdlerized the story of Alex Pussieldi and his associated scandals in Florida.

And that was about it. Miller wrapped up: "USA Swimming must act quickly, decisively, and evenly each and every time an allegation of abuse is brought to its attention. Immediate, timely, and enhanced scrutiny by an outside expert such as the FBI would make significant strides in placing USA Swimming on a path to rid its ranks of sexual predators."

Miller wasted no taxpayer dollars putting his communications director to the trouble of producing a news release for wide distribution. Instead, the office sent the FBI letter and response, accompanied by no cover announcement or commentary, to a handful of media outlets, mostly in California. Miller also did one Bay Area radio interview, in which he noted that he, himself, had grandchildren who swam competitively.

One of the recipients of the limited release, the *San Jose Mercury News*, rushed out a story whose focus was the FBI's reply of August 26, 2014 — barely more than 100 words, under the signature of Maxwell D. Marker, acting deputy assistant director of the Criminal Investigative Division. "The FBI's Violent Crimes Against Children Section has reviewed the information provided in your letter for potential violations of federal law," Marker wrote to Miller. With all the deference the FBI gives an average citizen who submits a random tip, this middle-tier official told the powerful congressman, "I appreciate your taking the time to bring forth information and your concerns on potential crimes."

The *Mercury News* coverage, headlined "FBI, USA Swimming officials talk on abuse," began: "FBI representatives met informally with USA Swimming officials in August to discuss ways the bureau could assist the sport's effort to protect children against sexual exploitation. A USA Swimming spokesman said Thursday the national governing body is not under investigation by the FBI. The meeting with the bureau occurred after Rep. George Miller, D-Martinez, requested the FBI launch an investigation into swimming's handling of child sexual abuse cases that have received national attention."

≈

Just before the holidays, in his last days in office, Miller's staff put out a statement intended to communicate continuity in the struggle to hold USA Swimming to account: "We are thrilled to announce that Congresswoman Jackie Speier, who has a long history of addressing concerns related to sexual assault on campus and in the military, with a particular focus on the needs of survivors, will be the new congressional lead on this issue."

If Miller was the quintessential neutered champion advocate, Speier proved worse. She was an emphatic minus for swimming's anti-abuse activists.

As Miller said, the choice of Speier as the House Democrats' point person on this issue did seem apt. She began her career on Capitol Hill as an aide to Congressman Leo Ryan, who was assassinated on an airstrip in Guyana in 1978 while trying to exit from a trip there to investigate constituents' reports about the encampment of followers of the demented cult leader Reverend Jim Jones. In the same ambush, Speier herself was shot and left for dead, but she was rescued and survived. During her time as a staffer in Washington, Speier also experienced her share of commonplace sexual harassment and boorishness from male counterparts and superiors. By 2015, Speier was an important voice for the #MeToo movement highlighting jobsite inequities in the military and elsewhere, which often rose to the level of what should be regarded as criminality.

Yet, for whatever reason, Speier chose not to contribute that voice when the GAO finally published the long-anticipated study Miller had set in motion, on the applicability of federal statutes to the youth sports abuse problem. Deferring to the upcoming launch of the U.S. Center for Safe Sport, the report was every bit the bloodless book report Miller would complain about in his 2017

Post interview — lacking evident purpose as well as bite. Unhappy with how the GAO left stuck in the mud the conversation about cleaning up swimming, activists urged Speier to follow up with a strong statement. No statement, strong or otherwise, was forthcoming. Nor did her office even reply to appeals for consideration of other next steps. This politician, who'd been expected to help them raise the heat, instead was freezing them out.

In 2016, while on a visit to the U.S. on other official business, Irish legislator Maureen O'Sullivan sat down with her counterpart Speier to discuss the status of the campaign to get George Gibney extradited. Early documents released by the American government in my Freedom of Information Act case, O'Sullivan said in a statement accompanying their meeting, "continue to raise troubling questions, the answers to which might spur the Irish government to seek Gibney's extradition and prosecute him — both on charges that were abandoned on dubious technical grounds years ago, and on new ones that have emerged. At least one case, in which Gibney raped and impregnated a teen swimmer in his charge during a training trip, occurred on American soil." Until he was brought to justice, O'Sullivan said, "there is no true vindication under law."

Speier killed this initiative kindly, saying only that she would continue to "monitor" the situation "and look for ways to constructively engage in this ongoing legal process."

In 2019 I returned from a trip to Ireland, during which I'd met with O'Sullivan and others involved in the Gibney campaign. I sent Speier a lengthy letter with information about, among other things, the status of a new investigation of Gibney by the U.S. Justice Department. This time, Speier's whip-smart staff rolled out a tactic too clever by well more than half: the congresswoman, having determined from the zip code on my letter's return address that I resided in the district of her colleague Congresswoman Barbara Lee, forwarded it to Lee — presumably on the grounds that it was an appeal for constituent services, such as troubleshooting a Social Security application. (I heard no further from Lee, either.)

In work whose stock-in-trade was the direction of the wind, a politico could articulate generic feminist concerns. Or she could choose deviation from bipartisan cowering before the Olympic brand by connecting those concerns to other matters, somewhat related and grounded in principle: the sexual abuse by coaches in youth sports programs. Jackie Speier's calculation, clearly, was that she mustn't do both. With friends like Miller and Speier, enemies of anti-abuse policies and practices barely had to bother showing up.

CHAPTER 16

GUTTER SPILLOVER

W hen it comes to recording the volume and breadth of coaches' sexual misconduct in swimming, there's no such thing as comprehensiveness. If it's Tuesday, then some coach somewhere, untethered to ethics or decency, is plotting to violate some young athlete in Lycra and under his sway. This vector of reality of the sports system — and of life — makes all the more delusional the promises of the consultants of Child Abuse Inc., now entrenched as a cottage industry, to double down on tried-and-false means to clean things up. In full truth, only two things could significantly alter these fundamentals and dynamics. The first: wrest administration of and discipline for abuse away from the organizations themselves, whose operating principle is money — not children's or anyone else's safety. Second and related: decouple educational and recreational swimming programs across the country from the jurisdiction of Olympic apparatchiks.

With the Woodmoor Waves in Monument, Colorado, the experience of swim parents Jeff and Cary Renwick taught them, the hard way, the limits of their own good-faith vigilance. This was the same club that had hired coach Charles Baechler, the defrocked judge whose no-contest plea to sexual assault in Washington State, followed by drunk-driving incidents in South Dakota, wasn't enough to set off background-check alarms.

The dad, Jeff Renwick, was a Navy veteran who became an airline pilot. The mom, Cary, swam collegiately at the U.S. Military Academy at West Point and represented the country at the 1995 Military World Games. Often, military types are assumed to be uniquely hostile to adjusting to updated standards on abuse issues. Reporting on the Renwicks and others, however, suggests something closer to the opposite. Military people can be exceptionally honorable about getting this area right — both in their own institutions and throughout a society in which they model a new generation of a multi-gender, multicultural citizenry's participation in activities not always historically distinguished by inclusiveness.

The Renwicks' particular encounter with USA Swimming's Kafkaesque execution of inverted priorities involved an assistant coach for Woodmoor, Sean Coffey. Among the charming items they found on Coffey's account at the legacy social media site MySpace was an exhortation to "party like a rockstar — FUCK LIKE A PORN STAR!!" Another was the question, "Have you ever wondered if your Mom kissed you goodnight after giving your Father a Blow Job?" Jeff Renwick said he brought this sighting to Waves president Sue Hippe "for the purpose of addressing three issues: appropriateness of the hiring choice, compliance with recommended hiring procedures, and resolution of legal liability issues if employment was continued. The team board admitted that no formal interview had occurred before Coffey's hiring, no references were called, and nothing but the mandatory criminal background check was performed." The board contacted USA Swimming's Susan Woessner, and according to Jeff, was counseled that, upon review of the submitted material, the assistant's employment looked A-OK.

At a meeting, board members told Renwick that if coaches wound up departing as a consequence of his initiative, "I would owe them new coaches. Whatever happened, the outcome was entirely on me."

Jeff and Cary reached out directly to USA Swimming. He met with Woessner in Colorado Springs. She conceded that the MySpace content was offensive and ill-advised, but demurred on whether it constituted a conduct code violation. Woessner emphasized that the national organization, by policy, didn't involve itself in local governance. And recommendations for screening employees were just that, "not mandatory."

In October 2011, Woodmoor quietly moved on from Sean Coffey, while offering to his possible future employers no trail of useful information. The club also served this notice to the Renwicks: "In the best interest of your family, the Woodmoor Waves and coaching staff, our decision as the Board of Directors has resolved to address your concerns of future liability by immediately terminating the relationship between the Woodmoor Waves Swim team and the Renwick family."

The Renwick kids joined a new team 20 miles away. When they competed in a meet that also included Woodmoor, the Waves boycotted it.

Chuck Wielgus closed USA Swimming's file on the matter with email advice to the Renwicks: "Do nothing and focus on a positive relationship with your children's new team."

On "Swimming Exposed," one of several websites launched by the sport's dissident participants and observers, Renwick shared these and other nuggets. In August 2012, he first noticed what appeared to be computer hacks on the site. He shared his suspicions with a local FBI cybercrime specialist and with a civilian member of the FBI's InfraGuard unit, a public-private partnership. The two experts came to a consensus that there was indeed a scripted outside attempt to access Swimming Exposed. But the FBI limited its involvement in prosecution of these kinds of cases to those with either more than $1 million in damages or child pornography.

The computer attacks persisted across a period of months. USA Swimming's lawyer Richard Young was contacted. Shortly thereafter, the "delete and destroy" portions of the attack script were found to have been removed, Renwick said, but other aspects of the cyber-spying continued.

The source of the aggression was the Internet Protocol (IP) address of USA Swimming's in-house server. An audit of Swimming Exposed traffic showed thousands of bad commands sent for every legitimate attempt to download a controversial web post by Bill Maxson, a financial planner from St. Louis who'd served both as a USA Swimming board chair and as president of its Barbados-based United States Sports Insurance Company. Critics said the page constituted Maxson's expression of enthusiasm for pornography. These commands were from a script of vulnerabilities primarily associated with Twitter, Renwick said, adding: "Any intelligent Information Technology type would know to hide the IP address and certainly not run it from USA Swimming's own server. Also, a person with even a basic grasp of computer security would not have targeted Twitter when the Maxson post was hosted separately. There were repeated, daily attempts to obtain user lists and passwords, as well as to gain control over the site through administrative controls. All failed due to the attackers' incompetence."

≈

Over the years, I had only a single face-to-face conversation with any USA Swimming official. That was a brief and unpleasant exchange with Karen Linhart, at the time the organization's head of public relations, at the Olympic Trials in Omaha in July 2012. The background of the encounter told a wider story.

In the first of what would be several ill-fated dealings I had with major media outlets, I'd been commissioned to write a long-form feature article about the swimming abuse issue for ThePostGame. com, then a "vertical" channel of the Yahoo Sports online network. The PostGame flew me to Omaha to gather local color and quotes. (Omaha was something of a swimming company town, whose most visible Fortune 500 corporation, Mutual of Omaha Insurance, was a major USA Swimming sponsor. Looming on the front lawn of the headquarters at Dodge and 34th Streets was a 12-by-25-foot sculpture of the head and shoulders of an Olympic swimmer, coming up for air and resplendent in red, white, and blue cap.)

These were the Trials at which Rick Curl's victim, the former Kelley Davies, would spot Curl coaching in the televised coverage — setting in motion her account in the *Washington Post*, and in turn, Curl's ban and criminal conviction and the call for a congressional investigation of USA Swimming.

Curl wasn't the only coach from the Curl-Burke Swim Club under the microscope during that period. There was also Noah Rucker, who'd been indicted the month before in Fairfax County, Virginia, on three felony counts of indecent liberties with a child in a custodial or supervisory relationship. The charges stemmed from 11-year-old allegations by a swimmer he coached at Madison High School in Vienna. At the time of his arrest, USA Swimming announced that Safe Sport director Woessner "initiated the emergency hearing process" for Rucker.

Since USA Swimming refused to grant The PostGame media credentials for the trials, I bought my own ticket into the arena then known as the CenturyLink Center. On the pool deck, I introduced myself to PR person Linhart and inquired as to the status and timeline of the Rucker emergency hearing.

"We're here for a competition, not to talk about that," Linhart snapped. "You're not authorized to be in this area. If you don't leave, I'll call security and have you ejected."

Back home, The PostGame, after editing and vetting my 5,000-word article for several weeks, ignored my request to schedule publication. I therefore arranged for another minor sports site to publish what promised to be a more comprehensive article than the already rumored scoop on Curl upcoming in the *Washington Post*. At that point, The PostGame belatedly stepped up and published its own version of my piece, without informing me or the other site, and a jurisdictional and rights mess ensued. (I choose here not to identify the rebound home of the article — for it would turn cowardly, too, and take down all my swimming articles there. My 2012 piece was rescued and republished at concussioninc.net/?p=10681.)

≈

As noted, Mark Schubert's Mission Viejo Swim Club was where swimming's loosey-goosey culture flourished. It was the site of signature incidents, along with random, coincidental ones contributing to the narrative of widespread abuse. In 2013 the *Orange County Register* reported on a coach there, Ad'm Dusenbury, and his sexual activities with a 16-year-old swimmer. USA Swimming responded by investigating Dusenbury for more than a year before eventually adding him to the banned list. Yet there he still was, speaking at that year's ASCA forum in Las Vegas.

Mission Viejo was one of the many settings of Rick Curl's molestations of his rising star Kelley Davies. It was also the site of two events that were more innocent but something of bookends of the history told here. In 2018, the former Irish swimmer Gary O'Toole, who'd helped expose George Gibney more than a quarter of a century earlier, recalled being taken by the coach to a five-week summer camp in Mission Viejo back in 1980, when he was 12. O'Toole remembered getting homesick one day and being verbally comforted by the coach. Later that night, Gibney snuck into the boy's bedroom, sat on the edge of the bed with an apple he'd brought Gary, and talked to him. "Immediately, alarm bells went off," O'Toole told the Irish podcast *Off the Ball.* "I said I was fine and he should leave." O'Toole, who described himself as naive up to the moment when, as an adult, he came to realize the breadth of Gibney's crimes against others, added, "I didn't put two and two together [about that night] until a long time later."

In the late 2000s, my daughter's coach in Northern California, Jesse Stovall, accompanied his star swimmer "Ivory" to Mission Viejo in the Southland. The Stovall-Ivory case was told in the book's Introduction. During this trip, Stovall gave the girl, then 15, a thrilling — and illegal — turn behind the wheel of his car. The next year was when he raped her during that national meet in Orlando, Florida.

≈

Just as Rick Curl wasn't the only abuser at his huge swim club, so was he not the only swimming coach in Montgomery County, Maryland, found to have committed sex crimes against athletes in his charge. In 2014, Christopher Thomas Huott, then 53, was arrested after being accused by a former student, Danielle Bostick, of abuse years earlier at what was then called the Silver Spring Swim Club. That happened in the 1980s. Convicted and sentenced to ten years, Huott did his time in the same state prison where Curl was incarcerated.

Reflecting on her life-damaging experience with Huott, Dani Bostick wrote: "Ah, the eighties: Huge foam goggles, Euro-cut suits for boys, backstroke turns that involved touching the wall and spinning, and mix tapes on Sony Walkmans for pre-race pep. Finding out how fast you went involved asking three timers who chose the time in the middle and got really excited if two of their three matched up. On-deck massages from coaches were commonplace.

Also common were coaches providing transportation for swimmers to early morning workouts and traveling alone with athletes to meets."

Bostick said "what should have been viewed as predatory and inappropriate was viewed — at worst — as quirky. At best, he seemed like another dedicated coach enjoying his profession."[3]

≈

The *Washington Post* ran with Mark Schubert's leak of the private investigation of Sean Hutchison and Ariana Kukors in Fullerton. Additionally, the newspaper reported on Rick Curl and Christopher Huott, and its editorial page set in motion the investigation of USA Swimming by Congressman George Miller. Yet the *Post*, whose journalistic forte was the ways of government operations, never cleared the space to follow up effectively on Miller's weak, grossly inadequate probe. Part of the reason may be that the *Post* itself, at the time, was a commercial stakeholder in the swimming industry through an online subsidiary, ReachForTheWall.com, which published mostly promotional news of the swimming scene around the nation's capital.

≈

Very few of the known survivors of youth swimming coach abuse in the U.S. are persons of color. One reason is a considerable racial divide in American aquatics infrastructure. Historically, the integration of recreational swimming was warped by eroticized mythology and fears. In many communities, and not just in the Jim Crow South, municipal pools were segregated; and in some cities where

---

3   Bostick also delivered a TED talk on the phenomenon of abuse survivors' struggles with post-traumatic stress. The 2018 video of it can be viewed at www.ted.com/talks/dani_bostick _breaking_the_silence_about_childhood_trauma.

such customs and practices got overturned by post–*Brown v. Board of Education* law, the municipally supported facilities became neglected, reduced hours of operation, fell into disrepair, and closed. Some commentators have even identified the fallout as a contemporary public health and lifestyle disparity crisis: they note a tragic gap between the basic, safety-centric swimming skills of white children, who enjoy more routine access to instruction, and those of urban African-American kids, who suffer from dramatically fewer swimming lessons per capita.

Attempting to buck this trend was the Oakland Undercurrents program in California. In 1997 a coach there, Ben Sheppard, who was a student at the University of California in Berkeley, started the Oakland Community Pools Project, which operated and funded a range of Undercurrents programs, including a swimming school and several teams. In 2009, USA Swimming hired him as a diversity consultant.

Two years later, abuse allegations against Sheppard surfaced. In 2013 he was added to the permanent banned list.

≈

Rick Curl found temporary refuge Down Under, on a remote swim-friendly continent with numerous additions to the global coach abuse saga.

In 2015, Australia's *Daily Telegraph* reported that Brian King was being investigated by Swimming Australia for his treatment of children at the Rackley Swim Schools. According to reports, this coach forced one kid to bark like a dog, and brought another to the precipice of suicide. Swimming Australia also cited King for falsifying credentials, "which assisted him in obtaining a number of high-profile jobs, including alongside top coach Denis Cotterell and at Penn State University," the *Daily Telegraph* said.

By then, Penn State — where Jerry Sandusky, an assistant to legendary football coach Joe Paterno, preyed on boys for many years — had become something of a rhetorical shorthand in public consciousness for institutional cover-ups. King got to the U.S. on an American Swimming Coaches Association fellowship — naturally. He was at Penn State in 2009–10 under head swimming coach John Hargis, who let King go after he was caught in a sexual relationship with one of his swimmers, multiple sources said. (Hargis himself departed Penn State in 2013 to become associate head coach at Auburn, then was head coach at the University of Pittsburgh for six years through 2022.)

By the time Swimming Australia got around to taking action against King, he was spotted defying his six-month suspension with a gig as a "consultant" on pool decks back in his native country, such as the Oasis Point Pool in Banora. His putative mentor, Denis Cotterell, was an Australian Hall of Fame coach who had a lucrative contract to work with the Chinese national team, which produced Sun Yang, a gold medalist and record holder at multiple freestyle distances. (Sun Yang's achievements were tainted by his ban of eight years — a sentence that got halved on appeal — for doping violations.)

Then there was Scott Volkers, the former Australian national women's coach who was accused of molesting three swimmers in his charge, ages 12 to 14, in 2002: Julie Gilbert, Kylie Rogers, and Simone Boyce. In 2015 they addressed a royal investigative commission, which was also told of mistakes in the original criminal investigation by the director of public prosecutions of Queensland State. A report by the Crime and Misconduct Commission criticized the dropping of the charges by prosecutor Leanne Clark, who in intervening years had fallen upward in the judicial system, to the position of judge. Press reports said the former head of the Queensland Academy of Sport told the royal commission hearing that Volkers kept his coaching post at the time simply "because he was good at it."

Volkers got the charges against him dismissed in 2020. In the meantime he worked with the Fiat-Minas team in Brazil. In that capacity, he made a stop in the Arena Pro Swim Series — at the George F. Haines International Aquatic Center in Santa Clara, California.

≈

Sexually abused by her middle school phys ed teacher in the San Francisco Bay Area suburb of Moraga, Kristen Lewis Cunnane went on to become an All-American swimmer at UCLA. After barely missing the 2004 Olympic team, she joined the women's coaching staff at UC Berkeley, and she wrote a memoir of her long struggle to overcome the trauma visited upon her by a childhood molester, and to put the teacher behind bars.

At Cal, Cunnane worked under Teri McKeever, arguably the profession's all-time most accomplished female coach. The list of the more than a dozen Olympians developed by McKeever — the first woman to serve as head coach of the U.S. Olympics women's swim team when she directed it in London in 2012 — included Natalie Coughlin, Missy Franklin, and Jessica Hardy. In 2023, McKeever was fired by Cal after a 30-year run, following an investigation of multiple swimmers' allegations about her misconduct. Though the accusations didn't include sexual abuse, details of thrown equipment, disregard of injuries, and mental cruelty, driving at least one of her athletes close to suicide, made for a disturbing coda to a celebrated career. Litigation — both by McKeever's victims and by McKeever herself, claiming wrongful termination — will likely carry multiple Olympic cycles past the publication of this book.

≈

Rowdy Gaines, who won three gold medals in Los Angeles in 1984 and is the long-time analyst for NBC Olympic coverage, has been called "swimming's greatest ambassador." In the business world, he was also, at minimum, a duped partner in a fraud scheme that revealed the challenges of trying to turn this niche sport into a major-league behemoth. While the color of water is clear, the color of money is green. They mix fitfully.

Arenas and stadiums can house multiple team sports, concerts, and conventions. But pools mostly just sit there, eating up mainte-nance costs. The commercial attractions for such spaces are few and far between; the faces of the marquee performers there are mostly submerged; their celebrity spans are truncated. That's why swimming spectatorship revolves around the brand, which is national pride, and the episodic extravaganza, which is the Olympics. At the level of logistics, how do associated development costs get underwritten? In swimming, the coin of the realm is mass fantasy. Local clubs, fish-ing for the next Michael Phelps, offer up age-group programs whose values and priorities are under the thumb of USA Swimming and the U.S. Olympic and Paralympic Committee. Parents of kid swimmers, en masse, provide the thousands of hours of volunteer labor to keep competitive swimming's pistons firing year-round. With precious few exceptions, the facilities they use are public pools, leased to local USA Swimming teams at rates well below cost.

Now and then, swimming visionaries — or delusionists — take experimental runs at private profit models. Rowdy Gaines was part of one of them, which went by the name of the National Swimming Center Corporation. Oleaginously, NSCC was yet another paper "nonprofit." In its short and sleazy life, this entity represented itself variously as a partner of USA Swimming, or of its philanthropic arm the USA Swimming Foundation, or of both. In 2013, NSCC's prin-cipals, would-be Texas developers Fred Yeo and Andy Sarwal, were convicted of federal bank fraud. In order to secure a $39-million credit line, which was almost completely tapped out when they were caught, Yeo and Sarwal had lied about having $7 million in liquid bank assets.

The basic NSCC scheme was to make deals with a string of mid-sized cities and towns, which almost, but in the end didn't, buy its snake-oil concept. Another entity involved in the chicanery was GlobeVest LLC, a Colorado company. In a nutshell, GlobeVest and NSCC sought to get municipalities to deed public land for the developers, who in turn would use it as collateral for financing projects tying new aquatic centers to hotels. After the bust of Yeo and Sarwal, swimming officials stopped using the NSCC name but continued to explore the NSCC modus operandi.

In 2010, the city of Cape Coral, Florida, on the Gulf Coast, rejected an NSCC plan for an $85-million pool-hotel-convention center, though not before sinking many tens of thousands of dollars into feasibility studies. Later, city officials likened the plan to a Ponzi scheme. The Cape Coral prospectus listed Rowdy Gaines, who resided in Lake Mary, Florida, as an NSCC board adviser. Gaines never responded to multiple requests to explain his role.

A swimming character from the Pacific Northwest, Brandon Drawz, joined the NSCC board in 2011, months before he was publicly announced as its chief operating officer. The next year he joined the SwimMAC program in Charlotte, North Carolina.

A coach with big-business aspirations and a lot of baggage in his management of both personal affairs and club finances, Drawz enjoyed nine lives as a USA Swimming muck-a-muck. At one point he served on the national board and was considered a Chuck Wielgus protégé. In June 2007, while coaching Oregon's Mt. Hood Swim Club, local swim sources said Drawz had a dispute with a colleague, Bud Taylor, that turned violent, and Drawz, then 35, decked the 67-year-old Taylor with a punch. (In a 2019 conversation with me, Drawz said the fight never happened and he was cleared by an Oregon Swimming investigation.)

Two months after that, Drawz chaperoned Mt. Hood juveniles to a swim meet in Indianapolis. There, he had an alcohol-fueled fight with his girlfriend, was charged with domestic violence, battery, public intoxication, and resisting arrest, and spent a night in jail while the kids on his team went unsupervised out of town.

After leaving Mt. Hood, Drawz landed at SwimMAC (formerly Mecklenburg Aquatic Club), a large and prestigious program in Charlotte. With his twin hat at NSCC, he tried to put together a deal for a new SwimMAC complex tied to the construction of a Doubletree by Hilton hotel and conference center. The plan, with backing from "special assessment district bonds" from the city of Mooresville, 30 miles north of Charlotte, didn't come to fruition. In 2015, SwimMAC dumped Drawz amidst whispers of financial impropriety.

Drawz told me: "Unfortunately, against the advice of outside colleagues, I took the job thinking I could work for a notoriously unscrupulous coach." (Drawz was referring to David Marsh.) "Finally, after several complaints from various employees, I had no choice but to report multiple ethical violations by the coach to the [board of directors]. . . . Additionally, I offered to resign and stay on as a consultant as the club had many great items in the works, but coach Marsh was afraid I would sabotage his chance at being the Head Olympic Coach in 2016 and let me go. He and his crew launched a full-scale attack against me in which they provided and circulated fabricated 'evidence' to discredit me. Unfortunately for those attacking me, the financial and competitive success of the club while I was its Executive Director speaks for itself — to my knowledge, my tenure at the club was the only time SwimMAC *ever* made money since coach Marsh's arrival seven years prior."[4]

---

4   A long-time college coach, now associate head coach at Cal in Berkeley, Marsh did indeed wind up serving as head coach of the 2016 women's team at the Rio de Janeiro Games.

Regarding NSCC, Drawz said he "was recruited for my expertise in building and operating facilities as well as attracting and running events. I never made any money from this group. Although I don't recall when, I and some of the other members of the group were informed that two of our board members were under investigation for some sort of financial issues. That was the end of my involvement with NSCC, and to this day, I have no idea what the issues were with these individuals. Sadly, several people put a great deal of time and effort into creating some unique projects. Unfortunately, we all lost time and money for our efforts as well as being embarrassed by our lack of understanding of our main investors' dealings."

In 2015 Drawz was up for a post with Georgia Swimming. A former chair of this regional affiliate of USA Swimming, Gary Theisen, said that after deciding not to hire Drawz because of information gathered about him, Georgia Swimming turned the information over to the national group for investigation. According to Drawz, the USA Swimming investigation cleared him.

Drawz was a close friend of Paris Jacobs, a Washington-Baltimore area aquatics entrepreneur who in 2001 started the Machine Swim School at the Madeira School, a girls' boarding school in McLean, Virginia. She later developed an associated physical complex, described as Fairfax County's first privately owned, purposely built swim center, and with Colorado partners franchised "SwimLabs, LLC." In 2018, with long-time American Swimming Coaches Association executive director John Leonard in his 70s and winding down, Jacobs added the title of chief operating officer of ASCA to her portfolio.

Jacobs and Drawz worked together on various commercial swimming ventures. One involved marketing an innovative pool design. Another was organizing a professional swimming league. In 2019 the two were spotted at a business lunch, at the Olympic Training Center commissary in Colorado Springs, with Craig Ungar, USA

Swimming's chief operating officer. Critics of swimming's record on coach abuse and child safety were incensed that Drawz had been rehabilitated again in the sport's leadership circles. In light of the Indianapolis episode in particular, these critics protested his even having been allowed to set foot inside the training center.

CHAPTER 17

THE NEW SOLUTIONS WERE
THE SAME AS THE OLD SOLUTIONS.

The United States Center for Safe Sport didn't become fully operational until Congress passed enabling legislation, a tweak of the Ted Stevens Olympic Amateur Sports Act. That 1978 law remains the youth sports system's last fundamental change: a transition to the national sport governing bodies under the Olympic Committee of functions of the old Amateur Athletic Union. The throughline of the incremental initiatives ever since have never shaken two elements: consolidation of private authority over youth sports programs, both Olympics-oriented and otherwise; and absence of independent oversight, via something like the government sports ministry found in many other countries.

In November 2017, Senator Dianne Feinstein, a California Democrat, led the bipartisan group who pushed the Protecting Young Victims from Sexual Abuse and Safe Sport Authorization Act through the Senate. Feinstein had become the legislative face supporting USA Gymnastics victims in reports at places like *60 Minutes* on CBS News. On January 29, 2018, the House of Representatives passed the Senate version of the bill with a minor amendment. The Senate ratified the amendment the very next day, and President Donald Trump signed the Safe Sport Act into law. In one assessment, the Politburo-scale near-unanimity of both the Senate (94 in favor, 3 opposed) and House (406 to 3) votes was a measure of national consensus around the abuse issue. What might be more acutely analyzed was the legislation's humdrum essence: it changed nothing of consequence in terms of who was in charge of policing abuse in youth sports. The task of overseeing the safety of the kids therein would continue to be an entity associated with the Olympic movement — hence one protective of, above all else, the Olympic movement.

On board endorsing the Safe Sport Act was a who's who of Child Abuse Inc.: the National Center for Missing and Exploited Children, the National Crime Victims Center, the National Child Abuse Coalition, the Child Welfare League of America, the National Center for Victims of Crime, the National Children's Alliance, Childhelp, the National Survivor Advocates Coalition, the National Children's Advocacy Center, Lauren's Kids, the Rape Abuse & Incest National Network, the American Academy of Pediatrics, and the National Association to Protect Children. The enthusiasm of this herd of independent minds stemmed from the law's expected standard features, such as mandatory reporting. Accompanying their embrace was obliviousness to what was simply the construction of a shiny new chicken coop guarded by the foxes.

Not among the organizations making Senator Feinstein's touted sponsor list was the Women's Sports Foundation. Champion Women could, however, be found there. This was the group started by Nancy Hogshead-Makar, the foundation's former director of advocacy, after her 2014 Diana Nyad–branded petition campaign forced Chuck Wielgus to stand down from induction into the International Swimming Hall of Fame (though he continued raking in seven figures a year as head of USA Swimming). Hogshead-Makar revealed that her split from the foundation came about after it inserted a clause into her contract renewal offer that would have barred her from advocating about abuse at Team USA — that is, the various Olympic sports squads.

At a certain point, as in all aspects of cultural and political life, a society gets the youth sports system it more or less wants, perhaps deserves. With the possible exception of the perpetrators themselves, no one could be said to be in favor of abuse. Certainly, no one believes the families of young athletes relish abuse. But whether the constituency of sports parents, as an effective bloc, is ever moved to say or do anything of substance, until and unless the worst outcomes land on their own individual kids, is another question. The ethos of American youth sports is to keep one eye on college athletic scholarships, and the other on Olympic glory and riches. When all else fails, the prospect or the fantasy of both is valued. These are the bottom lines of American youth sports. If a dollop of genuine safety measures can manage to get sprinkled in, then fine. If not, then attentiveness to safety becomes defined as episodic outrage whenever a particular case surfaces — preferably one involving a coach no one has ever heard of — in isolation and usually too late. There's no evidence that many parents are seriously focused on separating the needs of children and adults, nor on challenging the hegemony of an inscrutable, one-size-fits-nobody assemblage of 501(c)(3) "nonprofit" national sport governing bodies anointed in Colorado Springs.

≈

Following up on the passage of the Safe Sport Act, February 2018 was the month of hearings on the USA Gymnastics scandals, spearheaded by the chair and the ranking member of the Senate Commerce, Science, and Transportation Subcommittee on Consumer Protection, Product Safety, Insurance, and Data Security. Respectively, these senators were Republican Jerry Moran of Kansas and Democrat Richard Blumenthal of Connecticut. Blumenthal had one thing in common with John Leonard, the boss of the American Swimming Coaches

Association: Blumenthal, too, had lied throughout his career about having served in the Vietnam War, during which he'd actually settled into a safe stateside gig with the Army Reserves. Despite getting busted for this stolen valor by opposition research during his 2010 Senate campaign against Linda McMahon, the CEO of World Wrestling Entertainment, Blumenthal handily won election, based on his popularity as the long-time attorney general of Connecticut.

During that campaign, Blumenthal arranged, through me, to fly in the father of Chris Benoit, a WWE star who'd gone postal in 2007, murdering his wife and their young son before taking his own life. Benoit was the exclamation mark of a staggering generational death toll among performers in the pro wrestling industry, caused largely by a combination of prescription drug abuse and traumatic brain injury. To Mike Benoit, the father, Blumenthal promised to carry forward the fight to improve occupational health and safety standards in that peculiar and popular entertainment — an initiative not without risk for a Connecticut politician, since WWE was headquartered there. As attorney general, and in convenient alignment with his campaign against McMahon, Blumenthal did launch an audit of her and husband Vince McMahon's company for abuse of independent contractor classifications, which shut off employees from health care and other basic benefits (while also reducing payroll taxes paid into state coffers). As soon as Blumenthal got elected, though, the state investigation of WWE evaporated. Six years later, when Linda McMahon was nominated to Trump's cabinet to head the Small Business Administration, Blumenthal yukked it up with her during her Senate confirmation hearings.

At the 2018 commerce subcommittee hearings, for which swimming abuse survivors and advocates descended on Washington, the expected featured testimony came from a procession of USA Gymnastics witnesses. USA Swimming witnesses weren't called. As with ESPN and its rambling interviewees in 2013–14 who somehow passed on mentioning that Congressman Miller had an ongoing investigation at that very moment, stage managers for the senators explained to the spectators from the swimming world that their hearings "ran out of time" for additional testimony from victims in their sport.

USA Swimming's chief executive, succeeding the deceased Chuck Wielgus, was now Tim Hinchey, a veteran administrator in professional soccer, basketball, and hockey. Coincidentally, Hinchey had graduated from Monte Vista High School in Danville, California, just ahead of Debra Denithorne-Grodensky, the swimmer to whom the monster coach Andy King had proposed marriage when she turned 16. While Grodensky was in Washington for the Senate hearings, Hinchey messaged her on Facebook. He then flew her to meet him in New York, where they discussed a proposal for Grodensky to join the USA Swimming staff in Colorado, in an abuse-fighting position he told her she could conceive and design. Nothing came of the feeler. Grodensky eventually would conclude this had been a maneuver to sever her from a group suing USA Swimming.

Grodensky had this reflection on her experience and decades of advocacy around abuse: "While I was part of a lawsuit that resulted in a significant monetary recovery, I've come to realize that civil litigation is a limited vehicle when it comes to forcing fundamental change. The money that changed hands as a result of my case brought a measure of accountability for survivors, but it didn't do much in terms of improving the system going forward. That was always my real goal — and that's a job for Congress."

Another (non-sexual) abuse survivor, Kim Fairley, wrote an award-winning memoir, *Swimming for My Life*. She'd swum for the Cincinnati Marlins, the team coached by Hall of Famer Paul Bergen, who damaged Deena Deardurff, Melissa Halmi, Fairley, and others. Fairley framed the problem this way: "It took me decades to have the courage to state publicly that my coach's behavior was abusive and dangerous, scarring many of us for life. This is, in part, because this kind of abuse has been pervasive and ignored for years as a part of the swimming culture. When swimmers are breaking more records and swimming faster than they'd ever imagined possible, a totalitarian approach doesn't seem like a red flag."

≈

Late in 2020, Congress passed the Empowering Olympic, Paralympic, and Amateur Athletes Act. The law called for the appointment of a "Commission on the State of the USOPC," which would issue a report recommending further amendments to the Amateur Sports Act. The chair of the Senate Commerce Committee, Washington State Democrat Maria Cantwell, appointed four commission members, including co-chair Dionne Koller, director of the University of Baltimore's Center for Sport and the Law.

"The USOPC exists to protect athletes and uphold the integrity of sport," the senator said. "There are many issues that plague sports, from unequal pay and treatment to sexual abuse. Having the right members on this Commission ensures that these issues can be properly addressed and remedied, so that Olympic and Paralympic athletes can feel safe in their sports environment." These commissioners would use "their knowledge and experience in the sports world to advocate for diversity and inclusion, and against abuse and inequality."

From the start, what remained unclear was whether the commission would tackle youth coach sexual abuse as a foreground issue or as just an appendage in service of elite women athletes' more consensual and cherished goal of equal pay in relation to their male counterparts. In 2019 Cantwell introduced the Equal Pay for Team USA Act. Late in 2022 she celebrated its passage by the Senate, 50 years after the enactment of Title IX. The House soon followed, and President Joe Biden signed the bill into law in the first days of 2023.

Later that year, in an email interview for my coverage of the commission for the Salon news site, chair Koller pushed back at the idea that her mandate even included a critique of the U.S. Center for Safe Sport. By then, accounts of the center's embarrassing lapses were running rampant not only at the sites of independent journalists, but also at such places as Deadspin, ESPN, and *USA Today*. Many of the mainstream stories focused on the painfully slow progress of the agency's work, caused by its huge backload of cases — suggesting that properly robust funding was needed more than a reconsideration of whether such an entity was the best vehicle, in the first place, for combating abuse at NGBs. Many of those who did pile on, additionally, against Safe Sport's incompetence, unprofessionalism, conflicts, and corruption were the very same voices who'd set in motion the stampede to pass the Safe Sport Act. No media-recognized spokesperson for the cause went so far as to advocate root-and-branch reform of the Amateur Sports Act. Not then, not ever.

And, of course, gymnastics and swimming weren't the only sports poisoned by sexual abuse. Some degree of the problem afflicted almost every sport, with different paradigms and patterns depending on whether they were individual or team sports, as well as on the ages at which their female athletes, especially, peaked athletically and vis-à-vis their bodily development into objects of sexual desire.

One activist closely following the work of the Commission on the State of the USOPC was Eva Rodansky, a former speedskater. Rodansky's experience dated back to what she said was whistleblower retaliation against her by U.S. Speedskating. That happened in 1995, when she was 17 years old and complained about an abusive coach who was running a junior development program in Salt Lake City. Following that fiasco, which derailed her career, she returned to the sport in 2001, at which point she clearly racked up enough high finishes in major competitions to qualify for the U.S. team for the 2006 Winter Olympics. But she got passed over. The evident reason was that the national team coach at the time, Mike Crowe, played favorites based on the fruits of his sexual harassment. Later, ahead of the resolution of multiple allegations against him, Crowe migrated to Canada, where he became head coach of that national team. When his abuse history was reported by the Canadian Broadcasting Company just before the start of the 2018 Winter Olympics, Speed Skating Canada placed Crowe on leave, and shortly thereafter, fired him.

Rodansky's story was the tip of the USA Speedskating iceberg. Famously, its roster of credibly accused abusers also includes Andy Gabel, the all-time longest active American Olympic skater before he graduated to administration of the sport. For the 2002 Winter Olympics, Gabel oversaw both the short-track speed skating and figure skating programs. In 2013, the first reports surfaced of his sexual misconduct and he left U.S. Speedskating. One of his victims, three-time American champion Bridie Farrell, now a public advocate for abuse survivors, sued Gabel, the NGB, and USOPC. An associated controversy over Gabel's membership in the sport's hall of fame has paralleled that involving Paul Bergen, Jack Nelson, the belatedly blocked Wielgus, and others in swimming.

Unlike many others' input to the commission, Rodansky's contained not proposed Band-Aids for the Olympic programs' rampant abuse problem, but a vision of the youth sports system's foundational flaws. One of the bullet points of her submission: "Moving away to train is ... dangerous for young teen athletes, especially young women."

In conversation with me, Koller characterized criticisms of the commission for not aggressively probing Safe Sport as "confusing," and suggested that the commission's work was being unfairly lumped together with various other internal and external examinations of USOPC. The commission wasn't tasked by Congress, she said, with seeking specifics about the processing of abuse complaints. Koller said she didn't write Senator Cantwell's statement referencing the commission's mandate on abuse, "and Senator Cantwell does not control" the commission, "though she did appoint me. What the Commission is obligated to follow is the statute enacted by Congress, which outlines ten areas of study. None specifically instruct the Commission to investigate SafeSport, though one of the areas references 'recent reforms,' which may be interpreted as including the establishment of SafeSport, and in fact some members of the Olympic community have responded to our requests by providing information and feedback about SafeSport."

As the commission report deadline approached, a survey by staff indeed seemed to compel at least lip service to examination of the Safe Sport agency's myriad shortcomings. Stakeholders' scathing comments painted "a picture of a center in potential crisis," according to a draft analysis released on the eve of a September hearing at which Ju'Riese Colon — successor to the center's founding CEO, Shellie Pfohl — was summoned to testify. "We have pioneered a shift to a safer sports culture over the last six years," Colon insisted.

Some critics said USA Diving, which was navigating a class action by athletes alleging abuse, was worse than USA Gymnastics and USA Swimming. All 23 members of the U.S. Women's World Cup soccer team, and four members of the men's team, were among the more than 100 athletes signing a letter to Congress arguing that the U.S. Center for Safe Sport was "failing," *USA Today* reported.

≈

The Commission on the State of the USOPC issued their report early in 2024, just as this book was going to press. On instant analysis, it was clear that chair Koller was a savvy hand in the bureaucratic infighting of the nation's capital, and had strategically chosen to tamp down expectations that the commission would tackle Safe Sport in any depth. To Koller's credit, she was no Victor Vieth, who a decade earlier had put out a namby-pamby review of USA Swimming's Safe Sport program that pandered to the Olympic money people and leveraged the carrot-nibbling precincts of Child Abuse Inc. more than the principles of youth athlete safety from coach abuse.

The congressional commission covered many topics, of which Safe Sport was only one, with the meat of the discussion filling a mere six of the report's 277 pages. But it was the Safe Sport recommendation that rightly grabbed immediate headlines. While the commission didn't advocate a complete teardown of Amateur Sports Act architecture, it did note, with historical sharpness, that the current system had sprung from an unfortunate obsession with the U.S. Olympic medal haul (something Koller had referred to, in a law review article years earlier, as the primacy of "national prestige"). There were 12 total recommendations, two of which went to the core of the abuse crisis. No. 3 called for congressional action to wrest the U.S. Center for Safe Sport away from the funding sources and the de facto control of the NGBs and the Olympic Committee, by providing it with direct federal appropriations and an administrative structure to make the functions of investigating and disciplining coach sexual abuse truly independent.

Even more fundamental and significant, perhaps, was recommendation No. 1: *"Congress should allow USPOC to focus on high-performance athletes and create a new federal office to develop youth and grassroots sports."*

It had taken 14 years to get to even this point of incremental reform, if you started the clock with Chuck Wielgus's miserable take in media investigations of USA Swimming's widespread abuse, followed by his procession of PR-focused solutions – and then the adoption, by USOPC as a whole, of swimming's so-called "model" approach. And even now, in the wake of the commission report, there was no guarantee that Congress would act quickly, or for that matter at all, on these root recommendations. The country was beset with arguably more pressing problems, such as saving its very democracy, and the Olympic lobby seemed unlikely to give up on its own bastardized vision of Safe Sport without a fight. Also remaining was the ever-open question of whether sports parents, addicted to the lure of scholarships and glory, would have a clue as to what's truly best for their children, and stand together as a political force in support of any kind of reform.

In an analytic bullseye, the commission noted that the current system had "emerged in large part as a result of public attention to what was believed to be poor U.S. Olympic showings against Soviet-bloc nations." The report went on to call the Amateur Sports Act "a uniquely American balance" of public-private oversight, one due for a facelift.

Safe Sport specifically, the report opined, "does not adequately employ trauma-informed practices," a flaw that exacerbates the reluctance of victims to file claims out of fear that the process will be re-traumatizing. The agency "has never been able to find its footing. It must not, however, be allowed to become an enduring example of failure."

Crucial to positive change would be a reorientation of Safe Sport along the lines of what had evolved for the U.S. Anti-Doping Agency. The report praised USADA as a rousing success. Tactfully, this rundown didn't mention how USADA's CEO, Travis Tygart, had cut his teeth as an abuse cover-up lawyer for USA Swimming.

ACKNOWLEDGMENTS
AND NOTES

R espectful of the personal stories of abuse survivors, many of which were outrageous and deserved unqualified sympathy, I also felt that the topic of this book needed to be pitched more broadly, to cover the warps in the American approach to youth sports programs, which are what allow the problem of coach abuse to persist so loathsomely and blithely. In football, boys get brained, and under the cover of enhanced Title IX opportunities in other sports, girls get raped. Why? In trying to answer this question, I was guided by a combination of the most compelling and revealing narratives and the identification of key villains — but above all, as they say, by following the money.

For a little more than two years starting in late 2012, I partnered content at my blog with another freelance journalist, Tim Joyce, who on his own had already pushed out important new information on the subject in articles at the *Forbes* magazine site Real Clear Sports. One of our great "Eureka!" moments together was the time we huddled on the phone in a conversation we resolved not to end until we'd figured out who was the coach identified only as "AP" in a heavily redacted USA Swimming dossier on a coach in Florida whose Peeping Tom videotapes of some of his athletes revealed wider scandals. Tim was the one who solved that puzzle by alighting on the sparse contemporaneous news coverage in Fort Lauderdale of one Alex Pussieldi.

Some of the material in this book was workshopped at third-party publications. I'm grateful to Randy Shaw, publisher of the San Francisco alternative news site Beyond Chron; to Andrew O'Hehir, executive editor of Salon; and especially to the late, lamented, and innovative Irish site Broadsheet.

In 2015, after Congressman George Miller's "investigation" of USA Swimming laid an egg, I was determined to carry on with my own reporting. I decided to zero in on the George Gibney story. Simultaneously, Broadsheet was becoming the first news outlet in Ireland to say out loud that Gibney's barrister in the important Supreme Court case there that threw out his prosecution had been heard by a panel of justices including the lawyer's sister. This was an object lesson in the casual nepotism of a small country — mirroring the incest and corruption of the swimming world — as well as a case study in the limitations of media scrutiny of official malfeasance in a place without First Amendment protections.

Long story short, Broadsheet began picking up some of my writings, as the latest reprise of the George Gibney saga played out in my Freedom of Information Act legal fight with the U.S. Department of Homeland Security for records from Gibney's immigration file. Olga Cronin, who'd compiled an exhaustively authoritative Gibney timeline for Broadsheet, became a good friend — someone with whom I'd hoist pints at The Bailey, a pub in Dublin once owned by the father of John Ryan, Broadsheet's publisher. John was another great supporter and treasured friend, who generously underwrote two trips in which, in addition to pursuing the Gibney truth, I was able to inhale the magic of the Emerald Isle — the second one along with my daughter Lia.

Michael Smith, who runs Ireland's *Village* magazine, also published a major article of mine on Gibney. (And to our amusement, Michael and I discovered that many years ago I'd been a word processing temp at New York law firms just before he was a proofreader at some of the same places.) The lively Irish sports podcast *Off the Ball* had me on now and then.

Thank you to all my sources, many of whom wished not to be named. You know who you are. In the cases of non-victims — coaches and officials inside swimming who wanted to speak out for the purpose of improving things, without leaving their fingerprints — they came and went. Mostly went. Somewhere in the middle of the pandemic, my main "Deep Throat" mysteriously stopped even acknowledging receipt of my email messages. I hope he's OK. Muckraking can be lonely work, but it can also be rewarding, in mostly non-monetary ways, if your boss — in this case, myself — doesn't pay you enough to pull punches.

For the first of two times in my career, the Reporters Committee for Freedom of the Press helped out importantly — here by lining up emergency pro bono legal help, from the BakerHostetler law firm in Washington, when one of the figures of an investigation made a heavy-handed attempt to silence me. Please go to www.rcfp. org to find ways to support this fine organization.

≈

Only one major U.S. news organization gave the George Gibney story any substantial coverage prior to the BBC's popular and cheesy *Where Is George Gibney?* podcast in 2020. Perhaps counterintuitively, that outlet was Fox News, which in 2016 featured an interview of me by correspondent Tamara Holder for a regular segment of hers called "Sports Court," which covered my FOIA fight for Gibney's immigration records. (The segment is still viewable at www.foxnews.com/video/4744406376001#sp=show-clips.)

This was her only plunge into the swimming scandals, but Tamara Holder was just getting started making waves. Though the details wouldn't emerge for a while, she was herself one of the cluster of sexually assaulted and harassed women at Fox News who would trigger tens of millions of dollars of civil lawsuit settlements by the network, often tied to non-disclosure agreements. Some of that story was told in the movie *Bombshell*.

In 2015, Francisco Cortes, vice president of Fox News Latino, cornered Tamara in his office, poured them shots of tequila, unzipped his pants, and tried to get her to perform oral sex on him. She fled the room.

Months after my appearance on that Sports Court segment, Tamara was one of the token liberals frequently seen on the round-table debates, or shoutfests, that were part of Fox presidential election coverage. On one such segment, she was across the table from Omarosa Manigault, a Black spokeswoman for the Donald Trump campaign who would go on to become a White House adviser before leaving unhappily. In the middle of the discussion, Manigault said on the air, out of nowhere, in a clip that sent Twitter fluttering: "Tamara, you come on here with your big boobs . . ."

In February 2017, Fox paid $2.5 million to settle Tamara's claim in the sexual assault by Cortes. She said to the *New York Times*, "I was told by agents and lawyers that if I opened up, I would for-ever be 'toxic' and my career would be over." They were right: she couldn't get another job on television.

Tamara Holder returned to her roots, as a civil rights attorney specializing in sexual assault cases. In Chicago, her image peers out from a prominent billboard advertisement for her firm.

THE AUTHOR

UNDERWATER is Irvin Muchnick's fifth book for ECW Press. The others are

- *WRESTLING BABYLON: Piledriving Tales of Drugs, Sex, Death, and Scandal*
- *CHRIS & NANCY: The True Story of the Benoit Murder-Suicide and Pro Wrestling's Cocktail of Death* (now in its third and "Ultimate Historical Edition")
- *CONCUSSION INC.: The End of Football As We Know It*
- *WITHOUT HELMETS OR SHOULDER PADS: The American Way of Death in Football Conditioning*

Called a practitioner of "magnificent investigative journalism" by the late dean of sportswriters, Frank Deford, Muchnick writes about the often neglected dark side of our sports entertainments. A former assistant director of the National Writers Union, he was named respondent of the 2010 United States Supreme Court case *Reed Elsevier v. Muchnick*, affirming the copyright and economic rights of freelance writers. Born in St. Louis, Muchnick lives in California.

This book is also available as a Global Certified Accessible™ (GCA) ebook. ECW Press's ebooks are screen reader friendly and are built to meet the needs of those who are unable to read standard print due to blindness, low vision, dyslexia, or a physical disability.

At ECW Press, we want you to enjoy our books in whatever format you like. If you've bought a print copy or an audiobook not purchased with a subscription credit, just send an email to ebook@ecwpress.com and include:

- the book title
- the name of the store where you purchased it
- a screenshot or picture of your order/receipt number and your name

A real person will respond to your email with your ePub attached. If you prefer to receive the ebook in PDF format, please let us know in your email.

Some restrictions apply. This offer is only valid for books already available in the ePub format. Some ECW Press books do not have an ePub format for us to send you. In those cases, we will let you know if a PDF format is available as an alternative. This offer is only valid for books purchased for personal use. At this time, this program is not offered on school or library copies.

Thank you for supporting an independently owned Canadian publisher with your purchase!